ECONOMIC SIMULATIONS *IN* SWARM:
Agent-Based Modelling and Object Oriented Programming

Advances in Computational Economics

VOLUME 14

The titles published in this series are listed at the end of this volume.

Economic Simulations *in* Swarm:
Agent-Based Modelling and Object Oriented Programming

edited by

Francesco Luna
Università di Venezia Ca'Foscari, Venice, Italy
Oberlin College, Ohio, USA

and

Benedikt Stefansson
University of California Los Angeles, USA

Kluwer Academic Publishers
Boston/Dordrecht/London

Distributors for North, Central and South America:
Kluwer Academic Publishers
101 Philip Drive
Assinippi Park
Norwell, Massachusetts 02061 USA
Telephone (781) 871-6600
Fax (781) 871-6528
E-Mail <kluwer@wkap.com>

Distributors for all other countries:
Kluwer Academic Publishers Group
Distribution Centre
Post Office Box 322
3300 AH Dordrecht, THE NETHERLANDS
Telephone 31 78 6392 392
Fax 31 78 6546 474
E-Mail <orderdept@wkap.nl>

 Electronic Services <http://www.wkap.nl>

Library of Congress Cataloging-in-Publication Data
Economic simulations in Swarm: agent-based modelling and object oriented
programming / edited by Francesco Luna and Benedikt Stefansson.
     p.cm. -- (Advances in computational economics ; v. 14)
  Includes bibliographical references and index.
  ISBN 0-7923-8665-5
    1. Economics--Computer simulation. 2. Economics--Mathematical models. I. Luna,
Francesco, 1963- II. Stefansson, Benedikt. III. Series.

HB143.5 .E25 2000
330'.01'13--dc21   99-056041

Printed on acid-free paper.

Printed in the United States of America

Contents

List of Figures

List of Tables

Preface

In 1991, the Center for Computable Economics was established at UCLA with the financial support of the Latsis Foundation. We hoped to promote the modeling of adaptive market processes and, eventually, of the macro-dynamics of systems composed of multiple such markets, using computer simulations as a tool. The editors of this volume, Francesco Luna and Benedikt Stefansson, have been part of this effort from the beginning at UCLA as well as later when the locus of it moved to the Computable and Experimental Economics Laboratory at the University of Trento, Italy.

This approach to the often complex dynamics of complex systems is gradually gaining ground in the profession as a complement to traditional analytical methods. It is, we believe, to play an increasingly important role in future years. But, so far, it has been a Tower of Babel. For this work to cohere and a cumulative body of knowledge to build up, groups of workers using the same language and simulation platforms with interchangeable parts have to form. At CCE and now at CEEL, we have encouraged the use of the Swarm platform developed at the Santa Fe Institute.

This book provides an accessible introduction and tutorial to Swarm and presents a rich sample of recent economic models done in Swarm. It is my hope that it will help attract a growing number of young economists to the Swarm community and in this way give added impetus to research on complex adaptive economic systems.

Axel Leijonhufvud
Professor Emeritus of Economics - UCLA
Professor of Monetary Economics - University of Trento

Contributing Authors

Peter Bruhn Master of Science in Computer Science from the University of Illinois at Urbana-Champaign (UIUC) in 1997 as a DAAD scholar. He is currently working on a PhD dissertation for the joint degree program Economics and Computer Science ("Wirstschaftsinformatik") at Darmstadt University of Technology, Germany. He is a scholar of the Konrad-Adenauer-Foundation (KAS).

Charlotte Bruun Associate Professor of Economics at the Department of Economics, Politics and Public Administration of the University of Aalborg, Denmark. Her main scientific contributions are in Monetary Economics with simulation studies on pure-credit economies and Macroeconomics in a Keynesian approach. An early and enthusiastic supporter of Agent-Based Economics, before discovering Swarm wrote her programs in Object-Oriented Pascal.

Marco Corazza Assistant Professor of Mathematics for Economics at the Department of Applied Mathematics of the University of Venice "Ca' Foscari", Italy. His main research interests are in quantitative finance (with particular attention to deterministic chaos and non-standard stochastic processes for financial return behavior), the dynamics of economic markets, and operation research modeling of hospital management

Timothy E. Jares Assistant Professor of Finance at the University of North Florida. He received his PhD from the University of Nebraska in August 1998. His research interests include asset pricing and business valuation models, efficient markets, experimental markets, and agency theory and contracting problems. One of his papers is forthcoming in the *Journal of Real Estate Research*.

Fu Ren Lin Associate Professor of Management Information Systems at the Department of Information Management of the National Sun Yat-sen University in Taiwan. He received a PhD degree in Business Administration (Information Systems) from the University of Illinois at Urbana-Champaign in 1996. His research interests include supply chain management, business process reengineering, data mining, and electronic commerce.

Francesco Luna Assistant Professor of Economics at the University of Venice "Ca' Foscari". Visiting Professor at Oberlin College and consultant for the World Bank. A UCLA PhD, he has published on "computable" learning in Economics, on the emergence of institutions, and on the History of Economic Thought. His interests include computability theory, Macroeconomics, Industrial Organization and Transition Economics.

Luigi Mittone Assistant Professor of Public Economics at the Department of Economics of the University of Trento, Italy. Mittone collaborates with the Computable and Experimental Economics Laboratory of the University of Trento. His main fields of research are the experimental approach to tax evasion and the organizational effects of moral factors in non-profit organizations.

Paolo Patelli Ph.D. student in Economics at the Scuola Superiore Sant'Anna, Pisa Italy, and coordinator for the Computable and Experimental Economics Laboratory, University of Trento, Italy. His interests include Experimental Economics and Computational Economics. Patelli has been a computer consultant and instructor for private and academic institutions. He recently led the Tofee project, which aims at developing tools which allows users with little programming experience to create software to run economic experiments in the laboratory

Alessandro Perrone Currently working on a dissertation largely based on Swarm, will obtain his degree in Economics from the University of Venice "Ca' Foscari". A computer and software consultant for various private enterprises, he has also written numerous computer programs for the departments of Economics and Business Administration. One of Swarm's earliest "beta-testers" outside Santa Fe, Perrone maintains a FAQ section for the mailing list .Machintosh developer.

Daniele M. Sapienza Ph.D. student in Economics of Istitutions, Monetary and Financial Markets at Università di Roma II "Tor Vergata". He is currently writing his dissertation on Real Options and Oligopolist Strategies. He has recently joined McKinsey Italia as business analyst. His interests range from the History of Economic Thought, to Political Economy, to Finance, to Computational Economics. Sapienza was awarded several grants for his essays on the History of Economic Thought.

Michael J. Shaw Associate Professor at the Department of Business Administration and Mechanical and Industrial Engineering at the University of Illinois at Urbana-Champaign and faculty member of the Artificial Intelligence Group at the Beckman Institute. Shaw is interested in theoretical issues and empirical applications of electronic commerce, distributed and group artificial intelligence, neural networks and technology management. He has published extensively on these issues and sits in numerous editorial boards of professional journals.

Christoph Schlueter-Langdon Assistant Professor of Information Systems in the Marshall School of Business, University of Southern California. Before joining USC, he was a visiting scholar at the Beckman Institute. Schlueter-Langdon has worked as a technology strategist with Andersen Consulting's Strategic Services in the United States and in Europe. His research focusses on the economics of online value and chains, electronic commerce, information system strategy and decision support systems.

Benedikt Stefansson Candidate for Ph.D. degree in the department of Economics of UCLA. He has been invited to teach Agent Based Modeling and lecture on Swarm by numerous institutes and universities in France, Italy, and the United States, and has taught graduate courses on social science modeling with Swarm in the Department of Political Science at UCLA. He has recently joined the Center for Adaptive Systems Applications (CASA), a management consulting company which specializes in using computer models to solve business problems. His research interests are in Industrial Organization and Business Strategy.

Troy J. Strader Assistant professor of Management Information Systems in the Department of Logistics, Operations and MIS, Iowa State University. He received the PhD degree in Business Administration (Information Systems) from the University of Illinois at Urbana-Champaign in 1997. His research interests include electronic commerce, strategic impacts of information systems, and information economics.

Pietro Terna Associate Professor of Mathematical Economics and Economic Dynamics at the University of Torino, Italy, with an interest in artificial neural networks for economic and financial modeling and in agent based models of social interaction. Among the pioneers of Swarm for Economics, Terna has created and teaches a graduate course on simulations and agent based economics using Swarm as a pedagogical tool. He is the author and editor of numerous volumes on recent computational techniques for Economic analysis.

Introduction

Francesco Luna
And
Benedikt Stefansson

1.   AIMS AND AUDIENCE

The volume *Economic Simulations In Swarm*[1] has several goals:

1. it wants to propose a common language[2] to those economists who already employ simulations as one of their tools of analysis;

2. it will present for the first time such a language (Swarm) with a condensed, but rather exhaustive, tutorial;

3. it collects a rich variety of original contributions to economics, where simulations offer a natural mode of analysis of the dynamics of complex systems with heterogenous agents.

Computer Simulations[3] of economic systems are slowly gaining ground within the profession. Economists have become aware of the limitations of the standard mathematical formalism. On the one hand, when dealing with real world phenomena, it is often impossible to reach a "closed form" solution to the problem of interest. One possible approach is to simplify the problem so that an elegant closed-form solution is synthesized. The implicit assumption is that the simplification process has spared all relevant elements and discarded only unnecessary ornaments. In case this *a priori* seems too strong, the empirically oriented researcher may want to employ a simulation to study the dynamical properties of the system. On the other hand, what Frank Hahn once dubbed "pure theory" is suffering from "exhaustion," the purely deductive method seems to have reached a dead end. Hahn argues:

> [A] thriving subject will know at each stage of its development what the next crucial questions are. Pure theory is no exception. But is so happens that it is becoming ever more clear that almost none of them

can be answered by the old procedures. Instead of theorems we shall
need simulations, instead of simple transparent axioms there looms the
likelihood of psychological, sociological and historical postulates[4].

Perhaps, economics is destined to be *once more* an inductive discip-
line; whether it will be "softer" because of that (as Hahn implies) it is
difficult to say. Undoubtedly, however, in their inductive efforts, theor-
eticians will find simulations of artificial "worlds" more and more useful
to extract regularities and/or to push their "simple" thought experiments to "unforeseeable" outcomes. These results are very useful to
help the intuition of the researcher and often suggest original interpret-
ations of real world phenomena.

Unfortunately, too often the acceptability of the frame of analysis and
the transmissibility of its results are spoiled by the difficulty to *read* the
model and hence by the "unreplicability" of the results reported. It is
hence becoming pivotal to construct a common language, not dissimilar
from French for diplomacy or more recently English. Simulations will
have to be written **in** some Esperanto: it is obvious that the current Babel is against the emergence of a renewed enthusiastic effort in economic
theory.

As a curiosity, we have performed the following search in EconLit, the
largest collection of economic citations available in electronic form. We
have searched the database for the word "computer" starting in 1970
up to 1998. In the Seventies, the word appears on average 16 times
every year. In the Eighties "computer" is employed in titles or in the
abstracts 80 times per year on average, and in the first eight years of the
Nineties 257 times. Obviously a large part of this "citations" refer to the
computer *industry* which has attracted much attention in the economic
literature. Perhaps, more interesting is the result to the query "computer
simulation". For this we obtained 101 entries for the complete period
(January 1969-July 1999).

Again, a significant proportion of these references are not directly relevant to our argument as they relate to statistics and econometrics linked
to *Monte Carlo* simulations, but about half of these papers deal with
models defined algorithmically which *unfold* on a computer. The topics
contemplated by these contributions are diverse and range from history
and the philosophy of science[5], to business cycle theory[6], to income distribution analysis[7], to pricing mechanisms[8], to disequilibrium dynamics[9]
to marketing strategy[10] and to industrial organization in general[11].

However, even at a casual look at the text and reference lists of these
papers it is evident that very few of them "build" upon some computer
model produced by other researchers[12]. Again, this is in large part
due to the absence of a "common language" for economic simulations.

The programs are written in various languages at very different levels. Fortran, C, Pascal and recently C++ and Java; but also packages like Gauss, Mathematica, Mathlab, Maple are employed depending on the preference and preparation of the "programmer".

The obvious result is that there is no evident cumulative learning process, and that even extremely significant achievements remain isolated and soon forgotten. No "school" based on a family of models comparable to the real business-cycle approach can emerge. One possible solution would be to construct a very sophisticated model of an economic system. This should be so powerful and flexible as to encompass a very large number of scenarios by changing a series of parameters. Various researchers have taken steps in that direction. Among the most interesting and daring contributions we will remember Tesfation's *Trade Network Game* model[13], GLOBUS[14], and with a more limited scope, PAGE[15] STRATHA[16], HasiG[17], and Imp-Mac[18].

Swarm follows a different approach. It is somewhat in the middle between the two extremes of "do-it-yourself" and "just-pour-water". Rather than giving a ready-made structure, it offers a rich set of libraries (could we call them nouns and verbs ?) to be combined as the researcher thinks it more appropriate to present his/her model. This aspect guarantees the flexibility necessary to any "creative" effort. At the same time, the very use of those libraries will make each brick of the construction perfectly intelligible to the "reader". In particular, all graphical interfaces are tested and their use and interpretation is made patent; a series of pseudo-random numbers for very different distributions are given so that even those simulations relying on random numbers can be replicated.

In a paper written by the original Swarm development team, the authors define Swarm as a "multi-agent platform for the simulation of complex adaptive systems." In practical terms Swarm is a collection of software libraries. Scientists can use these libraries as building blocks to create Agent-Based simulation models. The libraries are written in Objective-C[19] and Tk/Tcl and have been ported to most flavors of the Unix operating system, in addition to Microsoft Windows and LinuxPPC on the Apple Macintosh[20].

Swarm was developed at the Santa Fe Institute in New Mexico by a number of researchers including Chris Langton, Roger Burkhart, Manor Askenazi, Nelson Minar, Glen Ropella, Marcus G. Daniels, Alex Lancaster, and Sven Thommesen. The Santa Fe Institute and a number of private and government sources have sponsored the development of Swarm, which is released under the GNU Library General Public License. Alla components of the software and development tools, in addition to documentation and sample applications are thus freely available both as executables and source code and may be redistributed free of charge.

The code to all programs presented in this volume and many other contributions in different disciplines can be found at `www.santafe.edu/` `/projects/swarm/` along with the source code for Swarm and precompiled versions for various operating systems.

The Swarm community is relatively large and growing. It is important to note that Swarm was not designed for Economics in particular but for all sciences that may need to simulate interactions among basic elements. Chemists and biologists are also involved as much as sociologists, anthropologists and social scientists in general. However, the first tested version of Swarm was released only two years ago and there is no structured manual for it.

For this reason, this book should be of interest to a relatively wide audience. To these potential readers more than being a simple manual the book will offer a rich series of examples, and a wealth of ready made technical solutions which cover a rich set of circumstances.

2.   COMPUTATION AND COMPUTABILITY

The title of this section, which reflects the interests of one of the editors –Francesco Luna– would like to draw the reader's attention to a particular methodological issue.

Kumaraswamy "Vela" Velupillai often points at the fact that mathematical General Equilibrium Theory grew on the tracks of the Hilbert "program" as later interpreted by the Bourbakian formalist school. Thus, economic theory adopted *real analysis* as its preferred tool of investigation.

However, there are three other branches in mathematical analysis known as *constructive* analysis, *computable* analysis, and *non-standard* analysis. It is, at least, intriguing to ask whether economics would be as we know it today, had Arrow and Debreu been trained in recursion theory or proof theory rather than in set theory. This counterfactual argument may be relevant in our case since computers were developed starting from the work of Turing, Church, and Post and their quest for a rigorous characterization of what is *calculable* in principle[21].

Clearly, a computer program is computable; it is some sort of algorithm and, accepting Church's Thesis, there exists a Turing Machine that simulates it[22]. Hence, it would seem that the fact of employing a computer automatically makes an economist an adept of *Computable Economics*. This is not the case. Very often, models implemented in a computer are based on theoretical models that are not computable in principle. The formal elegance and universality of a utility function based on a rational preference ordering is lost when a crude Cobb-Douglas function is coded because the simulation results are dictated by **that** particular function which translates into "trivial" rules of behavior.

Economic models of reality are metaphors and they are useful as long as they lead our actions successfully. For this reason I agree that it should not really matter how these metaphors are obtained and complete freedom should be granted when a researcher *thinks* of economic phenomena. However, we also know that policy measures have to be designed carefully, taking into consideration the institutional idiosyncrasies of the historical and geographical situations they have to operate upon.

The issue, then, is two-fold. On the one hand, we can wonder whether the results reached by computational models which are "obtained" from theoretically uncomputable ones, can be justified by invoking the theoretical ancestor, or even used as evidence against that very reference point. On the other hand, it is natural to ask whether there is any substantial gain (apart from a logical consistency) in designing theoretical models which are computable in principle and which, therefore, should "naturally[23]" lead to computational models.

One thing is clear, the "computer is here to stay" and its use in the economic profession, as in other fields, is ineludible. Some may argue that it should not be enough for an economist to use a computer to call himself a computational economist. Our hope is that the fact of using computational techniques however, may trigger the interest in the foundations of computer science and invite the economist to approach computability theory. Economic models in this way may also attain a mathematical consistency with the tool they are implemented in.

3. OBJECT-ORIENTED PROGRAMMING AND AGENT-BASED MODELING

Object Oriented Programming (OOP) is not really new, but has only recently become dominant thanks to the diffusion of languages like C++ and Java[24]. Why is Object Oriented Programming so popular? Theoretically speaking there is nothing that can be done with an object oriented language that could not be achieved in any of the other computer languages. However, when dealing with *agent-based models*, there are some evident advantages for the initial programmer and, later, for the "reader".

In particular, there are four essential properties characteristic of OOP: *abstraction encapsulation, inheritance,* and *poli-morphism*[25]. These properties allow the programmer to conceive an agent as a self-contained (encapsulated) object which is the "tangible" instance of some initial template (abstraction), and which has inherited some general features that define its essence without "hindering" its potential development. The fundamental component or object in Swarm is a collection of objects called *swarm*. This is a set of agents along with a well defined schedule of events those very agents will have to deal with. A swarm can represent the whole model: it has agents as well as time. Furthermore, each object in a swarm can be composed of a swarm. "A pond inhabited by single-celled animals each of them composed of a collection of organelles". Even better, from the point of view of an economist, an agent may have its own representation of the world. Hence, an agent, living in some environment, may have its own model-swarm of the reality.

Since Swarm was designed with the need of natural scientists in mind, it takes time and the notion of concurrency very seriously. In nature concurrency is governed by the laws of physics, but when one starts using a computer, simulation actions have to be taken in a well predefined order. The aim of the Swarm designers was that of forcing the experimenter to make explicit his/her assumption on the order of events (that in a real-world experiment would have been coordinated by nature itself). The result is extremely valuable for economics: by forcing the researcher to make explicit reference to time and ordered sequence of events, "real" dynamics is introduced and the interaction among agents or feedback mechanisms will take time to be performed and will be taken only after other well specified events have occurred. Furthermore, since each swarm can be made to observe its own schedule, it is easy to introduce in the system an *asynchronous* clock management. This will reflect a fundamental characteristic of real-world phenomena caused by the interaction of independent actors each one following its own motives and schedule. Certainly, such an option seems to suggest a way out of the *clock-work* dynamics which constrains many traditional economic models.

Another very interesting feature of Swarm derives once more from the fact that this platform was created with especially natural scientists in mind: the concept of observability is taken to the obvious extreme. Consider an experiment: there is some object on which the researcher wants to perform an experiment to observe what will happen. Well, of course, from a certain philosophical perspective if nobody is there to observe then perhaps nothing really happens, and from another perspective the fact that an observer is there may also change the nature and the outcomes of the original phenomenon. Anyway, if we abstract from these issues we can consider that the instrument for the observation and the object of the observation are distinct.

Swarm once more tries to replicate this state of affairs that comes automatically when dealing with nature. The program will build an Artificial World that then becomes the object of some Artificial Observer. It is important to remark that each of the two objects will "function" according to its own well and independently specified schedule. Hence, it is up to the Observer to decide what to look at, but also when to look at it. If later on the researcher realizes that there is another interesting feature of the phenomenon he/she has not considered, he/she has just to reposition the microscope or the camera, or, in our case, change some details in the Artificial Observer. The Object of the analysis keeps on working (living) independently of it.

On a more applied note, Swarm offers an already large library of classes that fit the needs of a lot of possible simulations. For example a two-dimensional grid is available and, as a sub-class, a cellular automata setting replicating the original "life" game is ready for use. On the other hand, because of the inheritance and encapsulation features described before, the grid can not only be sized at wish, but it can also be filled with objects that will behave according to rules that the researcher explicitly imposes.

It is hard to evaluate whether Swarm qualifies as *the* common language for simulation that we fancy about. Perhaps other researchers (in a garage?) are now working at something easier to use and more powerful. What is essential however, is to recognize the need for such Esperanto.

4.   CONTRIBUTIONS

First of all let us reiterate that Swarm is freely available under the terms of the GNU license at `www.santafe.edu/projects/swarm`. Similarly, the code for all the models presented in this collection of papers will be found at the same URL and at `www-ceel.gelso.unitn.it`.

This volume can be logically divided into two parts. The first part is devoted to a concise tutorial of Swarm by Benedikt Stefansson. The second part collects a series of papers, explicitly written for this book, which use Swarm to investigate the object of interest.

It is significant to notice that only few of the computer programs presented have been produced by professional programmers and the elegance in the written code varies substantially across contributions. We believe that rather than being a drawback, this shows with no doubt that *effective* communication can be reached even after a relatively short learning investment. Even "amateur" programmers will manage to implement their original ideas without having to master much more than a "broken English".

The first contribution of the collection, *Economic Experiments with Swarm: a Neural Network Approach to the Self-Development of Consistency in Agents' Behavior* by Pietro Terna, investigates with much sensibility, the methodological implications of agent-based models for social sciences in general and economics in particular. Methodology and techniques are "largely under construction" according to Terna, who proceeds to present a generalized *Environment-Rules-Agent* scheme as a tool to assist the researcher in the design of a "bottom-up" model. A package **bp-ct** is proposed as an easy way in building and running artificial laboratories for social scientists. The package is finally employed to produce a spontaneous no-auctioneer Hayekian market.

Charlotte Bruun and Francesco Luna present a model of *Endogenous Growth with Cycles in a Swarm Economy*. The term "Endogenous Growth" will appear misleading to the reader who expects to find a model of sustained growth in line with New Growth Theory. As a matter of fact, the artificial economy described eventually reaches a "steady state". However, the trigger for the *take off* is hard-wired in the behavior of self-interested agents who face a complex environment which they try to tame. The emergence of original entrepreneurs lead to the growth of this "Schumpeterian" economy. Business cycles are caused both by the failure of sub-efficient firms and by the change in wealth distribution in this pure-credit economy. The model appears flexible enough to address an ample spectrum of issues, by modifying only marginally the original code: one of the great advantages of the Object-Oriented paradigm.

Luigi Mittone and Paolo Patelli present a model of *Imitative Behavior in Tax Evasion*. Thanks to their simulation approach they manage to tackle effectively a series of criticisms addressed to previous models. Psychological motives and experimental results are taken into consideration and integrated in the simulation framework to analyze the effects of "framing" and of "moral suasion" on tax-evasion decisions. Furthermore, the authors construct a model of cultural evolution: tax evasion can become the general attitude under some particular imitative and monitoring/enforcing behavior.

The spontaneous emergence of financial intermediation is the object of *An Experimental Approach to the Study of Banking Intermediation: The banknet Simulator* by Massimo Sapienza. The author builds his model on a pre-existing one, "BankNet," initially designed by one of the original Swarm programmers as an "exercise". The model is then employed to analyze a somewhat different topic. Here is an example of the re-usability of Object-Oriented code and of the possibility of "building upon" a pre-existing model. Transaction costs, economies of scale, agents' heterogeneity, and strategic interaction are the "real world" features that, according to this model, lead to the endogenous creation of intermediaries. One of Swarm's library allows for the "real time" graphical representation of the credit links being established in the system. Such (completely decentralized) *emergent* phenomenon is hence monitored very effectively.

Moving to a different issue in finance, *Numerical Modeling, Noise Traders, and the Swarm Simulation System* by Timothy E. Jares investigates the persistence of noise traders observed in the real world, a phenomenon that contradicts the predictions of traditional models. The presence of such traders is shown to affect long-term prices. Wealth appears to play a secondary role with respect to the configuration and characteristics of market institutions. Noise traders are shown to disappear when their beliefs are not highly correlated so that fundamental traders will dominate.

Shifting now to Industrial Organization, *Nonlinear Stochastic Dynamics for Supply Counterfeiting in Monopolistic Markets* by Marco Corazza and Alessandro Perrone, studies the strategic interaction between a monopolist and a counterfeiter from a dynamical perspective. Initially, some closed form solutions are obtained for the model proposed. It has to be noticed that this model becomes not only *computable*, but also tractable thanks to the appropriate choice of the demand function. Still, the inherent complexity due to nonlinearities and the presence of stochastic disturbances requires a simulation investigation of the possible outcomes. The authors (for the first time) implement in Swarm a graphical representation of a state-space dynamics.

Using Swarm for Simulating the Order Fulfillment Process in Divergent Assembly Supply Chains is the title of the contribution proposed by Fu Ren Lin, Troy J. Strader, and Michael J. Shaw. The effective management of a supply chain requires the coordination of different and sometimes contradictory interests. A multi-agent simulator can turn out to be a powerful support in the decision-making process. In particular, the effect of information sharing on order fulfillment in divergent assembly supply chain is found to attain a substantial reduction in inventory costs while maintaining acceptable order fulfillment cycle times. In other words, information as a source of enhanced coordination and uncertainty reduction is a substitute for inventory.

Christoph Schlueter-Langdon, Peter Bruhn, and Michael Shaw present their *Online Supply Chain Modeling and Simulation*. They analyze one of the most dynamic markets of this last few years: the online services market. Digital interactive services are still an industry in its infancy and rapidly evolving. What are the most effective strategies to deal with entry decision in such an environment? The approach followed by the authors is to design an advanced "flight-simulator" implemented in Swarm to be used as a sophisticated aid to decision making. Also in this case it is interesting to discover that the original version of this model was built upon two pre-existing programs: the so called "Anazasi village" and the supply-chain model by Fu-Ren Lin.

The last contribution, *The Coevolution of Human Capital and Industrial Structure* by Francesco Luna and Alessandro Perrone is mainly designed as an exercise for the "interested reader". The model tries to depict the dynamical interaction between the structure of enterprises (as captured by their size) and human capital represented by the skills available in the pool of workers in the economy. A successful entrepreneur can share with her/his workers part of her/his profit. Once an imitation process is introduced among workers, these initially successful "professions" will spread among workers modifying the pool of human capital from which new entrepreneurs will draw their work-force. The ex-ante distribution of skills is hence modified and evolves "interactively" with the size distribution of firms. Certain regularities are pointed at and hypotheses formulated. Unanswered questions are left to the reader to be investigated.

5.   ACKNOWLEDGMENTS

This project was conceived in August 1998 when both editors were visiting the Santa Fe Institute as members of the "Working group on Adaptive and Computable Economics" organized and sponsored by Professor Axel Leijonhufvud. We would like to thank Professor Leijonhufvud for his continuous support. Professor Kumaraswamy Velupillai has always been prodigal of good advice and a source of inspiration. Dr. Christof Ruehl has given us encouragement during the preparation of the manuscript. Dr. Nicoletta Pireddu helped us with certain aspects of the editorial process. We would also like to acknowledge the effort made by all contributors who chose to sacrifice a good part of Summer 1999 to complete their work in time for the book to appear at the dawn of the new millennium. Our sincere thanks to Allard Winterink of Kluwer Academic Press for his precious help and gentle spur. Last but not least, we want to express our gratitude to Alessandro Perrone who contributed to this volume as author and as technical problem solver. His help with LaTeX was pivotal to all of us, and his work for the camera ready version of the manuscript made this project a finished product.

Notes

1. The code for *Swarm* as well as for all programs presented in this volume and many other contributions in different disciplines can be found at `www.santafe.edu/projects/swarm/` and downloaded free of any charge according to the GNU License

2. To avoid any misunderstanding in the rest of this introduction and volume, we will try to be precise about the use of the word "language". Clearly Swarm is **not** a *computer* language such as BASIC, FORTRAN, Objective C etc. When we say that Swarm may be proposed as a "common language," we imply a different, more general connotation of the word *language*: that of **semiotic code**.

3. We are grateful to Alessandro Perrone and Marcus Daniels for their comments on certain computer technicalities and to Kumaraswamy Velupillai for his comments on the computability issues touched in this introduction. All remaining imperfections are our responsibility

4. Hahn (1991), p.47

5. Ahrweiler and Gilbert (1998) offer a collection of papers on such a topic

6. For example Hudson (1996)

7. Yunker (1998)

8. Gupta, Stahl and Whinston (1997)

9. Jamal and Sunder (1996)

10. Moutinho (1994)

11. Grabowski and Vernon (1987)

12. A significant exception is given by Axtell and Epstein classic *Growing Artificial Societies* which has been "replicated" by many researchers in numerous simulating platforms. There exists also a Swarm version of their *SugarScape*

13. Tesfatsion (1997). For further details and a version of the code visit `www.econ.iastate.edu/tesfatsi/`

14. Bremer (1987)

15. Plambeck, Hope and Anderson(1997)

16. Preusse (1993)

17. Hagemeier (1993)

18. Marris (1991)

19. See Pinson and Wiener (1991), and `http://developer.apple.com/techpubs/macosxserver/ObjectiveC/index.html`

20. At the time of the writing, a version of Swarm with Java interface is under development. This will allow users to program Swarm simulations in Java, while the implementation of the libraries will not change.

21. All the more significant if we consider that, as K. Velupillai reminded us, one of the pillars of the origins of recursion thoery (and hence computability) was the quest for an answer to Hilbert's third question: decidability–the other ones being completeness and consistency. Answering the question about decidability required a definition of effective calculability.

22. The coded function may be partial so that for some input the computer may enter a loop

23. Without underestimating all complexity problems

24. Arguably Visual Basic is the most popular Object-Oriented computer language, but it has until recently not implemented some of the essential characteristics of Object-Orientation such as inheritance

25. For a precise definition and explanation of these concepts we suggest Pinson and Wiener (1991)

References

P. Ahrweiler and N. Gilbert, eds: 1998 'Computer Simulations in Science and technology Studies,' Springer Verlag, Heidelberg and New York.

S. Bremer ed.: 1987 'The GLOBUS model: Computer Simulation of Worldwide political and Economic Developments,' Westview Press, Boulder Colorado.

J.M. Epstein and R. Axtell: 1996 'Growing Artificial Societies', Brookings Institution Press and MIT Press. Cambridge, Massachusetts.

H.G. Grabowski and J.M. Vernon: 1987 "Pioneers, Imitators, and Generics–A Simulation Model of Schumpeterian Competition," Quarterly Journal of Economics, pp. 491-519.

A. Gupta, D. Stahl, and A. Whinston: 1997 "A Stochastic Equilibrium Model of Internet Pricing," Journal of Economic Dynamics and Control, 21, pp. 697-722.

H. Hagemeier: 1993 "The Computer-Simulation-Programme HasiG," in 'Cross Cultural Approaches to Home Management,' Foundation Der Private Haushalt Series n. 18, R. von-Schweitzer ed., pp. 165-176, Westview Press, Colorado.

F. Hahn: 1991 "The Next Hundred Years," Economic Journal, 101, pp. 47-50.

J. Hudson: 1996 "Bankruptcies, Firm Size and Unemployment: A Big Bank Theory of Economic Cycles," Small Business Economics, 8, pp. 379-388.

K. Jamal and S. Sunder: 1996 "Bayesian Equilibrium in Double Auctions Populated by Biased Heuristic Traders," Journal of Economic Behavior and Organization, 31, pp. 273-291.

R. Marris: 1991 'Reconstructing Keynesian Economics with Imperfect Competition: A Desk-top Simulation,' Elgar and United Nations University World Institute for Development Economics Research, Aldershot, U.K.

L. Moutinho et al.: 1994 'Computer Modelling and Expert Systems in Marketing,' Routledge Academic Press, London and New York.

L.J. Pinson and R.S. Wiener: 1991 'Objective-C. Object-Oriented Programming Techniques,' Addison-Wesley Publishing Company, Menlo Park, California.

E. Plambeck, C. Hope and J. Anderson: 1997 "The Page95 Model: Integrating the Science and Economics of Global Warming," Energy Economics, 19, 77-101.

H. Preusse: 1993 "The Computer-Simulation-Programme STRATHA: Household Simulation in the Family Life Span," in 'Cross Cultural Approaches to Home Management,' Foundation Der Private Haushalt Series n. 18, R. von-Schweitzer ed., pp. 144-164, Westview Press, Colorado.

L. Tesfatsion: 1997 "A Trade Network Game with Endogenous Partner Selection," in 'Computational Approaches to Economic Problems," H. Amman, et al. eds, Kluwer Academic Press, Dordrecht, the Netherlands.

J. Yunker: 1998 "Inheritance and Chance as Determinants of Capital Wealth Inequality," Journal of Post Keynesian Economics, 21, pp. 227-258.

To
Nicoletta,
Michele, Teresa,
Laura, Adriana

I
THE GRAMMAR

Chapter 1

SIMULATING ECONOMIC AGENTS IN SWARM

A short tutorial for economists and other social scientists

Benedikt Stefansson

Department of Economics, UCLA

1. INTRODUCTION

Markets for goods and services in modern economies are probably among the most complex dynamic systems which science has tried to analyze and model. It is well known that modern economics inherited a large share of its mathematical formalism and thus modeling apparatus from theoretical physics. This marriage is not always a happy one. Economic and social systems consist of agents which think and react. The elementary particles of matter do not observe, learn and influence each others decisions. Much is therefore lost in the translation from economic behavior to the mathematical language of modern economic theory.

Compared to mathematical models Agent Based Computational Models (ABCM) offer a more flexible method to study economic behavior in particular and social systems in general. In an ABCM each agent and other constituent parts of the economic or social system can be represented by algorithms and variables which define the artificial agent's behavior and record the evolution of his state over time. In some sense this approach lies between analytical modeling and empirical observation. The axioms and theorems of an analytical model usually lead to an unambiguous result, while scientists which work with ABCM must analyze the output of a simulation program to be able to reach a formal conclusion.

In would be quite premature to state that Agent Based Models now offer a clear alternative to traditional analytical modeling in economics. This area of research is still in its infancy. Most importantly a standard methodology has not developed, and practitioners differ in their focus and approach. One of the stumbling blocks in the development of a methodology and standard tool-box is the fact that practitioners must usually build their own tools from scratch. The number of programming languages, software packages and operating systems in use is almost as large as the number of modelers.

In 1995 the Santa Fe Institute in New Mexico launched the Swarm project with the objective to create a standard set of program libraries which could be used to simulate and analyze complex systems in the social and natural sciences. Dr. Chris Langton, the originator of the project, has said that the main motivation behind Swarm was to create a tool that would allow modelers to focus on their area of expertise rather than to spend time on writing software. The Swarm libraries should provide the elements which most Agent Based simulation programs have in common, and in particular the parts which non-programmers often find tedious to write, such as algorithms for graphical output and managing the user interface.

In short the Swarm software libraries allow users to construct simulations where a collection of heterogeneous independent agents or elements interact through discrete events. Any physical process or social system could potentially be simulated in Swarm, since it imposes no inherent constraints on the model world or patterns of interaction between model elements. Programs using Swarm have been developed in such diverse areas as biology, political science, economics, anthropology, chemistry and ecology.

Laboratory scientists usually conduct experiments with standard equipment, with characteristics known to other practitioners in the field. This standardization reduces the degrees of freedom and allows the experimenter to document his approach in a more precise yet compact form. Few papers in the natural sciences devote space to descriptions of the characteristics of standard equipment such as an oscilloscope or Bunsens burner.

In simulation programming however the situation is radically different. Like early astronomers hunting for stars on the firmament, modelers still "grind their own lenses" using home-grown solutions and tailor made algorithms. Although scientists may distribute program code, common repositories or libraries are seldom used in any systematic way to distribute shared methods and foster critical review. Even worse, individual solutions which often may influence model behavior in subtle ways are rarely documented in detail. In to many cases other scientists have no hope of being able to replicate experiments or carry the research further.

An additional aim of the Swarm project has therefore been to create a flexible but standardized collection of lower level tools and routines, so researchers can base their simulations on components which have been tested under different conditions and are known by other experimenters in the field. The base libraries are general purpose, but practitioners in individual fields of research can take these building blocks and construct higher level libraries which fit particular problem domains.

All components of Swarm and the code libraries they are based on is freely available under the GNU Library Public License[1] These components have already been implemented on a variety of different computer platforms and the code tested by numerous programmers. The documentation and replication of simulations based on the Swarm libraries should thus be a simpler task than with home grown solutions. Scientists can be certain that the work they build on has been studied by a wide audience and will remain accessible and in the public domain.

2.   WHAT SWARM PROVIDES

In short Swarm is a collection of objects which the programmer can use as building blocks and incorporate into his own programs. The starting point for a Swarm simulation is usually a collection of agents, each serving as a prototype (class) for a number of individuals (instances) which will populate the model world. To construct a working simulation we add various objects from the Swarm libraries.

The most important parts of the Swarm libraries which we will focus on in this tutorial are objects which manage the creation and destruction of objects, classes which keep track of a collection of objects, grids and lattices, a library which allows us to manage model events in an OOP framework and finally a number of Graphical User Interface (GUI) classes, including raster images and graphs. A more comprehensive list of the libraries follows:

defobj Root of the class hierarchy in the Swarm libraries. Defines basic creation and destruction methods for objects. Also provides classes which can archive (serialize) instances of objects and create instances based on data in different formats.

objectbase Defines two base classes, SwarmObject and Swarm. The former can be used to subclass agents which have the ability to be "probed" both through the GUI and internally in the program. The latter class can be used to subclass objects which manage the creation and destruction of agent populations and control the execution of events in the simulation.

activity Allows the programmer to create data structures which schedule events in the simulation and update the GUI. Events in the model and the user interface can be defined in separate schedules and merged to create a coherent whole.

collections Manages collections of objects, as arrays, lists or maps with an associated key (hash). Methods in these classes allow the user to send a message to all members of a collection, delete or add members, sort or shuffle the collection and iterate over a collection or retrieve individual members.

space Defines classes which allow us to store and retrieve either data or objects from a discrete 2d lattice. Provides classes which can apply algorithms to spatial data, read data from files and handle events in a user interface.

gui Classes which allow the creation of raster images, line graphs and histograms in addition to creating composite widgets for a user interface and respond to user interaction with the GUI.

analysis Provides 'wrapper' classes for an easier creation of line graphs of time series data and histograms. Also automates the task of collecting information and updating output on graphs or histograms dynamically while the simulation is running.

random An Object-Oriented library of random number generators and statistical distributions based on streams of pseudo-random numbers. Implements a number of algorithms for generating pseudo-random numbers and major statistical distributions, such as uniform, gamma, beta and Gaussian. Users can explicitly set and save state of random number generators to replicate simulation runs.

simtools Provides tools to 'load' objects from or 'save' objects to an ASCII file, also provides classes to read strings and numbers from files or print to files in OO framework.

As this listing indicates the Swarm libraries are too large to describe in detail in a beginner's tutorial. To enhance the usefulness of the tutorial the reader should try to keep the Swarm documentation set at hand and refer to it for further information on each class mentioned in the text, and also the many classes that we do not describe here. The documentation set is distributed with the Swarm software and freely available for download from the Swarm website. It is available both as a set of web pages (HTML) which can be read in a browser, such as Netscape Communicator or Microsoft Explorer or in various formats for creating a printed copy such as PostScript or DVI. The HTML version is in many ways more useful since it is extensively indexed and 'hyperlinked'.

In addition it might be a good idea to keep a reference work on the C language handy, and any decent university library should have at least a half-dozen books on this popular programming language. Objective-C is fortunately a very simple extension to basic C syntax. Books on it are therefore hard to find, but the main reference is actually available for free on the web from the Apple Inc. website. URLs for some resources are listed in the appendix.

3.   OBJECT ORIENTED PROGRAMMING

The principles of Object Oriented Programming (OOP) and the fundamental ideas that motivate work with Agent Based Computational Models (ABCM) are quite compatible. To implement an ABCM in an OOP language is probably easier than to write a similar model in a more traditional functional language such as Pascal or FORTRAN.

An agent in an agent-based model may be defined as an autonomous entity which is capable of interacting with other agents based on its own state and rules of behavior. In OOP an object is a data-structure containing variables, which register the state of the object, and functions which define the object's behavior. The functions - usually referred to as methods - contain instructions which describe how the object should react to changes in its state, respond to input or communicate with other objects.

A program written in an OOP language is simply a set of object definitions and rules which determine how the objects will interact. In practical terms, a programmer stores object definitions in text files which define both state (instance variables) and functions (methods) which determine the object's behavior. These text files, which are written in a humanly readable programming language, must then be translated by a compiler into machine instructions which can be executed by the computer's microprocessor.

At this point it is helpful to introduce some more specific terminology. Instead of the generic term 'object' we usually refer to the definitions of variables and messages, as a 'class'.[2] When a program is run and the computer allocates space in the Random Access Memory (RAM) for an object's variables and methods, we refer to each individual copy of the class as an 'instance'. Instances of a class only share the specification of variables and methods but do not share the same memory space. These objects are thus analogous to heterogeneous agents of a given type, which may over time diverge as they experience different histories.

Another fundamental concept in OOP is inheritance. Since the first programming languages were implemented programmers have incorporated previously written code into their programs. When a program contains an instruction to print output to the screen or to add two numbers, the compiler or interpreter which translate the programmer's instructions into machine code often substitute algorithms from programming libraries with the instructions to carry out the given operation. Inheritance in OOP takes this idea one step further. A class may inherit all variables and behavior from another class, thus saving the programmer the work of replicating instructions and variables while enhancing the class by adding new functionality. We refer to the class inherited from as the 'superclass' while the class which inherits these features is referred to as a 'subclass'. Inheritance can give rise to a virtual family-tree of super- and subclasses.

3.1   ON OBJECTIVE-C

The design of Objective-C was influenced by Smalltalk, one of the earliest and yet most powerful OOP languages. It is therefore a very clean and accessible implementation of the OOP paradigm. Objective-C is a superset of the C programming language, which enables the programmer to define classes and send messages to classes or instances, but it adds no new keywords to basic C. In addition to defining several macros which are interpreted by the preprocessor and compiler, Objective-C provides a couple of new variable types, most importantly the generic object type `id`.

The definition of a class in Objective-C consists of two files, the interface and the implementation. These files should carry the .h and .m extension respectively. It is a good idea to name the files associated with a class by the name given to the class. A class called `Agent` would thus be defined in the files `Agent.h` and `Agent.m`.

The interface declares the superclass of the given class, its instance variables and the methods which it implements. The implementation provides the code for each of the methods defined in the interface. Listing (1) shows the interface and implementation of a simple agent which knows its own 'name' and responds to a message `sayHelloTo:` by calling its argument and printing out hello followed by the callers name, which is retrieved by calling the method `get_name` on the caller.

As the listing shows the interface starts by importing header files for the superclass of the class being declared. The interface then starts with the `@interface` macro followed by a colon and the name of the object's superclass, which in this case is `SwarmObject`. This is followed by curly

Listing 1 Interface and implementation of simple agent

```
#import <objectbase.h>
#import <objectbase/SwarmObject.h>

@interface Agent: SwarmObject
{
  char * name;
}
- set_name: (char *) n;
- sayHelloTo: o;
- (char *) get_name;
@end

#import "Agent.h"

@implementation Agent

- set_name: (char *) n
{
  name = strdup(n);
  return self;
}

- sayHelloTo: o
{
  printf("Hello %s\n",[other get_name]);
  return self;
}

- (char *) get_name
{
  return name;
}
@end
```

brackets which delimit the list of instance variable declarations. As in standard C variables are declared by giving the variable type followed by the variable name. In this case the class defines one new instance variable, a pointer to a string called name. Finally there are the declarations of the methods which the class will implement. The file ends with the @end macro.

A method name can be any arbitrary string, followed by a colon, the variable type of the argument and the variable name that will be associated with the argument. If the method returns a pointer to an object - i.e. a variable of the type id - no return type needs to be declared for the method. Two of the three methods shown in listing (1) return id and thus their names start with a dash. The third method returns a pointer to a string and thus starts with - (char *). An Objective-C method can of course take any arbitrary number of arguments. Compare the declaration of a C function which takes three arguments and returns an integer and the equivalent Objective-C method:

```
// Declaration of a C function
(int)something(int a1, double a2, char * a3);

// Declaration of equivalent Objective-C method
-(int)something: (int)a1 with: (double)a2 and: (char *)a3;
```

The listing also shows the implementation of the Agent. This file imports the header file or interface and defines each method. It starts with the @implementation macro and ends with the @end macro.

The implementation of the sayHelloTo: method then shows how we call methods in Objective-C. The name of the target followed by the method name and its arguments is enclosed in square brackets. Again compare how we call a C function and the equivalent Objective-C method:

```
// Calling the C function
x = something(1,2.0,"Three");

// Calling the Objective-C method
x = [object something: 1 with: 2.0 and: "Three"];
```

Objective-C also supports protocols, which are in essence interfaces which can be implemented by more than one class. Although the two types of declarations are similar, protocols serve a different purpose than interfaces. A protocol file looks almost exactly like an interface, except that it starts with the @protocol macro (with no superclass attached) and only defines the types of messages which a class responds to but does not declare variables. A class can also declare that it supports more than one protocol. The purpose of this is to allow the compiler to verify at compile-time which types of objects are being created and the messages that they respond to. The reader will notice that Swarm code often contains variable declarations such as this:

```
id <SomeProtocol> anObject;
```

This declaration of variable `anObject` simply means that the instance associated with this variable implements `SomeProtocol`. The following line in the interface declares that the class `SomeClass` is a subclass of `SwarmObject` and also implements all the methods declared in `SomeProtocol`:

```
@interface SomeClass: SwarmObject <SomeProtocol>
```

There is really little more to say about Objective-C syntax. The strength of the language is its simplicity. This is also the main reason why so few textbooks about Objective-C have been published.

Considering the easy learning-curve it is in fact somewhat puzzling why Objective-C has remained less popular than its sibling C++ which has become one of the most popular programming languages in current use. This seems to be mostly a question of historical accident, another example of the infamous path dependence which permeates the software and computer industries.

Objective-C was chosen by the Swarm project for the main reason that it would have been much harder to implement the libraries in another language such as C++. In particular, much of the code in Swarm is based on the principle of late-binding, i.e. the class of an object which will be targeted by a message will sometimes not be known until at runtime. Objective-C is very flexible in this respect, while C++ requires rigorous typing of objects and variables at compile time. In addition Objective-C allows methods and their arguments to be handled as data, which is a fundamental feature required by some of the main libraries in Swarm such as `activity` and probes.[3]

4.   ABOUT THIS TUTORIAL

Programming, like most things, is best learned by practice. This chapter is not a generic introduction to Swarm, nor a detailed manual of the libraries. Instead it develops a series of models, and discusses the most important features of Swarm im terms of how the simulation utilizes the libraries. We hope that readers can learn from these examples and will practice programming with the Swarm libraries by modifying and tailoring the programs to their own ends. While the particular models presented here may interest some readers more than others, the code is fairly representative of a typical Swarm simulation and should suggest some interesting exercises and experiments.

The tutorial is based on simple and well documented models from the game theory literature, the Prisoner's Dilemma (PD) and the Iterated Prisoner's Dilemma (IPD). We will start by developing a very basic version of the PD model, followed by a basic version of the IPD. We then develop different versions of the IPD where agents either interact randomly in a 'soup' or where they live on a 2d grid. These examples show how one can easily implement an Evolutionary Algorithm or implement different 'topologies' of interaction.

Each of the following sections is intended to illustrate a particular important feature of the Swarm libraries. The following listing describes the features discussed in each section or subsection:

The base model: Creating simple classes A player class is created and a `main` function used to create two instances and run a game between the two players. Shows the basic steps needed to create an instance of a class based on the Swarm libraries.

Random: Generating random numbers Discusses the various random number generators and statistical distributions implemented in Swarm.

Swarms and Zones: Creation and death Implements an Iterated Prisoner's Dilemma. Shows the use of the `Swarm` class and `Zone` to control the creation and destruction of objects.

Collections: Managing groups of agents Develops a model where an Evolutionary Algorithm is applied to a population of players which engage in an IPD and propagate their strategy based on level of payoffs. Shows how the `collection` library and features of the `Swarm` class enable the programmer to handle collections of agents and other objects.

ObjectLoader and InFile: Reading parameters from file These two classes can be used to instantiate objects or set parameters based on information contained in an ASCII file.

Space and GUI: Grids, images and graphs Develops a version of the evolutionary IPD where players live on a grid and interact with their neighbors. Players imitate the neighbor with the highest payoff by adopting his strategy. Shows how the `space` library can be used to manage objects on a lattice and how the `gui` and `analysis` libraries can be used to create graphical representations of data.

Activity: Scheduling events and actions Continues the discussion of the spatial IPD. Shows how one can separate the objects in the GUI from the model, and how the `activity` library and the `Swarm` and `GUISwarm` classes are used to control the execution of events in the model and GUI.

Probes: Interacting with agents Builds on the spatial IPD from the previous sections and shows how to add code which provides means to probe agents on the grid or to change parameters in the model during execution.

4.1 A NOTE ON STYLE

The code examples presented in the text only represent a fraction of the programming code which is needed to implement the models. This is due to obvious space constraints, printing the listing for the entire code is impractical. The reader is however urged to download the code for the examples and to keep it at hand while reading the text. The programs can be obtained at the Swarm website, please see the appendix to this chapter for further details.

It should be noted that in many cases when the text refers to the code for a particular method only the body of the method is actually shown. This means that the method prototype or interface is not reproduced, nor the declarations of local variables.

5. THE BASE MODEL AND CLASSES

In the first example of this tutorial we will construct a program with two agents which play a standard Prisoner's Dilemma (PD) game. The object of the simulation is to find the equilibrium of the game; this by definition is a strategy for both players which satisfies the condition that neither player would want to deviate. In the simulation each player is assumed to know the payoff matrix but not his opponent's strategy. Players select a random strategy and then each agent checks if another strategy would increase his payoff. Once both players are satisfied the simulation stops. The simulation always converges in two steps or less.

The Prisoner's Dilemma is of course widely discussed in the game theory literature. Many books provide a more rigorous introduction to the model and provide examples of simulations of the Iterated Prisoner's Dilemma (Axelrod, 1984; Grim et al., 1998). For a history of the game and a discussion of its implications see Poundstone,1992.

At each stage game either of two players - the prisoners - choose an action a_i which can be either 'cooperate' (C) or 'defect' (D). Payoffs are structured such that for any action $a_j \in \{C, D\}$ by a fellow prisoner a player has an incentive to defect $(a_i = D)$, while if a prisoner could be certain that the other would cooperate he would also cooperate $(a_i = C)$ and both would be better off. The dilemma is that if both players expect the other player to act rationally and believe that the other player expects them to be rational, they will both be forced to defect and thus

Figure 1.1   Payoffs in the Prisoner's Dilemma game

	C	D		C	D
C	R, R	S, T	C	$3, 3$	$0, 5$
D	T, S	P, P	D	$5, 0$	$1, 1$

end up in a mutually disagreeable situation. Rationality and beliefs about rational behavior force the agents to end up in a suboptimal state.

The 2×2 payoff matrix which defines the utility which each player stands to gain for each strategy by himself and the other player is defined as in table (1.1). These payoffs must satisfy the following relationship: $T > R > P > S$ and $2R > T + S$. In the simulations presented below we will use standard numerical payoffs used widely in the literature, also shown in table (1.1).

The first example simulation uses the base libraries of Swarm, features of the defobj and the objectbase classes which may be considered the 'root classes' in the Swarm libraries.

The defobj class provides basic memory management for the creation and destruction of object instances, while the SwarmObject class provides the ability to 'probe' instance variables and methods. We will discuss probes at a later stage. In addition we will use instances of a random number generator and classes which provide uniformly distributed random numbers both from the random library. To implement the model in its simplest form we simply need to create a main function and write two classes, Prisoner which represents the players and Payoff which represents the payoff matrix.

5.1   PRISONER CLASS

The Prisoner class defines three instance variables and responds to five messages, in addition to variables and methods it inherits from its superclass, SwarmObject. The header file is shown in (2).

The initial: method returns the initial random move by the player and is implemented as follows:

```
- (int) initial
{
    move = [uniformIntRand getIntegerWithMin: 0 withMax: 1];
    return move;
```

Listing 2 Interface for the Prisoner class

```
@interface Prisoner: SwarmObject
{
  id  payoffs;
  double payoff;
  int move;
}
- reset;
- set_payoffs: p;
- (int) initial;
- (int) move: (int) o;
- (double) get_payoff;

@end
```

```
}
```

In this case we call on the object uniformIntRand which is an instance of the UniformInteger class, in the Swarm random library. The library contains about two dozen different random number generators which represent some of the most widely discussed and documented random number generators in the scientific literature on pseudo-random number generation. In addition the library provides classes which map a stream of random numbers coming from the generators into a specific distribution, such as the uniform, Gaussian and gamma distribution. The instances of the generator and distributions used here are created by calling a function initSwarmBatch() in the main.m function, which is discussed below. The UniformInteger instance is fed pseudo-random values generated by the random number generator and the object returns integer values with uniform probability from a given interval. In the code example the integer variable move can only take the value zero or one.

The move: method takes a move by the opponent (the other prisoner) as argument and returns a new move by the player, which has the choice of either sticking to his previous move or to change to the other available action. It is implemented as follows:

```
- (int) move: (int) o
{
  payoff += (double)[payoffs me: move other: o];

  if([payoffs me:  move other: o] <
     [payoffs me: !move other: o])
```

Listing 3 Interface for the Payoffs class

```
@interface Payoffs: SwarmObject
{
  int payoffs[2][2];
}
- createEnd;
- (int) me:(int) m other: (int) o;
```

```
    move = !move;

  return move;
}
```

The player here sends two messages to the `payoffs` object. It compares the payoff value of its previous move against the value of taking the opposite action. Since choice in this game is binary we can use the value for `!move` or 'not move' to indicate the opposite choice.[4]

The `Payoff` class is a type of utility or 'wrapper' class, which simply maps some functionality necessary for the simulation model to the OO paradigm. In this case we would like to be able to pass the payoff matrix around in the form of an object which can respond to simple messages about payoffs for different actions. This also ensures that payoff information is consistent across agents, since it is specified in one place which reduces the risk of errors.

The interface for the `Payoffs` class is shown in listing (3). The class overrides the `createEnd` method which is defined in `SwarmObject`, in order to set the payoff values for each element in the matrix. The only new method implemented is the `me:other:` method, which takes two arguments, action by a player and by his opponent and returns the payoff as an integer value.

The remaining element in this example program is the `main` function, which creates the agents and carries out the simulation. Listing (4) shows both the creation phase in the `main` function and the simulation itself. Here we start by calling a function from the Swarm libraries, `initSwarmBatch()` which takes as arguments command line arguments that the user may have passed to the program and processes them[5] In addition the function creates 'memory zone' objects which will be useful in allocating memory for objects used in the simulation, and initializes a random number generator and three objects which return uniform random numbers, respectively as doubles, integers or unsigned values.

5.2   AN ASIDE ABOUT CREATING OBJECTS

Swarm uses 'memory zones' to allocate space in the computer's memory for instances of classes. In fact Swarm overrides the memory allocation mechanism in Objective-C and defines methods in the defobj and objectbase classes which determine how instances are allocated, instantiated and made ready for use. The creation process is in fact divided into two parts, a beginning and an end. In most of the code examples presented here we will see objects created like this:

```
object = [SomeClass create: aZone];
```

This means that the instance object of SomeClass will request memory from the memory zone aZone. In some cases however we will see this:

```
object = [SomeClass createBegin: aZone];
[object set_some_parameter: value];
object = [object createEnd];
```

In this case the class can not create a functional instance without setting the parameter some_parameter. Hence the class restricts the programmer to calling a createBegin: method for the class, then set the parameter for the instance and finally call the createEnd method for the instance to return a usable object. As a matter of fact the create: method in the defobj superclasses is implemented by first calling createBegin: and then createEnd. This means that the following two ways of creating an instance are equivalent:

```
\\ Use create:
object = [SomeClass create: aZone];

\\ Use createBegin: and createEnd
object = [SomeClass createBegin: aZone];
object = [object createEnd];
```

In general when writing new subclasses of defobj or objectbase the programmer only needs to implement a createBegin: or createEnd method when some parameters need to be processed before the instance is used. To see an example of this look at the code for ModelSwarm in the next section of the tutorial. Also keep in mind that createBegin: is a class method instead of an instance method, and the prototype of the method is thus +createBegin instead of -createBegin. This is probably the only time that you will have to make a distinction between class methods and instance methods, so this issue does not warrant a detailed discussion. The Objective-C manual (see appendix to this chapter) provides further details.

5.3   THE MODEL LOOP

The second part of the main function retrieves the actions of the two prisoners and enters into a loop until the players have reached equilibrium. The logic applied in the algorithm is that an equilibrium is any choice by both players which satisfies the criteria that neither player wants to deviate. Hence we ask the players for their first choice, which they pick at random as shown above. We then ask both players to respond to the choice made by the other player - if both players stick with their earlier decision then their strategies are in equilibrium. If either player wants to deviate we ask again and so on until the criterion is satisfied.

5.4   RANDOM: GENERATING RANDOM NUMBERS

The Swarm random library is one of the most useful parts of the system. The library consists of classes which generate streams of pseudo-random numbers, called generators and classes which take these numbers and return distributions of values with a certain statistical property.

The libraries define dozens of generators which are based on some of the most popular algorithms from the literature on pseudo-random number generations. The user can choose to create and use an instance of one of these classes, or use an instance of the MT19937 class which is generated in the background when the the initSwarm() function is run in main.m as we have discussed before. This generator is based on the algorithm presented in Matsumoto and Kurita, 1998, which currently offers the longest period of any published pseudo-random algorithm.

An instance of a random number generator can be created as any other object in Swarm. The following message creates an instance of the MT19937 generator and sets the random seed to be 49:

```
generator = [MT19937 create: aZone setStateFromSeed: 49];
```

The seed is an unsigned (positive) integer (hence any integer between 0 and 2^{31} or $2,147,483,647$ to be exact, at least on most microcomputers which allocate 32 bits for an integer, leaving one bit for the sign). It primes the generator and since the algorithm is deterministic it will always generate the same sequence of random numbers. The sequence can thus be recreated by setting the same random number seed and

Listing 4 The `main.m` from pd-simple

```
// Call initSwarm() to process command line
// switches, allocate memory zone support
// and create random number support objects
initSwarmBatch(argc,argv);

// Create object to hold payoff matrix
payoffs    = [Payoffs createBegin: globalZone];
payoffs    = [payoffs createEnd];

// Create prisoners
prisoner1 = [Prisoner create: globalZone];
[prisoner1 set_payoffs: payoffs];

prisoner2 = [Prisoner create: globalZone];
[prisoner2 set_payoffs: payoffs];

// Get initial move by each prisoner
init_1 = [prisoner1 initial];
init_2 = [prisoner2 initial];

// See if these are equilibrium
move_1 = [prisoner1 move: init_2];
move_2 = [prisoner2 move: init_1];

printf("Initial play:        (%d,%d)\n",init_1,init_2);

// If not keep on looking
while((init_1!=move_1) || (init_2!=move_2))
  {
    init_1 = move_1;
    init_2 = move_2;
    move_1 = [prisoner1 move: init_2];
    move_2 = [prisoner2 move: init_1];
    printf("Play:                (%d,%d)\n",move_1,move_2);
  }

// Exiting while() must mean equilibrium is found
printf("Equilibrium found at (%d,%d)\n",move_1,move_2);

return 0;
```

replicating all calls to the generator. This is a very important point: If the programmer uses the same random number generator to generate all random numbers in the simulation the entire run can be replicated by setting the random number seed.

As noted above a `MT19937` generator instance is already revved up by the Swarm machinery and ready to go. The programmer can call this generator referring to the instance name which is a global variable: `randomGenerator`. By default it uses the same random number seed every time, hence if the programmer does not prime it the simulation will always produce the same result (absent any intervention by the user which changes the course of the model).

The user can also run the simulation using the -s option on the command line, as in `progname -s`. The software will then generate a fresh random number seed. This means that results may be different every time the program is run with the switch, but the user will not have any record of the random number seed and thus no possibility of replicating the run. To control the seed used by the `randomGenerator` instance put this statement in `main.m` immediately after calling `initSwarm()`:

```
[randomGenerator setStateFromSeed: 49];
```

Of course you can substitute any positive integer less than or equal to 2^{31} for the seed.

The second part of the random number library are the distributions. Each distribution takes a sequence of pseudo-random numbers from one of the generators and returns values with a particular property. In this example we create an instance of the NormalDist class which uses the `randomGenerator`:

```
normal=[NormalDist create:zone setGenerator:randomGenerator];
```

To fetch a random value with $\mu = 0.0, \sigma^2 = 1.0$ we would write:

```
value = [normal getSampleWithMean: 0.0 withVariance: 1.0];
```

The following list describes the distributions and gives the methods which return the random values:

BernoulliDist Method `getSampleWithProbability`: returns 1 with given probability.

BooleanDistribution Method `getBooleanSample` returns zero or one with even probability.

ExponentialDistribution Method `getSampleWithMean`: returns exponentially distributed samples with given mean.

GammaDist The `getSampleWithAlpha:withBeta:` method returns a sample value from a Gamma distribution with the specified alpha and beta values.

LogNormalDist To retrieve double-precision floating point values from this distribution call `getSampleWithMean:withVariance:` with specific mean,variance.

NormalDist To retrieve double-precision floating point values from this distribution call `getSampleWithMean:withVariance:`

UniformDoubleDist The `getDoubleWithMin:withMax:` method returns a double-precision floating point number in the interval with uniform probability.

UniformIntegerDist The `getIntegerWithMin:withMax:` method returns an integer in the interval with uniform probability.

UniformUnsignedDist A `getUnsignedWithMin:withMax:` method returns an unsigned integer in the interval with uniform probability.

The random number library also gives users a number of options to prime and control the generators; in addition the complete state of generators can be saved to disk and loaded from file. For further information please refer to the extensive documentation for this library.

6.   SWARMS AND ZONES: CREATION AND DEATH

In laboratory science an experiment consists of the phenomenon being observed and separate instruments to record measurements. The 'design philosophy' behind Swarm is to provide a similar structure for simulation programs, to separate the model from the objects which allow us to observe it.

In this second variant of the PD model we will add a third class to the simulation: the `ModelSwarm`. This class will take over the responsibility of creating instances of agents and running the experiment. Shortly we will also introduce an `ObserverSwarm` which will manage objects which handle graphical display of data and record information. By separating the two 'Swarms' we are able to make changes to either the model code or the output code without affecting the other.

Until now we have created the components of the model in the body of `main`. One of the advantages of using a separate class to create objects and run the model is that the Swarm libraries provide convenience methods to manage object memory allocation and deallocation.

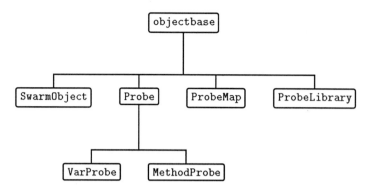

Figure 1.2 Some important classes in the `objectbase` library, not including `Swarm` which implements protocols from several libraries.

In the first example described above we saw how each object was created in the `globalZone` which was created by default when the function `initSwarmBatch()` was called. What this means in practice is that each class which is being instantiated requests memory space in the computer's Random Access Memory (RAM) from the object `globalZone` which is an instance of the `Zone` class in the `objectbase` library. This memory allocation is transparent to the user. The `Zone` instance also keeps a list of all the objects for which it has allocated memory, thus the memory zone can also manage the reverse operation of deallocating memory.[6]

The `ModelSwarm` class which we will introduce shortly will be a subclass of the `Swarm` class which inherits all the features of `Zone`, in addition to providing other functionality. It should be noted however that a `Swarm` is not a subclass of `Zone`. Creating an instance of `Swarm` also creates a special `Zone` where model components can be allocated. The upshot of this is that after an experiment has been created with all its constituent objects and components it can as easily be erased from memory - or 'dropped'. The programmer simply needs to send a `drop` message to `ModelSwarm` which will reclaim the memory allocated to all the model components and wipe the slate clean for the next experiment. This gives the programmer a very simple and intuitive method to create several different experiments or to generate different model scenarios based on changes in some condition or set of parameters.

In this section we will implement an 'Iterated Prisoner's Dilemma' game, where each pair of agents plays the stage game more than once. Strategy in this case no longer consists of a single action, but an 'action profile' which is contingent on what the players have done in the past. More specifically a strategy is given by three parameters, i, p and q.

Table 1.1 Typical strategies with one-step memory.

Name	i	p	q
All-C	1	1	1
Tit-For-Tat	1	1	0
Anti-Tit-For-Tat	0	0	1
All-D	0	0	0

Here $i \in (0, 1)$ gives the probability of cooperation on the first iteration of the stage game, while $p, q \in (0, 1)$ are the probability that the player cooperates after his opponent has cooperated and defected, respectively. This strategy thus retains a one-step memory.

If we restrict the probability of cooperation to be either zero or one the strategy space is reduced to eight different types. Of these eight strategies the four types shown in table (1.1) are widely discussed in the literature on the IPD.

6.1   PRISONER

To be able to initialize the Prisoner instances with different parameter settings we will need to make small changes in the implementation of the Prisoner class. In particular we will add a new method and corresponding instance variables to set the three parameters, i, p, q. In addition we will change the implementation of the initial| and move methods. The implementation of both the initial and move: methods is quite straightforward. As shown in listing (5) in each case we flip a coin and decide whether to cooperate or defect depending on the initial probability or contingent probabilities of cooperation.

Although the switch() block is verbose the code should be fairly transparent even to the casual reader. Note the use of the constants 'C' and 'D' which are defined as 1 and 0 respectively, but are used here to increase the legibility of the code. The code takes into consideration that i, p, q are probabilities and thus that cooperation or defection are contingent on the flip of a coin. In the model shown we restrict these two parameters to take either the value zero or one.

Listing 5 Prisoner's `initial` and `move:` methods in IPD

```
- (int) initial
{

  // Flip a coin to decide
  if([uniformDblRand getDoubleWithMin: 0.0 withMax: 1.0] < i)
      move = C;
  else
      move = D;

  return move;
}

- (int) move: (int) o
{
    // Record payoff
  payoff += (double)[payoffs me: move other: o];

  // Choose next move based on coin
  switch(o)
    {
    case C:
      if([uniformDblRand getDoubleWithMin: 0.0
                                 withMax: 1.0] < p)
        move = C;
      else
        move = D;
      break;
    case D:
      if([uniformDblRand getDoubleWithMin: 0.0
                                 withMax: 1.0] < q)
        move = C;
      else
        move = D;
      break;
    }

  return move;

}
```

6.2   MODELSWARM

To implement the model we start by delegating most of the operations previously carried out by the `main.m` to the `ModelSwarm` class which has the interface shown in listing (6).

Listing 6 Interface for ModelSwarm class

```
@interface ModelSwarm: Swarm
{
  id payoffs;
  id prisoner1;
  id prisoner2;
}

- buildObjects;
- run;
- toBinary: (int) n in: (int *) s;

@end
```

Here the `buildObjects` method simply replicates the creation phase in the `main.m` from the simple model above. As discussed above `ModelSwarm` also has the functionality of a `Zone` and thus the objects are now no longer created in `globalZone` but in the Swarm itself, as is shown in the following lines from the `buildObjects` method.

```
prisoner1  = [Prisoner create: self];
prisoner2  = [Prisoner create: self];
[prisoner1 set_payoffs: payoffs];
[prisoner2 set_payoffs: payoffs];
```

The `run` method contains the code necessary to run the model. The simulation consists of matching all possible combinations of the eight possible prisoner types. Since the three parameters i, p, q are binary there are only 2^3 different combinations of these parameters, and thus 64 combinations of players. We create a utility method `toBinary:in:` which allows us to map from the space of integers $(0, \ldots, 7)$ to the space of binary strings. Listing (7) shows the implementation of the `run` method.

The code consists of two nested loops, which iterate over the eight possible types for each player. A call to the `toBinary:in:` method returns the arrays `s1` and `s2` which contain the values for i, p, q for player 1 and 2 respectively. We next 'reset' the player objects and set the new parameters, thus cancelling the accumulated payoff and readying the

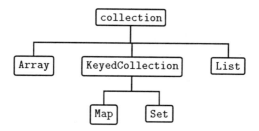

Figure 1.3 Some important classes in the `collection` library

object for the next round. Play proceeds in steps similar to the ones seen in the simple PD example above, players make the first move based in the parameter i and then interact three more times, each time based on the history of play and their type. Not shown are `printf()` statements in the code which output a report on the history of this interaction, and the accumulated payoff by each type.

7.   COLLECTIONS: MANAGING GROUPS OF AGENTS

We now have the setup for creating a model which involves a population, i.e. more than two agents. In particular we will now create a model in which a simple Evolutionary Algorithm (EA) is used to evolve a population of heterogeneous `Prisoners`. Prisoners will play the four iteration IPD with an opponent chosen at random from the population. In each match the prisoner who earns a higher payoff will pass his strategy to an offspring in the next generation with a high probability. This selection pressure along with the particular matching procedure will lead some strategies to gain a larger number of adherents in the population.

The model will consist of two 'loops', the outer loop which will iterate over generations of agents and the inner loop which matches one agent against another in random order. After each pair of agents has played the IPD which was developed in the previous section, the winner, i.e. the agent which received a higher payoff, is cloned and injected into the new generation. By setting the parameter `selectionPressure` to a value less than unity the looser gets cloned with positive probability. When the tournament is finished the old generation is erased and the next generation brought to play.

The model will only run the outer loop. A new class `GenerationSwarm` will run the inner loop. We therefore migrate most of the code from the run method in the model to the new swarm.

In this evolutionary version of the IPD we need a simple method to clone agents. Since the only feature of the players which needs to be

Listing 7 ModelSwarm run method

```
for(i = 0; i < 8; i ++)
 {
 for(j = 0; j < 8; i++)
  {
   // Convert integer values to binary strings
   [self toBinary: i in: s1];
   [self toBinary: j in: s2];

   // Reset player types
   [prisoner1 reset];
   [prisoner2 reset];
   [prisoner1 set_i: s1[0]
                 p: (double)s1[1]
                 q: (double)s1[2]];
   [prisoner2 set_i: s2[0]
                 p: (double)s2[1]
                 q: (double)s2[2]];
   // Get initial moves
   move_1 = [prisoner1 initial];
   move_2 = [prisoner2 initial];

   // Get moves on remaining steps
   for(k = 1; k < NUM_STEPS; k++)
     {
        init_1 = move_1;
        init_2 = move_2;
        move_1 = [prisoner1 move: init_2];
        move_2 = [prisoner2 move: init_1];
     }
   // Add payoff for last round
   [prisoner1 set_payoff:
[prisoner1 get_payoff] +
        [payoffs me: move_1 other: move_2]];
   [prisoner2 set_payoff:
[prisoner2 get_payoff] +
        [payoffs me: move_2 other: move_1]];
 }
}
```

replicated is the strategy it makes sense to break the player into two parts, the object which interacts with the environment and receives the payoff and an object which represents the strategy and can be copied from one agent to another.

We thus migrate the code representing the strategy from the `Prisoner` class to a new class titled `Strategy`. A strategy instance becomes an instance variable of a `Prisoner` and the player simply sends a message to the strategy to request the next move contingent on his opponents play. In fact while we will create n instances of `Prisoner` which will be replaced by a new set of n objects in each new generation, we only need to create one instance of `Strategy` for each different strategy type which is assumed to exist in the population. Players inherit their ancestor's strategy by simply setting the instance variable strategy to the same value as in their parent.

In the `buildObjects:` in `ModelSwarm` method we create the first generation of agents and the first instance of `GenerationSwarm`.

7.1   OBJECTLOADER AND INFILE: SETTING PARAMETERS FROM FILE

A new feature from the Swarm libraries which we will use in this example is the ability to read instance variable settings for class instances from a simple text file. This feature is provided by a class called `ObjectLoader` in the `simtools` library. The `ObjectLoader` is only one of many classes in the libraries which provide the programmer with means to instantiate object instances by reading in data from a file or even from a different process or communication link. While the other implementations are actually somewhat more sophisticated we will use `ObjectLoader` in these examples because it is based on a very simple file format which is easy to explain and understand.

In the code shown in listing (8) we use `ObjectLoader` in two different contexts. First we read the simulation parameters, which are instance variables in the `ModelSwarm` from a file, using the `load:fromFileNamed:` method in `ObjectLoader`. Note that we do not need to create an instance of the class, but simply call the class itself. This is an example of a so-called 'class method' which can be invoked without the creation of a class instance.

The second example of the use of `ObjectLoader` occurs within the loop where the instance variables for each instance of the `Strategy` class are read from a file. In this case we have stored the settings for each of the four varieties created in one file. This requires us to use the `load:from:` method in `ObjectLoader` which takes as a second argument an `InFile` ob-

Listing 8 ModelSwarm buildObjects method

```
// Load parameters from file
[ObjectLoader load: self fromFileNamed: "model.setup"];

// Create object to hold payoff matrix
payoffs = [Payoffs createBegin: self];
payoffs = [payoffs createEnd];

// Create Swarm for first generation
currentGeneration  = [GenerationSwarm create: self];

// Open the file to read in strategies
file = [InFile create: self withName: "strategies.setup"];

for(i = 0; i < numTypes; i ++)
   {
      // Load the strategy information and create object
      strategy      = [Strategy create: self];
      [ObjectLoader load: strategy from: file];

      // Create the players of this type
      for(j = 0; j < (populationSize / numTypes); j++)
{
  prisoner    = [Prisoner create: currentGeneration];
  [prisoner set_payoffs:  payoffs];
  [prisoner set_strategy: strategy];

  [currentGeneration addLast: prisoner];
}
   }

[file drop];
```

ject, not a text file like the `load:fromFileNamed:` method. In the line preceding the `for()` loop we create an instance of `InFile` and use it to open the text file containing the strategy definitions. Within the loop the `ObjectLoader` class repeatedly calls `InFile` retrieving the next set of variable names and values.

The `ObjectLoader` class expects to find a file which consists of a starting line with the string `@begin` and an ending line with `@end`. Between these two lines each line of the file should either consist of a comment, which is indicated by a '#' in the first column, or an instance variable name and a corresponding value. To define values for more than one instance in the same text-file one can simply insert each set of definitions with a leading @begin and a trailing @end. Each definition in strategies.setup, which gives the instance variables for four different strategies, looks like this (note that only one set of definitions is shown):

```
@begin
name all-D
i   0.0
p   0.0
q   0.0
@end
```

The ObjectSaver class allows the programmer to store the value of the instance variables in an object to file in the format that ObjectLoader reads. The following line of code would save values of the instance variables defined in object:

```
[ObjectSaver save: object toFileNamed: "filename"];
```

A class called OutFile is also defined in the libraries, it opens text files and responds to messages like putString: which prints a string to the file and putNewLine which inserts a newline character. The ObjectSaver and OutFile can be used in conjunction to save the state of more than one instance to the same file. The following code would save the state of all the strategies created in listing (8):

```
// Open the file
file  = [OutFile create: aZone withName: "filename"];
// Iterate over collection
index = [strategies begin: aZone];
while(strategy = [index next])
{
  [ObjectSaver save: strategy to: file];
}
[index drop];
// Close file
[file drop];
```

The Swarm libraries now also support a simple "Lisp-like" format for serializing objects, and a format based on the HDF5 data standard. These formats and the classes which support them are much more

Listing 9 Interface for GenerationSwarm

```
@interface GenerationSwarm: Swarm
{
  id nextGeneration;
  id players;
  id payoffs;
  int numSteps;
  double selectionPressure;
}

- (void) addLast: anObject;
- set_selectionPressure: (double) s;
- set_numSteps: (int) n;
- set_nextGeneration: n;
- set_payoffs: p;
- run;
- get_players;
- (double) get_payoff_average;
@end
```

powerful and versatile than the ObjectLoader and ObjectSaver. The creation and initialization of classes is not a separate operation, since the file format contains enough information for Swarm to create one or more instances of a class and set instance variable values. The HDF5 format is also quickly becoming a popular format for saving and manipulating large object collections or scientific data-sets, and is supported by a wide range of data-analysis and visualization tools. This will allow Swarm to cooperate with various kinds of other software, both for input and output. In the future the serialization protocols will also allow programmers to send objects over a pipe or stream, which would for example enable programs to run in a distributed computing environment, as objects can be sent to another computer on the local area network or accross the world.

7.2 USING LISTS AND ARRAYS

As listing (8) shows the ModelSwarm hands over the population of agents to the generation through the addLast: method. The interface for the subswarm is shown in listing (9)

The implementation of the addLast: method shows the use of an instance of List from the collections library to handle a population of agents.

```
- (void) addLast: anObject
{
  if(!players)
    {
      players = [List create: self];
    }

  [players addLast: anObject];
}
```

Here the list is created if it doesn't exist, and the first element is added using the addLast: method. Henceforth the elements are added one by one. The main feature of the List class is that the collection expands dynamically when needed and contracts if elements are removed. The disadvantage of this approach is that access to elements on the list is somewhat slower than with the Array class, which provides the same functionality as a C array in the context of an object. An Array does not expand dynamically and thus does not provide an addLast: method, elements are inserted with an atOffset:put: method which take as arguments the offset and object to be added.[7]

7.3   USING A MAP

The third important class in the collection libraries is Map, which allows us store and access members based on a key value. In an Array or List we must know the position of the member in the collection in order to retrieve it or search for it by traversing the collection element by element. Both classes implement an atOffset: method which takes a position as argument and returns the member at that position. The Map associates each member with a key object, which stores information concerning an arbitrary attribute. Examples are income (a floating point value), number (an integer) or color (a string). We can then retrieve the member by passing the key to the Map instance. A key object can be any class which implements the basic set: and get methods so that its value can be set and retrieved. In addition it must implement a compare: function which returns an integer $i \in \{-1, 0, 1\}$ based on whether the argument (assumed to be a key or object of the same class) is 'less than','equal to' or 'greater than' the key itself. In the case of non-numerical values the programmer must implement a compare: method which conforms to this

Listing 10 ModelSwarm report: method, using Map

```
// Create map
types = [Map create: globalZone];

// Iterate over the population and count
index = [[currentGeneration get_players] begin: self];
while(agent = [index next])
  {
    key  = [agent get_strategy];
    list = [types at: key];
    // If no list retrieved at key create and insert
    if(!list)
{
  list = [List create: globalZone];
  [types at: key insert: list];
}
    // All agents of a given type end up on list
    [list addLast: agent];
  }
[index drop];

// Start print out
printf("%04d ",i);

index = [types begin: self];
while(list = [index next: &key])
  {
    // Print out type and count of agents
    printf("%s:%d ",[key get_name],[list getCount]);
  }
[index drop];

// Drop the map and its associated keys, members
[types deleteAll];
[types drop];
```

behavior based on the particular context. Swarm provides a string class which stores key values as strings and implements a compare: method.[8]

7.4   USING INDEXES TO RETRIEVE MEMBERS

Listing (10) from the `report:` method in `ModelSwarm` shows how we can use a `Map` to count prisoners in the collection of each type.

In listing (10) we show how we use the type value as keys to construct a `Map` which contains instances of `List` as members, where each list contains in turn all the agents of a particular type. The listing also shows the use of an index, first to iterate over the collection of agents which is an instance of the `List` class, and then to iterate over the `Map` instance.

In both cases an index is created an initialized so that it points to the first member of the collection by calling the `begin:` method for the collection. The method `next` then iterates over a `List` or `Array` returning each member in turn, until it reaches the end. Since the `next` method returns 'nil' or 'false' once it reaches the end of the collection we can use a `while()` loop to iterate over the entire collection as the listing shows.

The comparable method for a `Map` index takes an argument, since it returns two pieces of information, the member and the key. To retrieve the key we need to declare a variable of the default object type (`id`) and pass the address of this variable (as in "`&varname`") to the `next:` method. See in the second `while()` loop in listing (10). The information that we are interested in is contained on one hand in the key and retrieved via the `get_name` method, and on the other as the number of members on the list and retrieved via the `getCount` method.

Note in particular that in order to use the `Strategy` instances as keys the class needs to implement a `compare:` method. The implementation of the method is as follows:[9]

```
- (int)compare: s
{
   return strcmp (name, [s get_name]);
}
```

Another type of index is the `PermutedIndex` which is a particular class which allows us to retrieve the members of a collection in a random order without replacement. We use this type of index in the `run` method in `GenerationSwarm` to match the players in random order. Listing (11) shows a part of this method, leaving out the code which has to do with the actual matching of the players which is replicated from the earlier IPD model.

Note that two indexes are created for the same collection. We iterate over both indexes, using one `while()` loop which retrieves the next random member from `index1` and then the next random member from `index2`. When both indexes are exhausted they return nil and we exit the loop.[10]

The last lines in the loop implement the 'Evolutionary Algorithm' which in this case takes a particularly simple form. Individuals with higher payoff from a match are copied to the next generation almost with certainty. This is done through the clone method in the `Prisoner` class. Also note that the new agents are cloned using the next generations memory zone, thus when this `GenerationSwarm` instance is dropped only the cloned players remain.

Sample output from the simulation consists of lines generated by the code in listing (10) which reports the number of agents of each type in the population and the average fitness of the current generation. Here we create an equal number of agents of each type given in table (1.1). The total population size is 1000 and the winner in each match is copied to the new generation with less than certainty. In a typical run it takes on the order of 10 generations before the All-D type has taken over the population. The reader can verify that although the number of iterations may be sensitive to parameters and initial conditions the perfectly grim strategy, All-D, will deterministically dominate the population after a finite number of rounds and once one type has taken over no change is possible since there is no injection of 'new genetic material'. The output produced by the `printf()` statements in the code looks something like this:

```
0000 TFT:250 aTFT:250 all-C:250 all-D:250
0001 TFT:201 aTFT:264 all-C:157 all-D:378
...
0009 all-D:1000
0010 all-D:1000
...
```

8. SPACE AND GUI: GRIDS, IMAGES AND GRAPHS

The Swarm libraries provide an impressive array of objects which can be used to provide a Graphical User Interface to the simulation. These objects can be divided into two groups, visualization tools such as line graphs, histograms and raster images and graphical probes, which are objects that visualize the state of the instance variables in an object and allow the user to access the objects variables and method through GUI widgets. This section will illustrate the use of the visualization classes while the next section will discuss the use of probes.

Listing 11 GenerationSwarm run: method, using PermutedIndex

```
// Run the tournament
index1 = [players beginPermuted: self];
index2 = [players beginPermuted: self];

while((prisoner1 = [index1 next]) &&
      (prisoner2 = [index2 next]))
   {
   <Code related to play deleted>

    payoff1 = [prisoner1 get_payoff];
    payoff2 = [prisoner2 get_payoff];

    if(payoff1 > payoff2)
      {
       winner = prisoner1;
       looser = prisoner2;
      }
    else
      {
       winner = prisoner2;
       looser = prisoner1;
      }

    // Propagate succesful strategies with higher probability
    if ([uniformDblRand getDoubleWithMin: 0.0
                                 withMax: 1.0]
                                     < selectionPressure)
       clone = [looser clone: nextGeneration];
    else
       clone = [winner clone: nextGeneration];

    [nextGeneration addLast: clone];
}
```

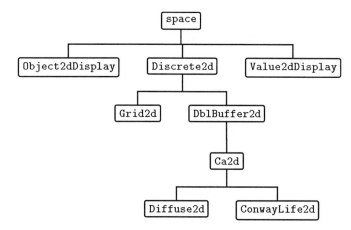

Figure 1.4 Some important classes in the space library.

As we saw in the previous section a random matching of the PD players in a 'soup' caused the grimmest strategy, which always defects, to take over the population. It might be interesting to know whether this particular matching method or 'topology of interaction' does indeed influence the result. To test this we will now substitute a different topology, or more specifically, we will arrange the agents on a two dimensional grid or lattice.

The Swarm libraries provide a library of classes to manage two dimensional discrete lattices, appropriately called space. The base class of this library is Discrete2d. The code in listing (12) creates a $X \times Y$ lattice and associates one Prisoner instance with each lattice point. Note that we give each Prisoner a randomly chosen Strategy instance, and a Location instance which is a new class which will be used here to keep track of the coordinates of each agent. By creating yet another class and associating it with the players we are able to use the previous incarnation of the Prisoner class with only minor changes.

The listing in (13) and (14) shows the interface for the new Location class and the changes we have made to the interface for Prisoner in order to be able to use the class in the spatial context. First note that Location has a get_neighbors method which retrieves the locations for the four agents on adjacent grid locations, looking north, east, south and west (the so-called VonNeuman neighborhood). If a player is located in the rows or columns on the edges of the lattice it only has two or three neighbors. Also note that the Prisoner class now has methods which allow it to play against neighbors and to figure out which of its neighbors has earned the highest payoff. The playNeighbors method thus implements the tournament code which earlier was in GenerationSwarm. The

---

Listing 12 ModelSwarm buildObjects method

```
// Create grid to hold player locations
grid       = [Discrete2d createBegin: self];
[grid setSizeX: gridSize Y: gridSize];
grid       = [grid createEnd];

i = 0;
for(y = 0; y < gridSize; y++)
  {
    for(x = 0; x < gridSize; x++)
{
// Select strategy at random
number    = [uniformIntRand
                    getIntegerWithMin: 0
                          withMax: numTypes-1];
strategy = [strategies atOffset: number];

// Create location
location = [Location createBegin: self];
[location set_grid: grid];
[location setX: x Y: y];

// Put location on grid
[grid putObject: location atX: x Y: y];

// Create the player
prisoner = [Prisoner create: self];
[prisoner set_payoffs:  payoffs];
[prisoner set_location: location];
[prisoner set_strategy: strategy];
[prisoner set_numSteps: numSteps];

// Add player to list
[players atOffset: i++ put: prisoner];

// Associate location and prisoner
[location set_object:   prisoner];
  }
    }
```

Listing 13 Interface for Location

```
@interface Location: SwarmObject
{
  id grid;
  id object;
  id neighbors;
  int xpos;
  int ypos;
}
- set_grid: g;
- set_object: o;
- setX: (int) x Y: (int) y;
- get_neighbors;
- drawSelfOn: r;
- (int) get_xpos;
- (int) get_ypos;
- get_object;
@end
```

Prisoner instance sends a message to its Location instance, and retrieves a list of adjacent locations. It then iterates over these locations, retrieves the player at that location and engages in an Iterated PD.[11]

8.1 SEPARATING THE OBSERVER AND MODEL

The objects which actually present graphical output from the simulation are created and controlled by a separate class ObserverSwarm which is a subclass of GUISwarm, which in most respects is identical to the Swarm class. Because events in the model and observer have to be synchronized, so that the information presented on screen is updated correctly and input from the user processed in a timely fashion (more on this later), we will use a unique feature in the Swarm libraries which allow us to integrate an 'action schedule' in both Swarms. The Swarm activity library provides a set of classes to schedule and trigger events in an OOP framework. To do the same with traditional for() or while() loops would be a rather messy process. In particular it would be quite difficult to separate objects and events in the observer and model since the two need to be synchronized cleanly.

Listing 14 Interface for Prisoner

```
@interface Prisoner: SwarmObject
{
  id payoffs;        // Payoff object
  id location;       // Location object
  id strategy;       // Strategy object
  id strategy_new;   // New strategy object
  double payoff;     // Current cumulative payoff
  int move;          // Last move
  int numSteps;      // Number of steps in IPD
}
- set_location: l;
- set_strategy: s;
- set_payoffs: p;
- set_numSteps: (int) n;
- mimicBest;
- reset;
- (int) initial;
- (int) move: (int) o;
- playNeighbors;
- findBestNeighbor;
- (double) get_payoff;
- get_strategy;
- get_location;
- (char *) get_color;
@end
```

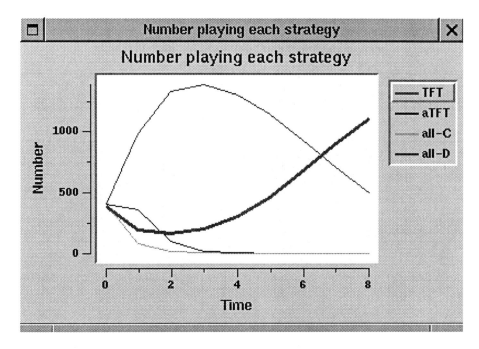

Figure 1.5 An instance of `EZGraph` with four sequences, which plot the time-series for the number of agents using each type of strategy in the population.

This section will describe the code in `ObserverSwarm` which creates the GUI while the next section will discuss the use of the Swarm `activity` library to schedule and coordinate events in the observer and model.

The `buildObjects` method in `ObserverSwarm` now carries out the operation of creating the model instance and issuing a call to the `buildObjects` method in the model. This is the first step in "merging the schedules" of the two Swarms, which we will discuss in the next section. In addition the `buildObjects` method in the observer creates instances of the following classes:

1. **ColorMap** Associates an integer number which can be used internally in the model a color value which is needed to output color on screen.

2. **ZoomRaster** Displays a 2d lattice on screen either by reading from a matrix of values or objects.

3. **Object2dDisplay** Reads information from a grid (in this case from the grid in the model) and feeds location and color information to the raster.

4. **EZGraph** Line graph which updates information dynamically from objects or collections of agents.

First we create the `ColorMap` instance.

```
colormap = [Colormap create: self];
index = [[model get_strategies] begin: self];
while(strategy = [index next])
   {
      [colormap setColor: [strategy get_number]
                ToName: [strategy get_color]];
   }
[index drop];
```

The colormap associates an integer number with colors in the palette used by the computer to display the raster image. This allows us to define a mapping between integers and colors, and to refer to each color in the model by a unique integer. In this case we have given each instance of the `Strategy` class both an ID number and a string to hold the name of the color which we wish to associate with that strategy. This uses a feature of the libraries which Swarm uses to create screen images, where color types are associated with names such as "blue", "pink", "orange" etc.[12] As the code shows we create an index over the `Array` holding the `Strategy` instances and read out the unique ID number and name of color for each strategy. This value is passed to the colormap through the `setColor:Name:` method.

The colormap also provides a method which allows one to associate specific RGB values with an integer, the `setColor:ToRed:Green:Blue:` method. This method can be useful when the number of colors we wish to define is large, or we want color intensities to reveal information about the level of some variable. When the RGB system is used each primary color value is a double-precision floating point value in the unit interval.

Next we create the `ZoomRaster` instance. This is a subclass of the `Raster` class which allows us to define a `zoomFactor` i.e. the number of pixels used to draw each grid location. Thus if `zoomFactor` = 10 each grid location is drawn as 10×10 pixels. Both superclass and subclass are created by passing a colormap as argument, setting the height and width (which corresponds to the x and y dimensions of the underlying grid) and a title which will appear in the upper bar of the raster window. Finally we need to send a `pack` message to the raster instance, which causes it to be drawn on screen.

```
// Create raster image of world
```

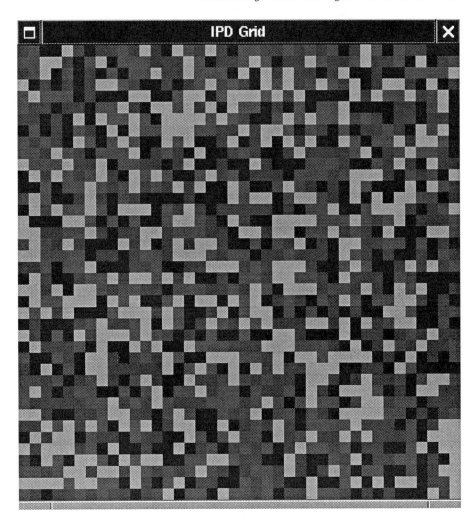

Figure 1.6 An instance of ZoomRaster which shows the distributions of player strategies in the population. Each player is located at a grid-point and the location is given a color according to the strategy which the player used.

```
raster = [ZoomRaster create: self];
[raster setColormap:    colormap];
[raster setZoomFactor:  zoomFactor];
[raster setWidth:       [model get_gridSize]
         Height:        [model get_gridSize]];
[raster setWindowTitle: "IPD Grid"];
[raster pack];
```

To actually display the grid on screen we need to create a bridge between the objects and the grid contained in the model and the raster. There are several ways to do this. In principle the raster needs to receive a drawPointX:Y:Color: message for each location which should be displayed, where the color is an integer number associated with a color definition in the colormap. One of the simplest ways to do this is to create an Object2dDisplay instance. This is a special class which takes as arguments a display widget (the raster), a lattice (the grid) and a message that will be issued to each object on the grid with the raster as argument. We will call this method drawSelfOn: and implement it in the Location class. First the code for creating the Object2dDisplay instance:

```
// Create object which will feed info to raster
display = [Object2dDisplay createBegin: self];
[display setDisplayWidget:        raster];
[display setDiscrete2dToDisplay: [model get_grid]];
[display setDisplayMessage:      M(drawSelfOn:)];
display = [display createEnd];
```

And then the implementation of the drawSelfOn: method in Location:

```
-drawSelfOn: r
{
  [r drawPointX: xpos Y: ypos Color: [object get_attribute]];
  return self;
}
```

Since this method will be called by the Object2dDisplay instance the argument to the drawSelfOn: method is the object given as argument to the setDisplayWidget: method above i.e. the ZoomRaster. The chain of method calls which are set in motion by these couple of lines in order to display the correct color in the correct location on the raster is as follows:

1. The Object2dDisplay calls the Discrete2d in the model and retrieves the Location instance with getObjectAtX:Y:.

2. The Object2dDisplay calls the Location with drawSelfOn: method giving the raster as argument.

3. The Location calls the Prisoner with the get_attribute method.

4. The Prisoner calls its Strategy with the get_number method and retrieves the integer which defines the color associated with this strategy in the colormap.

5. The `get_attribute` method returns the value to `Location` which sends a `drawPointX:Y:Color:` message to the raster. The raster retrieves the actual RGB color intensities associated with this value from the colormap and draws a rectangle on the screen at the given x, y coordinate, with the predefined zoom factor and appropriate color.

Finally we create a line graph which will plot the number of prisoners which are using each strategy at each time step. The Swarm libraries define an `EZGraph` class which allows one to create a graph of an arbitrary number of time series, which are updated automatically at specific intervals. After creating the instance we must define the title of the graph, and labels to be displayed on each axis. In order for information to be fed to the graph we also must define one or more "graph sequences" which are objects that read data from an object or members of a collection. These sequence objects can also perform some transformation of the data read from a collection, such as counting the number of agents responding or calculating the average, minimum and maximum. In the listing we create an index over the strategy collection and create a sequence for each instance which will plot the number of agents using the strategy. The `createSequence:withFeedFrom:andSelector:` takes as argument a string which will appear on the graph to identify the time series, an object which will be called to get the data (the list of agents associated with the strategy) and a method selector which will be used when the object is called. To call each member of a collection of agents we would have used either the `createAverageSequence:withFeedFrom:andSelector` or sibling messages where we can substitute the string "Min","Max" or "Count" for "Average" with the expected result.

```
// Create graph of number of agents with each strategy
graph = [EZGraph createBegin: self];
[graph setTitle: "Number playing each strategy"];
[graph setAxisLabelsX: "Time" Y: "Number"];
graph = [graph createEnd];

// Find the objects which will feed information
index = [[model get_types] begin: self];
while(list = [index next: &strategy])
  {
    [graph createSequence: [strategy get_name]
       withFeedFrom: list
        andSelector: M(getCount)];
  }
[index drop];
```

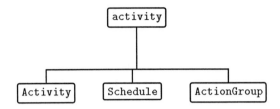

Figure 1.7   Some important classes in the activity library

The classes discussed here come from three different libraries in Swarm. The ColorMap and ZoomRaster with numerous other display classes reside in the gui library, while the Object2dDisplay comes from the space library and EZGraph from analysis. The EZGraph class is actually a wrapper around a number of classes which fetch and filter data which gets passed on to the graph. A more rudimentary class is Graph in the gui library. It allows the creation of graphs which do not display time series but some other form of x, y data in the form of a line graph.

9.   ACTIVITY: SCHEDULING EVENTS AND ACTIONS

In the spatial IPD model which we are developing we have separated the observer and model although we want events on both sides of the divide to be nicely synchronized. This is where the activity library in Swarm comes into play. The second major feature provided by the Swarm and GUISwarm class, in addition to memory management through Zone, is that these classes can integrate and manage activity plans. These plans are simply lists of events, where some target object must be called at a specific time-step with a specific message and arguments. These method calls then trigger action in the model or observer.

The most important classes in the activity library are Schedule and ActionGroup. Both are fundamentally collections of special objects which store the required information to trigger a method on a specific target. The main difference between the two is that a Schedule associates a particular time step with each action, while an ActionGroup is simply a list of targets and methods with no time associated with each event. The philosophy behind this separation is that an ActionGroup should list events which can happen "simultaneously" while a Schedule defines a specific time-line where actions are triggered in a well defined order.

In practice the events that are listed in an ActionGroup are actually executed in the order in which they were defined, and since Swarm does not yet implement execution in parallel on multiple processors, these events are always executed in sequence. It can however be a useful abstraction to think of ActionGroups as being executed in parallel, and more importantly to make sure that agents are not changing the state of other agents while an ActionGroup or two events on the same time-step are being executed.[13]

In addition to providing these utilities to define the order of events which will be triggered during the execution of a program the activity library provides means to merge the schedules of one or more Swarms. These rather complex operations are carried out with a minimum of fuss, only require a few method calls by the programmer. To understand the principle at work here we can first look at the new main function for the spatial IPD:

```
int
main(int argc, const char ** argv) {
  ObserverSwarm * observerSwarm;

  initSwarm(argc, argv);

  observerSwarm =  [ObserverSwarm create: globalZone];
  [observerSwarm buildObjects];
  [observerSwarm buildActions];
  [observerSwarm activateIn: nil];
  [observerSwarm go];

  return 0;
}
```

Note in particular the fact that there is no reference to ModelSwarm here, since the model is actually created inside the ObserverSwarm. In the discussion of the buildObjects method in the previous section we also saw that the method call to buildObjects in the model was carried out by the observer. Also note the method calls to buildActions and activateIn: in the main. The purpose of the buildActions method is to create the Schedule and ActionGroup instances which define the sequence of events in the observer, and to send a buildActions call to the model to trigger the creation of the same kind of objects in it. The activateIn: method then actually merges the schedules into the activity machinery which is already present in the background.

9.1   BUILDING SCHEDULES

The buildActions method in ModelSwarm looks like this:

```
modelActions = [ActionGroup create: self];
```

```
[modelActions createActionForEach: players
                         message: M(reset)];
[modelActions createActionForEach: players
                         message: M(playNeighbors)];
[modelActions createActionForEach: players
                         message: M(mimicBest)];
[modelActions createActionTo:      self
                 message:          M(update)];

modelSchedule = [Schedule createBegin: self];
[modelSchedule  setRepeatInterval: 1];
modelSchedule = [modelSchedule createEnd];


[modelSchedule at: 0 createAction: modelActions];
```

The sequence of events here parallels what we have seen in previous incarnations of the program where for() loops were used to trigger actions. The schedule is programmed to send each player a reset message at the beginning of each time-step. Subsequently the schedule will send a playNeighbors message to all players and finally invoke mimicBest which triggers a search for the most successful neighbor by each prisoner. Finally the model will receive a message to update information on the number of prisoners playing each strategy.

The method creates one ActionGroup and a Schedule. Both classes implement methods which will send a particular message to each member of a collection or target a single object. Compare these examples:

```
// Target each member of collection
[schedule        at: t
 createActionForEach: list
           message: M(step)];
// Target a single object
[schedule        at: t
     createActionTo: object
           message: M(step)];
// Target an ActionGroup
[schedule        at: t
       createAction: actionGroup];
```

In both cases the schedule or action group stores the information on the target and message in a special data structure. Defining an event on a Schedule however also requires additional information, namely the time-step at which a particular action should be triggered. The last line above shows the use of the at:createAction: method, which targets an ActionGroup and uses the default step as the method name to be called.

In the spatial IPD example we want to define the sequence of actions at each time-step and then let the schedule repeat itself. Conveniently Schedules can be created with a repeat interval, which determines the number of time-steps since the invocation of the first action on the schedule before it should be rescheduled. The repeat interval is thus the number of time-steps from the invocation of the first action before the schedule is supposed to repeat itself. Hence the interval must always be larger than the number of time-steps that must elapse from the first action on the schedule until the last action is executed. Otherwise the schedule would start repeating before the last action was invoked.

All references to time-steps in the context of schedules are relative. The execution of a schedule starts when it is activated, and the schedule defines the relative time between the time of activation and the time the event should take place. Take as an example two schedules which both define two events, one at 0 and the other at 5. If one schedule is activated at time-step 0 in terms of the overall simulation, while the other is activated at time-step 3 the events on one schedule will be executed at time-step 0 and 5 in absolute terms while the the events on the second schedule will be executed at time-step 4 and 9, because events on the schedule will be executed starting on the time-step after it has been activated. A schedule thus defines the relative time between events, while activation determines the absolute time of execution.

In the examples shown in this chapter all schedules are activated in the beginning and thus both relative and absolute time-steps are the same. In the IPD example all of the events on the schedule take place for the first time at time-step 0 and are rescheduled immediately one time step later at 1. Subsequently they will be rescheduled for time step $2, 3, \ldots$ and so on. We could also set a longer repeat interval, which would simply mean that all the agents in the model would lie dormant for some number of time-steps between execution of the ActionGroup.

Let us also look at the buildActions method in ObserverSwarm. It is quite similar, although the targets and messages are different.

```
[super buildActions];
[model buildActions];

displayActions = [ActionGroup create: self];
[displayActions createActionTo: display
                    message: M(display)];
[displayActions createActionTo: raster
                    message: M(drawSelf)];
```

```
[displayActions createActionTo: graph
                       message: M(step)];
[displayActions createActionTo: actionCache
                       message: M(doTkEvents)];

displaySchedule = [Schedule createBegin: self];
[displaySchedule  setRepeatInterval: 1];
displaySchedule = [displaySchedule createEnd];
[displaySchedule at: 0 createAction: displayActions];
```

Note that the second statement in the method sends a `buildActions` message to the model. The observer then creates one action group and a schedule.

The targets on this schedule have been discussed above with exception of the `actionCache` which is an object created by default by virtue of the fact that the observer is a subclass of `GUISwarm`. This object processes events in the GUI, for example allowing users to click on buttons which 'Start' and 'Stop' the simulation. If we were not to issue a call to this object at the beginning and end of each time-step the interface would not respond to any user interaction. In some cases this is actually a desired effect - since redrawing the GUI is resource intensive. Often it is possible to speed the execution of a simulation significantly by "slowing down" the GUI, i.e issuing calls to the GUI objects and to `actionCache` with a large repeat interval.

9.2   DYNAMIC AND ASYNCHRONOUS SCHEDULES

A last but crucial point to mention regarding schedules and action groups is that both classes can be used to schedule events dynamically during the simulation run. This allows us to implement programs where all events are asynchronous and generated endogenously within the simulation. For example a prisoner in the IPD might choose to face his opponents again if his payoff has shown an upward or downward trend. We could start with a schedule that is completely empty, and have agents schedule the next match by sending a message to the schedule object, asking for a message call to be invoked at a future time-step with the agent as target. Another example would be a simulation of firms which manufacture some type of durable good where firms schedule actions to replenish stocks when inventories are about to be depleted.

In order to implement asynchronous dynamic scheduling the programmer simply needs to pass a reference to one of the schedules to the agents in the model. Using the manufacturing example, the firm objects could have an instance variable schedule which points to a schedule created in one of the swarms. Let us assume that the firm implements a produce method. Once some event signals that stocks are about to be depleted the firm would send the following message:

```
[schedule at: t createActionTo: self message: M(produce)];
```

where t could be any future time. The global macro getCurrentTime() returns the current time-step in absolute terms. Then t must be this time plus some interval greater than 0. The schedule would receive these messages from the firms and integrate the pending events into the global schedule of the application, thus ensuring that after the required number of time-steps the firm in question would receive a produce message. Obviously this feature is even more useful when the object calling the schedule is not the target for the future message call.

9.3   ACTIVATING SCHEDULES

We have already noted that the following line in **main.m** creates instances of a memory zone, random number generator and random number distributions:

```
initSwarmBatch(argc,argv);
```

We did not mention at that time that another side effect of this function is the creation of objects which can take schedules and action groups and merge them into one coherent list of activity in the program. Here we actually use a sibling function initSwarm() which does all this and in addition provides the means to create a GUI display.

While these activation messages may seem rather mysterious they are actually based on a very simple principle. Think of the ObserverSwarm in this case as a 'top-level' Swarm and the ModelSwarm as a 'sub' Swarm. The schedules of events in the ObserverSwarm is first activated, i.e merged into a unique list. By calling activateIn: on ModelSwarm its schedules are activated. Subsequently the ModelSwarm is activated in the ObserverSwarm which basically means that the activity machinery merges the schedule of events in the two Swarms into a single coherent list of actions. Finally the ObserverSwarm is activated in 'nil' which only means that the merged schedule in the observer becomes the top-level schedule of the simulation, which now is composed of a lists of events in both Swarms.

We can see how this is done in practice by looking first at the activation method the observer:

```
-activateIn: (id) swarmContext {
```

```
[super activateIn: swarmContext];
[model       activateIn: self];
[displaySchedule activateIn: self];
return [self getSwarmActivity];
}
```

The second statement activates the model in the observer and the third statement activates the single schedule defined in the observer. As a practical matter this means that schedules of events defined by the model will precede any events defined by displaySchedule. The activateIn: method in ModelSwarm looks like this:

```
-activateIn: (id) swarmContext
{
  [super activateIn: swarmContext];
  [modelSchedule activateIn: self];
  return [self getSwarmActivity];
}
```

Here the second statement activates the only schedule defined in this Swarm, while the method as a whole will ensure that the schedule will get integrated into the schedule of the top-level Swarm. In both Swarms we also need to call the activateIn: method in the superclass (i.e. in Swarm). This is a prerequisite which ensures that a series of objects will be created to enable schedules to be created, merged and invoked.

10.   PROBES: INTERACTING WITH AGENTS

Probes are one of the most interesting aspects of the Swarm toolkit. As the name indicates probes are objects which interface with other objects, which in practice means that they can read and change the value of instance variables from an object or invoke its methods. Probes can also be associated with a graphical widget on the screen, which allows the user to interact with objects through the GUI, both monitoring and changing their state in real time. This gives the programmer the ability to create a graphical display on the fly for any agent or object in the simulation.

We have actually already seen probes at work in previous sections of the tutorial. Readers who have compiled the code of the last example will have noticed that a widget with several buttons appears on the screen each time that the simulation is run. These buttons are actually probes to methods in the Swarm activity machinery which allow the user to start, stop and step through the simulation. Probes are also often invoked in the background without a graphical display. When we create the EZGraph in the last example, the class creates an instance of a class called MessageProbe in order to invoke a method on each member of the collection of players and process the requisite data for the graph.

The probe library consists of a number of classes:

1. **VarProbes** Able to read and change the value of an object's instance variables.

2. **MessageProbes** Able to invoke an object's methods, with required arguments and read the result.

3. **ProbeMaps** Collections (instances of Map class) of message and variable probes for a given class.

4. **ProbeLibrary** Class which keeps track of which probes and probe maps have been defined for the objects in the simulation and allows us to access and change these.

Probes are actually part of the objectbase library. All subclasses of SwarmObject and Swarm can be probed, i.e. they are created with a ProbeMap instance which contains probes for all the instance variables and methods in the class and its superclass. We can retrieve any of these probes by calling the object's ProbeMap, and also change the map so that it contains only probes of some subset of the object's instance variables and methods.

Let us now look at examples of how we can use probes in the context of the spatial IPD which was developed in the last two sections. We will first define a custom ProbeMap for the ModelSwarm which contains probes to two new methods which allow the user to change the names of the setup files which contain the model parameters and the definitions of the IPD strategies. Secondly we will define a custom ProbeMap for the Prisoner class and give the ZoomRaster widget the ability to respond to mouse-clicks on the raster image by displaying a graphical ProbeMap of the agent at the corresponding x, y location.

The code which defines the custom ProbeMap for ModelSwarm can be defined in the createBegin method of the class as follows:

```
obj = [super createBegin: aZone];
obj->gridSize       =40;
obj->numTypes       =4;
obj->numSteps       =4;
obj->strategy_file  =strdup("strategies.setup");
obj->parameter_file =strdup("model.setup");
```

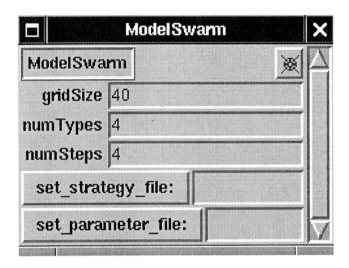

Figure 1.8 Customized `ProbeMap` display for `ModelProbe` class, created in text. The probe is displayed when the simulation starts and allows users to change parameters before model starts, as is explained in the text. Clicking on the label `ModelSwarm` in the upper left corner with the right mouse-button will open the complete `ProbeMap` for the model, while clicking on the rectangle with the icon in the upper right corner will close the probe window. To change a value the user simply types in the input field and hits 'Enter', and to execute a method clicks on the appropriate button.

```
// Create a custom probe map for this class
probeMap = [EmptyProbeMap createBegin: aZone];
[probeMap setProbedClass: [self class]];
probeMap = [probeMap createEnd];

// Add the probes we want to show up on screen
[probeMap addProbe:
 [probeLibrary
  getProbeForVariable: "gridSize"
              inClass: [self class]]];
[probeMap addProbe:
 [probeLibrary
  getProbeForVariable: "numTypes"
              inClass: [self class]]];
[probeMap addProbe:
 [probeLibrary
  getProbeForVariable: "numSteps"
              inClass: [self class]]];
[probeMap addProbe:
```

```
[[probeLibrary
   getProbeForMessage: "set_strategy_file:"
              inClass: [self class]]
        setHideResult: 1]];
[probeMap addProbe:
 [[probeLibrary
   getProbeForMessage: "set_parameter_file:"
              inClass: [self class]]
        setHideResult: 1]];

// Now install the new probe map in the probeLibrary
[probeLibrary
 setProbeMap: probeMap
         For: [self class]];
```

Note in passing that the first lines of the method contain new instance variables for ModelSwarm, namely the names of files containing strategy definitions and model parameters respectively. We have given these variables a default setting which correspond to the constants used in the previous section.

The statements after the definition of the default values for the object's instance variables are concerned with the creation of a custom probe map with several variable and message probes. First we create an instance of EmptyProbeMap which does not contain any probes at creation time. The probe map must be associated with a particular class, hence the setProbedClass: message and this parameter must be set before we call the createEnd method for the class. The next three lines retrieve VarProbes for each of three instance variables in ModelSwarm and add these probes to the EmptyProbeMap instance. Note that we need to call the probeLibrary instance to retrieve the probes as in:

```
probe = [probeLibrary getProbeForVariable:  "varname"
                               inClass: someClass];
```

This method takes as arguments a string with the name of the instance variable and the name of the object's class, which is retrieved by calling the method class in ModelSwarm. The next two lines repeat the same procedure but for two MessageProbes for the new methods which we have added to ModelSwarm.[14]

The final line sends a message to the probeLibrary instance telling it to install a new probe map for ModelSwarm based on the map just defined. This ensures that any time that a probe map is retrieved or displayed for this object it will only contain the variable and message probes we have defined.

It is important to remember that ProbeMaps are simply subclasses of the Map class, and thus we can for example create an index of a probe map to iterate over an object's probes, or check whether a particular variable or method is defined in the object. This can be a very powerful feature in a simulation with heterogeneous populations of agents. The programmer can for example choose which methods are invoked at runtime, build method calls on the fly and figure out which methods an object responds to by querying its probe map.

In order to actually display the probe map defined in the code above we need to add some code that sends a message to probeLibrary instructing it to display the ModelSwarm probe map. The following lines in the buildObjects method in ObserverSwarm will cause the probe to be displayed before the user has a chance to push a button on the control panel that is displayed by default when the simulation starts. This allows the user to input new filenames for the setup files if he chooses so. Otherwise the default file names will be used. Note that the following listing only shows the first part of the buildObjects method since changes to the rest of the method are discussed below:

```
...
// Necessary for zone etc.
[super buildObjects];
// Create model
model = [ModelSwarm create: self];
// Create probe display for model
[probeDisplayManager createProbeDisplayFor: model];
// Stop GUI
[controlPanel setStateStopped];
// When user presses 'Start' or 'Next' build objects
[model buildObjects];
...
```

The call to create the probe display could of course be made from the model but this would violate the principle of separation between model and observer. As is we can still run the model without enabling a graphical display, but if the message call was included in ModelSwarm the program would crash unless the GUI was running.

The next feature we would like to add to the GUI is the ability to probe the agents in the model by clicking on the raster image. This is fortunately a trivial task in Swarm. The ZoomRaster must first be told how to process mouse-clicks. The following code (added to buildObjects in ObserverSwarm) defines a target and method which the raster will trigger for mouse clicks at a specific x, y location on the lattice:

```
[raster setButton: ButtonRight
          Client: display
         Message: M(makeProbeAtX:Y:)];
```

Here we tell the raster to process mouse-clicks with the right mouse button by sending a message to the display object instructing it to retrieve the object at a particular location and creating a probe. While the message sent to the client object can be defined, by the raster will attempt to pass the x, y coordinates of the mouse-click as arguments to any message we define.

The `Object2dDisplay` class implements a `makeProbeAtX:Y:` method. As expected the method sends a message to the object at location x, y and asks it to create a probe display on screen. As we saw in the code example from a previous section which showed how the `Object2dDisplay` instance was created, the object is connected to the `Discrete2d` instance in the model which contains the `Location` objects. As a result a mouse-click in this context would create a probe display for the `Location` instance at a particular x, y coordinate.

We could however also process the mouse-click and actually return a probe to the `Prisoner` instance at the location, which is probably more useful for the user of the program. The following code illustrates how this can be done and provides an example of how a subclass of one of the classes in the Swarm libraries (apart from `SwarmObject` or `Swarm`) can override a particular method in the superclass.

The procedure is as follows:

1. Ceate a subclass of `Object2dDisplay` called `ModObject2dDisplay` which adds no new variables or methods but redefines the `makeProbeAtX:Y:` method.

2. Substitute the new class for `Object2dDisplay` in the code, simply creating an instance of `ModObject2dDisplay` instead of its superclass.

The code in listing (15) shows the full implementation of the new class, where the substitute definition of the `makeProbeAtX:Y:` method will create a probe of the resident at a particular grid location instead of a probe to the `Location` object.

Here the first statement retrieves the resident object (the `Prisoner` instance) and substitutes the prisoner on the grid for the `Location` instance. The second statement creates the probe, by invoking the same method in the superclass of `ModObject2dDisplay`. This will simply execute the original method in `Object2dDisplay`. Finally the third statement puts the `Location` object back in its place, retrieving it from the `Prisoner` via the `get_location` method.

Listing 15 Implementation of Mod2dObjectDisplay

```
@implementation ModObject2dDisplay

- makeProbeAtX: (unsigned)x Y: (unsigned)y
{
  id obj;
  id tmp;
  // Switch the location object with the resident (prisoner)
  obj = [discrete2d getObjectAtX: x Y: y];
  tmp = [obj get_object];
  [discrete2d putObject: tmp atX: x Y: y];

  // Use the method in the superclass
  [super makeProbeAtX: x Y: y];

  // Now switch back so location is on grid for next time
  obj = [tmp get_location];
  [discrete2d putObject: obj atX: x Y: y];

  return self;
}
@end
```

11.   AFTERWORD

The Swarm libraries allow researchers to develop simulations in a short amount of time. However, the process requires knowledge of a general purpose programming language and some familiarity with a command line shell, compiler and debugger. These are not trivial issues for most students or scientists who are loath to devote too much time to tasks which carry little weight within their chosen profession. The question which any interested party must therefore answer is the following: Can I gain an additional insight using an Agent Based Computational Model which I could not obtain otherwise? Some economists and other social scientists believe that for a number of key problems the answer to this question is affirmative.

Hopefully this brief tutorial will help readers to evaluate the costs and benefits of using the Swarm libraries, and ease the learning curve for those who conclude that the investment is worthwhile.

12.   APPENDIX

In writing this tutorial I have benefitted from feedback from students at a number of universities in Europe and the United States where earlier versions of this material have been presented. I would however like to single out past and present members of the Swarm development team, in particular Chris Langton, Roger Burkhart, Manor Askenazi, Nelson Minar, Glen Ropella, Marcus G. Daniels and Alex Lancaster for their assistance and work on the development of Swarm. I also owe a great debt of gratitude to Professor Lars-Erik Cederman of the Department of Political Science at UCLA who developed an earlier version of the Prisoner's Dilemma tutorial and to Professor Axel Leijonhufvud of the Department of Economics, University of Trento, Italy for his unrelenting encouragement and support.

All code in this tutorial is available from the Swarm website which also contains current and past versions of the Swarm libraries, example applications and the Swarm documentation set. These files and documents can be accessed at the following URL:

`http://www.santafe.edu/projects/swarm`

The website also contains numerous references to simulations which use Swarm, additional training material, names of Swarm users and an archive of mailing-lists for the discussion of matters relating to the libraries, including problems which beginners may face.

An Objective-C manual is available from the Apple Inc. website. Updated URLs are to be found at the Swarm website or by searching Apple's homepage:

`http://www.apple.com`

Notes

1. For a description of this license please see the file Copying in the Swarm distribution or visit the GNU website at `http://www.gnu.org`.

2. In some OOP languages, such as Objective-C, a class is defined in two separate files, a file containing the declarations of the class' variables and methods, called the 'interface' and a file containing the actual programming instructions for the class methods, called the 'implementation.'

3. At the time of the writing of this document a new version of the Swarm libraries is due to be released, where programmers will be able to use the Java programming language to code their own agents and call Swarm library classes from Java objects. This release will not alter the fact that the libraries are implemented in Objective-C - with the exception of the user interface which is based on Tcl/Tk. A native Java version has not been planned.

4. The C language and its derivatives define 'false' or 'untrue' as '0' and 'true' as any positive value. In the binary logic implemented in the language the negation of '0' is '1', and the negation of '1' is '0'.

5. In standard C and Objective-C any arguments which are given when the user types in the program name in the shell are passed as arguments to main, in the form of an array of strings (argv) and an integer (argn) which gives the number of arguments (including the program name). If the user types in 'progname -t' then argv[1], the second element of the argv array, would take the value "-t" and argn the value 2. Parsing this information is left to the programmer, but the Swarm libraries provide special classes which can handle this task.

6. Computer programmers use the term 'memory leak' to describe subtle errors in code, where objects or data structures which will not be used again are left in memory indefinitely. Objective-C and C++ do not provide automatic 'garbage collection' i.e. that memory which is used by objects which will never be called again is automatically reclaimed. OOP languages of more recent vintage, such as Java, provide means for automatic garbage collection.

7. Using the library class Array instead of a normal C array is recommended, the advantage of using objects in this case is that basic error checking and verification is put in place. As many a programmer knows array overflows are one of the most frequent sources of errors in C programs.

8. The compare: method in this case is implemented using a standard function from the C string library, strcmp.

9. The int strcmp(s1,s2) function from the string library in the standard C language compares the two strings s1 and s2. It returns an integer less than, equal to, or greater than zero if s1 is found, respectively, to be less than, to match, or be greater than s2.

10. Note that there is no provision in the code that an object is not matched against itself. While it would be a simple matter to test whether the two objects are the same, it would take a few lines of code to provide means of finding a different match and yet to make sure that all members get matched with at least one adversary.

11. In the previous section each prisoner was matched against another prisoner twice (unless the random order matched the prisoner against himself). In this case a player will also get matched against his neighbor twice, since a player i which has a player j in his neighborhood is also in the neighborhood of player j. One simple method to ensure that players do not get matched twice is to have each prisoner keep track of his opponents via a list. Potential opponents found on this list will be rejected. After each round the list is cleared.

12. On Unix systems the names are defined in a file called rgb.txt which is usually found in the directories associated with the X11 library.

13. As an aside about the types of problems that a programmer must be aware of, in the spatial IPD we have to make sure that agents do not copy a strategy from one of their neighbors until all agents have been matched with their neighbors. Finding the most successful strategy in the neighborhood is not a valid operation until results are in from each tournament. If agents started copying strategies before other agents had a chance to play we would end up with a diffusion process which was entirely different from the one we intended to implement. Furthermore, since the display is only updated once every time-step we need to keep information about strategies that were used during the current step around until it is no longer needed. The simple solution to these problems is to define a variable in Prisoner called strategy_new which holds a reference to the strategy that will be used in the next round. A refresh method is then called at the beginning of each round which copies the value of strategy_new to strategy, the instance variable that references the current strategy.

14. The nested method calls cause the probes to be set to hide the result of their invocation, since we are not interested in showing this on the screen. When the result of a method call is of interest to the user the programmer should call setHideResult: with the argument 0, i.e. 'false'.

References

Axelrod, R. (1984). *The Evolution of Cooperation*. Basic Books, New York.

Grim, P., Mar, G., and Denis, P. S. (1998). *The Philosophical Computer - Exploratory Essays in Philosophical Computer Modeling.* MIT, Cambridge, MA and London.

Matsumoto, M. and Kurita, Y. (1998). Mersenne twister a 623-dimensionally equidistributed uniform pseudo-random number generator. *ACM Transactions on Modeling and Computer Simulation*, 8(1):3–30.

Poundstone, W. (1992). *Prisoner's Dilemma.* Doubleday, New York.

Chapter 2

INSTALLATION: AN APPENDIX

Alessandro Perrone

Department of Economics

University of Venice "Ca' Foscari"

30120 Venice, Italy

alex@unive.it

1. INTRODUCTION

Swarm [1] libraries run on a wide range of Computer Operating systems. Swarm is available on the following architectures: Windows Nt/95/98 and Unix[2]-like Systems. It has been tested on the following operating systems:

- Linux on Intel Box

- LinuxPPC

- FreeBSD [3]

- Solaris [4]

- SGI Irix[5]

- OSF[6]

- HP/UX[7]

- Windows NT/95[8] through Cygnus Win32[9] package

Theoretically, Swarm can be compiled on almost all Unix-like Operating systems. Installing Swarm is not an easy operation: Swarm has become, during these years, a full complex set of packages.

Since its beta-version it has been modified several times to give the package a professional aspect.

This appendix is only an aid to people who want to build the libraries on their own home computer, and to enter the "Fabulous world of Swarm".

Swarm is distributed in two forms: source code and binary. The binary distributions provide an environment in which user applications can be compiled and linked, without building the Swarm kernel from source. In this appendix we'll explain how to compile Swarm Libraries yourself, because the author is against the *binaries installation*, due to the fact that the files created in other systems may contain or not certain libraries (in Unix shared libraries are very delicate to manage). For a more complete references, refer to Swarm documentation[10] or Paul Johnson's SwarmFAQ[11]

This appendix is composed of four sections:

- Swarm and its dependencies.

- How to install the package on a generic Unix System.

- How to install the package on a generic Windows system.

- Compiling and Running Swarm Applications

2.   SWARM AND ITS DEPENDENCIES

Before compiling Swarm libraries, the user has to dowload and compile some other software which contains some "routines" needed by the Swarm Package. Swarm need of two kind of resources:

- prerequisite software

- needed software

The `prerequisite software` are some packages which your OS environment shoud already contain (maybe not in right version), and **needed software** are ackages the User should compile before compiling Swarm libraries. Here is a short description of each component of both the prerequisite and needed software.

All these pieces of software are downloadable freely, and their source code are readily available in Santa Fe' ftp site and in many web sites on Internet.

2.1   PREREQUISITE SOFTWARE

- **egcs-1.1** or **gcc-2.8.1**. It is a C compiler which offers portability to a great number of systems and fairly good optimization. It has C,C++ Objective-C compiler inside it. It permits, roughly speaking, to compile a source code, to render it "executable" so the user can run it. The **egcs** or **gcc** calls the C preprocessor, the C compiler, the assembler, and the linker. The C preprocessor expands macro defnitions and also includes header files. The compilation phase creates assembly laguage code corresponding to the instructions in the source file. The assembler creates the machine-readable object code. Then the linker searches specified libraries for function in your program's object modules, and, finally, it creates an executable file.

- **xpm**[12]. The XPM library adds pixmap (coloured bitmap) support to X11. XPM is a common X library, many systems already have it installed.

- **gdb**[13]. it is the debugger written from GNU [14] A debugger is a tool which can help you find bugs in your code. It will allow you to follow your program as it executes to see what happens at each step. The program can be stopped on any line or at the start of any function and various types of information can be displayed, such as the value of a variable or the sequence of function calls that got you where you are. If your program causes a segmentation fault, GDB will show you where it happened. Advanced users can alter the values of variables to experiment with temporary bug fixes and view the contents of the program stack. The purpose of a debugger such as GDB is to allow you to see what is going on "inside" another program while it executes–or what another program was doing at the moment it crashed.

- **make**. This utility keeps track of which modules of a program have been updated, and helps to ensure that when you compile a program you use the latest versions of all program modules.

2.2   NEEDED SOFTWARE

- **tcl/tk**[15] It is a general-purpose scripting language developed originally by Dr. John Ousterhout, and now by a group of people at Sun. It is similar in nature to Perl, but has a much cleaner syntax and also has the famous Tk GUI built in. Tcl is an extendable control language of which Tk is a widget set extension: "Tcl interpretes the scripts and tk makes the windows, menus, scrollbars, bottons". Tcl stands for "Tool Command Language". Tk is actually an extension onto Tcl, so that Tcl will work quite happily without Tk (although pretty much everyone who uses Tcl also uses Tk).

- **BLT**. It was created by George Howlett with some help of Michael McLennan, both at AT&T Bell Labs Innovations for Lucent Technologies. BLT is an extension to the Tk toolkit, adding new widgets, geometry managers, and miscellaneous commands. It adds a lot of useful commands and widgets to Tcl\Tk, which made it one of the most popular extensions over the past years. Just in case you're wondering what BLT stands for: to the best of my knowledge, it's an "acronymic pun" (probably based on "Bell Labs Technologies") and translates into "Bacon, Lettuce & Tomato" (c.f. "bltwish"'s builtin logo: "pack [button .b -bitmap BLT]")

- **libpng** It was written as a companion to the PNG specification, as a way of reducing the amount of time and effort it takes to support the PNG file format in application programs.

- **libffi** or **ffcall**. Ffi stands for Foreign Function Interface. Some programs may not know at the time of compilation what arguments are to be passed to a function. For instance, an interpreter may be told at run-time about the number and types of arguments used to call a given function. Libffi can be seen in such programs to provide a bridge from the interpreter program to compiled code. The libffi library provides a portable, high level programming interface to various calling conventions. This allows a programmer to call any function specified by a call interface description at run time..

- **zlib**. It is a general purpose data compression library.

- optionally, **hdf5**. It is a database oriented toward scientific data. It provides efficient, parallel access to named objects, which may be very large.

3.   HOW TO INSTALL THE PACKAGE ON A GENERIC UNIX SYSTEM

To Install Swarm on a Unix box system, follow these steps

- Download from santafe's ftp site (ftp://ftp.santafe.edu/pub/swarm/need software) all the needed software

  - tcl 8.0
  - tk 8.0
  - BLT2.4g
  - libpng-1.0.3
  - libffi-1.18 or - ffcall-1.4
  - zlib-1.1.3

    − optionally, hdf5-1.0.1

and swarm-1.4.1.tar.gz

- Check that the prerequisite software are in the right version. This mean that you have to check that your OS contains[16] :

  − the right compiler *gcc-2.8.1*[17] or *egcs-1.x*[18];

  − the right version of XPM[19];

  − the right version of *make* program[20]

- Compile all the needed software. To compile the software, please, read the INSTALL file present in each packages. On various Unix Systems, to build the applications, just type `./configure` (to "build" the `Makefile` and to tell the compiler where to the binaries) then `make` and finally `make install` (to install the package)

- Compile the Swarm package `./configure`
  ```
  make
  make install
  ```

This is not intended to be an exaustive manual on how to install Swarm. For further information, please refer to Swarm Home Page or to Swarm-FAQ.

4.   HOW TO INSTALL THE PACKAGE ON A GENERIC WINDOWS SYSTEM

This is a 2 step process.

- Download the Cygnus Cygwin library. Learn about it at Cygwin's Web site: `http://www.cygnus.com` They have links to information and `ftp` sites. Go to a site and get the package "full.exe" for Cygwin Beta-20. Make a directory in an out-of-the-way place such as c:\tmp\cygnus and download it in there. Go to c:\temp\cygnus and double-click on full.exe. I let it install itself into c:\cygnus and recommend "newbies" do the same, since installation on other disk drives caused a big problem for users of previous versions

- Download the Swarm stuff. Make a directory c:\tmp\swarm and then go to ftp://ftp.santafe.edu/pub/swarm and get these 2 files and save them in c:\temp\swarm: swarm-1_4.exe and swarmapps-1.4.tar.gz

  (Windows muffs the second file name and saves it as swarmapps-1_4_tar.gz. Don't worry about it).

Go to c:\tmp\swarm and doubleclick on swarm-1_4.exe. Say OK, and follow the boxes. If you accept the defaults the Swarm library will be installed in c:\Swarm-1.4. When it asks if you want to reboot, say yes. After the reboot, look in your start menu, see the Swarm item and its "bash" subitem, choose that and you see an "X terminal" in which you can type unix commands and do unix stuff.

4.1   POSSIBLE INSTALL PROBLEMS

- During Swarm installation process, you may get the message "Severe: could not find PATH in autoexec.bat". That crashes the install-ation. If you see this, use explorer to look in c:\ for the file autoexec.bat. Do you find it? Do you have PATH in there? If not, create one with a text editor and add a line like this: PATH=C:\WINDOWS;C:\WINDOWS\COMMAND Then in ex-plorer, go back to c:\temp\swarm and double click on swarm-1_4.exe to try installing again.

- If you do not have a directory called c:\tmp, you will get an error message about it when you first run the swarm-term. So why not just create one?

5.   COMPILING AND RUNNING SWARM APPLICATIONS

Swarm applications are distributed separately: You will need to down-load and unpack applications independently. The apps are set up to be unpacked in a sibling directory to the Swarm libraries: if you unpack an application elsewhere, you will need to change the definition of the SWARMHOME environment variable. All you need to do to compile an application is type *make,* and it will compile and link. Applications are the best current roadmap for the Swarm code: much of what is pos-sible with Swarm is demonstrated in the sample applications. The most important applications are:

- **template**. Template simulation. The code itself here is trivial, but provides a nice base for new Swarm programmers to start from.

- **tutorial**. A step-by-step tutorial to using Swarm. The tutorial starts with a simple implementation of a cellular automaton in ordinary "C" and proceeds up to a full-blown GUI-oriented Swarm application in Swarm Objective C.

- **heatbugs.** Heatbugs, a simple complex system. The code here is thoroughly commented for use as a guide to swarm programming.

- **mousetrap.** Mousetrap is a discrete event simulation of a room full of mousetraps loaded with ping-pong balls. The triggering of one of the traps sets off a chain reaction supposedly similar to fission. It is also thoroughly commented.

- **market.** Market is an Objective-C wrapped piece of legacy code originally written in C. It is a useful example of how to convert legacy code into Swarm; but, it is not very instructive on Swarm programming in general.

Acknowledgments

I'd like to thank the editor, Francesco Luna, for the possibility he offered me to write this chapter/appendix.

I will also be deeply indebted with Prof. Masssimo Warglien: without him I'd never have known of the Swarm Project.

Notes

1. Swarm is copyrighted by Santa Fe' Institute, and released to the public under the GNU General Public Licence

2. Unix is a registered trademark of Unix System Laboratories, Inc.

3. FreeBSD is a trademark of FreeBSD, Inc.

4. Solaris is a trademark of Sun Microsystem, Inc.

5. SGI is a trademark of Silicon Graphix, Inc.

6. OSF is a trademark of Digital Equipment, Inc.

7. HP/UX is a trademark of Hewlet Packard, Inc.

8. Windows is a trademark of Microsoft, Inc.

9. Win32 is a trademark of Cygnus, Inc.

10. *http://www.santafe.edu/projects/swarm*

11. *http://lark.cc.ukans.edu/~pauljohn/SwarmFaq/SwarmOnlineFaq.html*

12. A reasonably modern version is needed: last one is version 3.4h. The library is available from ftp://ftp.x.org/contrib/libraries/xpm-3.4h.tar.gz

13. Not all version can be used with Swarm code. The working version of gdb which supports *Objective−C* language, is available at Santa Fe' ftp site (ftp://ftp.santafe.edu/pub/swarm)

14. Gnu stands for Gnu's not Unix. For futher info on various projects of GNU, connect your browser to the following URL http://www.gnu.org or http://www.fsf.org

15. Last version of Swarm works with Tcl/Tk 8.0x

16. If your system does not contain the right version of one of the packages, you have to download it from Santa Fe' ftp site and then to compile it. REMEMBER, to compile these software you HAVE TO BE SUPERUSER on your system

17. Just type at the prompt *gcc -v*

18. Just type at the prompt *gcc -v* or *egcs -v*. Compiling the compiler is not an easy operation, and it took some time. Refer to INSTALL file in the package for further info, or see the Alex's SwarmJournal

19. This is a bit difficult, because the name of file does not contain the right version, so my advice is to compile yourself this library to be sure it is in the right one

20. Just type at the prompt *make -v*

References

Minar, N., R. Burkhart, C. Langton, and M. Askenazi. 1996a. Swarm documentation [electronic document] (accessed 10/20/96); available from http://www.santafe.edu/projects/swarm

Minar, N., R. Burkhart, C. Langton, and M. Askenazi. 1996b. The Swarm simulation system: A toolkit for building multi-agent simulations. Technical Report 96-04-2, Santa Fe Institute, Santa Fe, NM.

Ousterhout John , 1994. Tcl and the Tk toolkit, Adison Wesley.

Sobel Mark G. , 1997. A practical Guide to Linux

Perrone A. SwarmJournal, available at http://www.dma.unive.it/~alex/ /swarm

II

..AND SOME PROSE

Chapter 3

ECONOMIC EXPERIMENTS WITH SWARM:
A NEURAL NETWORK APPROACH TO THE SELF-DEVELOPMENT OF CONSISTENCY IN AGENTS' BEHAVIOR

Pietro Terna
University of Turin,
Department of Economics and Finance G.Prato,
corso Unione Sovietica 218bis, 10134 Torino, Italy
terna@econ.unito.it

Abstract   We underline the usefulness of agent based models in the social science perspective, also focusing on the main computational problems due to the structure of our models: to simplify the task we introduce a generalized Environment-Rules-Agents scheme. Finally, within Swarm, we introduce a neural network tool (Cross Target method), useful in building artificial laboratories, for experiments with learning, self-developed consistency and interaction of agents in artificial worlds, in order to observe the emergence of complexity without a priori behavioral rules.

1.   INTRODUCTION

The goal of this work is that of proposing a tool, the **bp–ct** package written in Swarm, as an easy way in building and running artificial laboratories for social scientists.

Section 2., "Agent based models in the social science perspective", introduces some considerations on agent based models and underlines their usefulness in the social science perspective, considering also the wide field of computational economics; Section 3., "The ERA scheme", deals with the main computational problems due to the structure of our models and introduces a generalized Environment–Rules–Agents scheme (ERA), here primarily used to build the bp–ct package; Section 4., "Neural networks", briefly explains the idea of networks of processing elements as learning computational tools; in Section 5., "The Cross–Target (CT) method", we show the construction of artificially intelligent agents founded upon neural network based algorithms, which can be modified by a trial and error process without a priori behavioral rules; in Section 6., "The Swarm bp–ct package", the new package is explained.

Finally, in Section 7., "An experiment with the CT scheme of actions and effects, to obtain a spontaneous hayekian market", an experiment is built and run, obtaining a no–auctioneer hayekian market; Section 8. plans for "Future improvements".

2.   AGENT BASED MODELS IN THE SOCIAL SCIENCE PERSPECTIVE

Choosing the agent based model paradigm we enter a wide unexplored world where methodology and techniques are largely "under construction." We are here working in the bottom–up direction, putting together pieces of software (our agents) which can react to stimuli from the environment or from other agents. Why to do so?

An interesting overview comes from the following Web sites: Syllabus of Readings for Artificial Life and Agent–Based Economics[1]; Web Site for Agent–Based Computational Economics[2]; Agent–Based Economics and Artificial Life: A Brief Intro[3]; Complex Systems at the University of Buenos Aires[4]; Computational Economic Modeling[5]; Individual–Based Models[6]. We can also refer to works in the social simulation perspective Conte *et al.*, 1997, artificial intelligence Russel and Norvig, 1995 and in economics Beltratti *et al.*, 1996; also of interest is The Complexity Research Project of the London School of Economics and Political Science[7].

At present, the best plain introduction to agent based modeling techniques is reported in the introduction to the Sugarscape model Epstein and Axtell, 1996. As Epstein and Axtell (Chapter 1) note:

> Herbert Simon is fond of arguing that the social sciences are, in fact, the hard sciences. For one, many crucially important social processes are complex. They are not neatly decomposable into separate subprocesses–economic, demographic, cultural, spatial–whose isolated analyses can be aggregated to give an adequate analysis of the social process as a whole. And yet, this is exactly how social science is organized, into more or less insular departments and journals of economics, demography, political science, and so forth (...)
>
> The social sciences are also hard because certain kinds of controlled experimentation are hard. In particular, it is difficult to test hypotheses concerning the relationship of individual behaviors to macroscopic regularities, hypotheses of the form: If individuals behave in thus and such

a way–that is, follow certain specific rules–then society as a whole will exhibit some particular property. How does the heterogeneous micro–world of individual behaviors generate the global macroscopic regularities of the society?

Another fundamental concern of most social scientists is that the rational actor–a perfectly informed individual with infinite computing capacity who maximizes a fixed (nonevolving) exogenous utility function–bears little relation to a human being. Yet, there has been no natural methodology for relaxing these assumptions about the individual.

Relatedly, it is standard practice in the social sciences to suppress real–world agent heterogeneity in model–building. This is done either explicitly, as in representative agent models in macroeconomics Kirman, 1992, or implicitly, as when highly aggregate models are used to represent social processes. While such models can offer powerful insights, they filter out all consequences of heterogeneity. Few social scientists would deny that these consequences can be crucially important, but there has been no natural methodology for systematically studying highly heterogeneous populations.

Finally, it is fair to say that, by and large, social science, especially game theory and general equilibrium theory, has been preoccupied with static equilibria, and has essentially ignored time dynamics. Again, while granting the point, many social scientists would claim that there has been no natural methodology for studying nonequilibrium dynamics in social systems.

The response to this long, but exemplary, quotation, is exactly social simulation and agent based artificial experiments. This means being capable of starting from the basis, with humility, to have our agents interacting, to observe what emerges (if something does) from their action. Partially this is the same exercise done when we explore the wide world of computational economics; computational economics is a complement of the theory Judd, 1996, since verifies and explains theoretical issues numerically solving and iterating equations, with true or guessed parameters. But, as Judd points out, we have here also the possibility of using computational (or agent based, my addition) results as results at all, as they would be theorems:

The increasing power of computers presents economic science with new opportunities and potential. However, as with any new tool, there has been discussion concerning the proper role of computation in economics. Some roles are obvious and noncontroversial. Most will agree that computation is necessary in econometric analysis and offers some guidance in policy discussions. Theorists will admit that examples are useful in illustrating general results. However, the discussion frequently gets heated when one raises the possibility of using the computer and computer–generated "examples" instead of the classical assumption–theorem–proof form of analysis for studying an economic theory. In economic terms, the first roles for computation are complements to and a useful ingredient in standard research activities; however, the activity of computational theory appears to be a substitute for conventional theoretical analysis. In this essay, I will focus on the potential role of computational methods in economic theory and their relation to standard theoretical analysis, asking "Are they complements or substitutes?"

But how to build an agent based model? Basically, we have to construct Gilbert and Terna, 1999a computer model in which agents (pieces of software) operate (behave).

First, we must consider the agents as objects: i.e., pieces of software capable of containing data and rules to work on the data. The rules provide the mechanisms necessary to react to messages coming from outside the object.

Second, we have to observe the individual agents' behaviour via the internal variable states of each agent–object and, at the same time, the results arising from their collective behaviour. One important feature of the software is therefore to synchronise the experiment clocks: we have to be sure that the observations made at the aggregate level and the knowledge that we are picking up about the internal states of the agents are consistent in terms of the experimental schedules.

Now let us suppose that a community of agents, acting on the basis of public (i.e. common to all agents) and private (i.e. specific to each agent) information and of simple internal local rules, shows, as a whole, an interesting, complex, or "emergent" behaviour. There are two kinds of emergence: unforeseen and unpredictable emergence. An example of unforeseen emergence occurs when we are looking for an equilibrium state, but some sort of cyclical behaviour appears; the determinants of the cyclical behaviour are hidden in the structure of the model. Unpredictable emergence occurs when, for example, chaos appears in the data produced by an experiment. Chaos is obviously observable in true social science phenomena, but it is not easy to reverse engineer in an agent–based simulation.

3.   THE ERA SCHEME

Swarm is a natural candidate to this kind of structures, but we need some degree of standardization, mainly when we go from simple models to complex results. Here a crucial role for the usefulness and the acceptability of the experiments is played by the structure of the underlying models. For this reason, we introduce here a general scheme that can be employed in building agent–based simulations.

The main value of the Environment–Rules–Agents (ERA) scheme shown in Figure 3.1 is that it keeps both the environment, which models the context by means of rules and general data, and the agents, with their private data, at different conceptual levels. To simplify the code, we suggest that agents should not communicate directly, but always through the environment; as an example, the environment allows each agent to know the list of its neighbours. This is not mandatory, but if we admit direct communication between agents, the code becomes more complex.

With the aim of simplifying the code design, agent behaviour is determined by external objects, named Rule Masters, that can be interpreted as abstract representations of the cognition of the agent. Production systems, classifier systems, neural networks and genetic algorithms are all candidates for the implementation of Rule Masters.

We may also need to employ meta–rules, i.e., rules used to modify rules (for example, the training side of a neural network). The Rule Master objects are therefore linked to Rule Maker objects, whose role is to modify the rules mastering agent behaviour, for example by means of a simulated learning process. Rule Masters obtain the information necessary to apply rules from the agents themselves or from special agents charged with the task of collecting and distributing data. Similarly, Rule Makers interact with Rule Masters, which are also responsible for getting data from agents to pass to Rule Makers.

Agents may store their data in a specialized object, the DataWarehouse, and may interact both with the environment and other agents via another specialized object, the Interface (DataWarehouse and Interface are not represented in Figure 3.1, having a simple one to one link with their agent; they are used in the bp–ct package and in its derivatives).

Although this code structure appears to be complex, there is a benefit when we have to modify a simulation. The rigidity of the structure then becomes a source of invaluable clarity. An example of the use of this structure can be found in the code of the Swarm application bp–ct in which the agents are neural networks; also the specialized code related to the hayekian experiment reported in Section 7., being built upon bp–ct, uses the same structure. The codes of these packages can be obtained both at CEEL site of Trento (http://www-ceel.gelso.unitn.it) and directly from the author (may be also from the anarchy section of the Swarm site).

A second advantage of using the ERA structure is its modularity, which allows model builders to modify only the Rule Master and Rule Maker modules or objects whenever one wants to switch from agents based on neural networks, to alternatives such as production systems, classifier systems or genetic algorithms.

In Swarm terms, the Environment coincides with the ModelSwarm object, while the ObserverSwarm object is external to this structure.

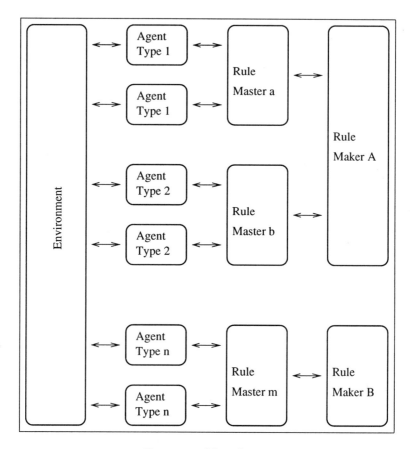

Figure 3.1   The scheme.

The bp–ct code represents a basic package from which we can derive any sort of application, via: (i) the modification of Interface objects if we are keeping unchanged the neural network choice and the CT (Section 5.) framework or we are using any internal system of rules producing inputs and targets for the neural networks; (ii) the substitution of external training and verification sets, if we are using the package as a backpropagation tool in the neural network field; (iii) the modification of RuleMaster and RuleMaker objects, if we are shifting to other paradigms, as described above.

4.   NEURAL NETWORKS

The choice of neural networks Rumelhart and McClelland, 1986 as standard tool for the implementation of bp–ct relies on the capabilities of these vectorial functions, specified in equation (3.1), as structures very close, in econometric terms, to nonlinear multidimensional regression functions.

$$y = f\left(\mathbf{B}\ f\left(\mathbf{A}\mathbf{x}\right)\right) \tag{3.1}$$

We can imagine a class of simple Artificial Neural Networks (ANN), the multilayer perceptron or feed forward network, as a system of connections linking several processing units of the kind shown in Figure 3.2. The processing element (PE) can be considered as an over simplified sketch of a natural neuron, where the parameters w_{kj} represent the strength of the synapses. The a_j values ("activations") are the inputs of the PE or neuron, which calculates their weighted sum (this operation explains the use of the conventional name "weight" to designate the parameters of a function in the ANN jargon). The same operation, in matrix algebra, is done by the product $\mathbf{A}\mathbf{x}$, where the $\mathbf{x}$ vector contains the a_j activations and the matrix $\mathbf{A}$ the w_{kj} parameters. The PE produces an output applying a non linear transformation to the weighted sum, as th.. i shown in equation (3.2), where k is the parameter that determines the closeness of the function to a crude step function.

$$f(z) = \frac{1}{1 + e^{-kz}} \tag{3.2}$$

A simplified form of ANN, not used here, does not consider the external transformation function and assumes the form $\mathbf{B}\ f(\mathbf{A}\mathbf{x})$.

Each row of $\mathbf{A}$ and $\mathbf{B}$ contains the weights of a PE. In Figure 3.3 we have an example of a network with an input layer of four PEs (from 1 to 4), an internal or hidden layer with three PEs (from 5 to 7) and an output layer with two PEs (from 8 to 9). Note that without the hidden layer the ANN would be a trivial non linear structure of the form $f(\mathbf{A}\mathbf{x})$.

As an example: the matrix $\mathbf{A}$ (2 rows and 3 columns) in Figure 3.3 contains the w_{kj} values of the PEs from 8 to 9, such as w_{97} in the Figure; the matrix $\mathbf{B}$ (3 rows and 4 columns) contains those of the PEs from 5 to 7; the $\mathbf{x}$ vector contains the four values of the input PEs, which are here simply the receptors of the stimuli arriving to the ANN from outside.

It is useful to consider also an input PE and a hidden PE as a constant value (e.g. always 1) to allow the definition of a w parameter operating as a bias value in the $-kz$ exponent of the logistic function (3.2), where $z = \sum_{s=1}^{m} a_s w_{ks}$, obtaining the correction $-k\left(z + b\right)$ with $b = w_{k0}$, directly as $-k\tilde{z}$ with $\tilde{z} = \sum_{s=0}^{m} a_s w_{ks}$. Formally this structure can be expressed as in equation (3.3).

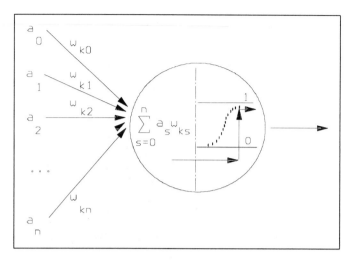

Figure 3.2   A Node or Artificial Neuron

$$y = f\left(\mathbf{B}\left(1, f\left(\mathbf{A}\left(1, \mathbf{x}'\right)'\right)'\right)'\right) \tag{3.3}$$

To find the **A** and **B** values (i.e. the ANN parameters) we have to use a numerical approximation with a simplified gradient method, the so–called backpropagation method (which comes from "propagating back" the error measures from the output layer to the hidden one), starting with random parameters and adapting the performances of the ANN function on the basis of a set of training examples. Other methods also exist, but the backpropagation (the bp part of the name of our code) is used here for its simplicity and robustness. A detailed explanation of the bp method is contained in the comments of the RuleMaker.m file of the bp–ct code.

The process of parameter determination is also called "learning", because the quality of the result is obviously related to the number of numerical iterations of the trial and errors correction cycle upon the examples (patterns, always in the ANN jargon). Generally a second set of examples, the verification set, not used in the learning phase, it is instead employed to check the performances of the ANN function.

The particular way neural networks work and are trained, makes them able to reproduce the performance of any function as "universal approximator" White, 1990.

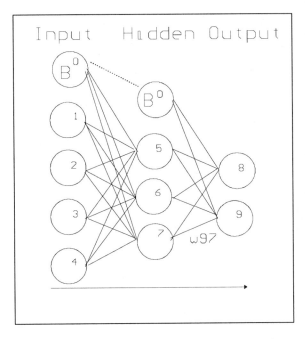

Figure 3.3 A simple Artificial Neural Network

5.   THE CROSS–TARGET (CT) METHOD

5.1   SKETCHING THE IDEA

To develop our agent based experiments, we introduce the following general hypothesis (GH): an agent, acting in an economic environment, must develop and adapt her capability of evaluating, in a coherent way, (1) what she has to do in order to obtain a specific result and (2) how to foresee the consequences of her actions. The same is true if the agent is interacting with other agents. Beyond this kind of internal consistency (IC), agents can develop other characteristics, for example the capability of adopting actions (following external proposals, EPs) or evaluations of effects (following external objectives, EOs) suggested from the environment (for example, following rules) or from other agents (for examples, imitating them). Those additional characteristics are useful for a better tuning of the agents in making experiments.

To apply the GH we are employing here artificial neural networks; we observe, anyway, that the GH can be applied using other algorithms and tools, reproducing the experience–learning–consistency–behavior cycle with or without neural networks.

An introductory general remark: in all the cases to which we have applied our GH, the preliminary choice of classifying agents' output in actions and effects has been useful (i) to clarify the role of the agents, (ii) to develop model plausibility and results, (iii) to avoid the necessity of prior statements about economic rational optimizing behavior Beltratti *et al.*, 1996.

Economic behavior, simple or complex, can appear directly as a by–product of IC, EPs and EOs. To an external observer, our Artificial Adaptive Agents (AAAs) are apparently operating with goals and plans. Obviously, they have no such symbolic entities, which are inventions of the observer. The similarity that we recall here is that the observations and analyses about real world agents' behavior can suffer from the same bias. Moreover, always to an external observer, AAAs can appear to apply the rationality paradigm, with maximizing behavior.

Complexity can be more frequently found out of the agents – in the framework emerging from their interaction, adaptation and learning – than within them; exactly in the same way, also rationality (and Olympic rationality) can be found out of agents, simply as a by–product of environment constraints and agents bounded capabilities. The same for optimization, as a by–product of interaction and constraints, emerging externally to the agents mind.

The main problem is: obviously agents, with their action, have the goal of increasing or decreasing something, but it is not correct to deduce from this statement any formal apparatus encouraging the search for complexity within agents, not even in the *as if* perspective. With our GH, and hereafter with the Cross Target (CT) method, we work at the edge of Alife techniques to develop Artificial Worlds of simple bounded rationality rationality AAAs: from their interaction, complexity, optimizing behavior and Olympic rationality can emerge, but externally to the agents.

Finally, we want to consider learning from the point of view of the bounded rationality research program Arthur, 1990:

> In designing a learning system to represent human behaviour in a particular context, we would be interested not only in reproducing human rates of learning, but also in reproducing the style in which humans learn, possibly even the ways in which they might depart from perfect rationality. The ideal, then, would not simply be learning curves that reproduce human learning curves to high goodness–of–fit, but more ambitiously, learning behaviour that could pass the Turing test of being indistinguishable from human behaviour with its foibles, departures and errors, to an observer who was not informed whether the behaviour was algorithm–generated or human–generated.

In order to implement this ideal target without falling in the trap of creating models that are too complicated to be managed, we consider artificially intelligent agents founded upon algorithms which can be modified by a trial and error process. In one sense our agents are even simpler than those considered in neoclassical models, as their targets and instruments are not as powerful as those assumed in those models. From another point of view, however, our agents are much more complex, due to their continuous effort to learn the main features of the environment with the available instruments.

The name cross–targets (CTs) comes from the technique used to figure out the targets necessary to train the ANNs representing the artificial adaptive agents (AAAs) that populate our experiments.

Following the GH, the main characteristic of these AAAs is that of developing internal consistency between what to do and the related consequences. Always according to the GH, in many (economic) situations, the behavior of agents produces evaluations that can be split in two parts: data quantifying actions (what to do) and forecasts of the outcomes of the actions. So we specify two types of outputs of the ANN and, identically, of the AAA: (i) actions to be performed and (ii) guesses about the effects of those actions.

Both the targets necessary to train the network from the point of view of the actions and those connected with the effects are built in a crossed way, originating the name Cross Targets. The former are built in a consistent way with the outputs of the network concerning the guesses of the effects, in order to develop the capability to decide actions close to the expected results. The latter, similarly, are built in a constant way with the outputs of the network concerning the guesses of the actions, in order to improve the agent's capability of estimating the effects emerging from the actions that the agent herself is deciding.

CTs, as a fulfillment of the GH, can reproduce economic subjects' behavior, often in internally ingenuous ways, but externally with complex results.

The method of CTs, introduced to develop economic subjects' autonomous behavior, can also be interpreted as a general algorithm useful for building behavioral models without using constrained or unconstrained optimization techniques. The kernel of the method, conveniently based upon ANNs (but it could also be conceivable with the aid of other mathematical tools), is learning by guessing and doing: the subject control capabilities can be developed without defining either goals or maximizing objectives.

5.2   TECHNICAL DETAILS

We choose the neural networks approach to develop CTs, mostly as a consequence of the intrinsic adaptive capabilities of neural functions. Here we will use feed forward multilayer networks as introduced in Section 4.

Figure 3.4 describes an AAA learning and behaving in a CT scheme. The AAA has to produce guesses about its own actions and related effects, on the basis of an information set (the input elements are $I_1, ..., I_k$). Remembering the requirement of IC, targets in learning process are: (i) on one side, the actual effects – measured through accounting rules – of the actions made by the simulated subject; (ii) on the other side, the actions needed to match guessed effects. In the last case we have to use inverse rules, even though some problems arise when the inverse is indeterminate. Technical explanations of CT method Beltratti *et al.*, 1996 are reported below.

A first remark, about learning and CT: analyzing the changes of the weights during the process we can show that the matrix of weights linking input elements to hidden ones has little or no changes, while the matrix of weights from hidden to output layer changes in a relevant way. Only hidden–output weight changes determine the continuous adaptation of ANN responses to the environment modifications, as the output values of hidden layer elements stay almost constant. This situation is the consequence both of very small changes in targets (generated by CT method) and of a reduced number of learning cycles.

The resulting network is certainly under trained: consequently, the simulated economic agent develops a local ability to make decisions, but only by adaptations of outputs to the last targets, regardless to input values. This is short term learning as opposed to long term learning.

Some definitions: we have (i) short term learning, in the acting phase, when agents continuously modify their weights (mainly from the hidden layer to the output one), to adapt to the targets self–generated via CT; (ii) long term learning, ex post, when we effectively map inputs to targets (the same generated in the acting phase) with a large number of learning cycles, producing ANNs able to definitively apply the rules implicitly developed in the acting and learning phase.

A second remark, about both external objectives (EOs) and external proposals (EPs): if used, these values substitute the cross targets in the acting and adapting phase and are consistently included in the data set for ex post learning. Despite the target coming from actions, the guess of an effect can be trained to approximate a value suggested by a simple rule, for example increasing wealth. This is an EO in CT

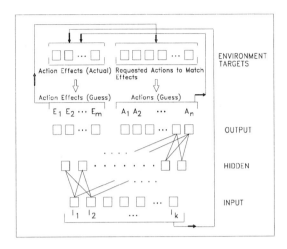

Figure 3.4   The Cross-Target (CT) scheme.

terminology. Its indirect effect, via CT, will modify actions, making them more consistent with the (modified) guesses of effects. Vice versa, the guess about an action to be accomplished can be modified via an EP, affecting indirectly also the corresponding guesses of effects. If EO, EP and IC conflict in determining behavior, complexity may emerge also within agents, but in a bounded rationality rationality perspective, always without the optimization and full rationality apparatus.

Now we may introduce some technical explanations about CTs, with the aid of the general scheme of Figure 3.4, observing that (i) the inputs of the model are mainly data coming from the environment or from other agents' behavior, (ii) they can be dependent or independent from the previous actions of the simulated artificial subject, (iii) targets are known only when actions take place.

The CT algorithm is a learning and acting one: action is necessary to produce the information by which we can construct targets to train the ANN that simulates the subject. A training set cannot be constructed here in the usual way because rules linking inputs and outputs of the ANN have 'to be discovered' by the experiments led by AAAs.

Learning and acting take place in four steps each 'day'; a day is the sum of the four steps required to perform a full cycle of estimation of outputs and of backpropagation of errors, correcting the neural network weights. Initial weights are randomized in a given range.

Looking at Figure 3.4, the four steps can be introduced in the following sequence.

1. Outputs of the ANN: the actions to be accomplished, reported in the right side of Figure 3.4, and the effects of these actions, reported in the left side of the same figure, are guessed following inputs and network weights.

2. Targets for the left side of the network: the targets for the effects supposed to arise from actions, as guessed in the left side of the output layer in Figure 3.4, are figured out by the independently guessed actions. In this way, guesses about effects become more close to the true consequences of actual actions.

3. Targets for the right side of the network: the differences measured in step (2) among targets and ANN outputs on the effect side can be inversely interpreted as starting points for action modifications, to match the guessed effects. So they are used to build the targets for the mechanism that guesses the actions. Being the inverses of the formulas shown below often undefined, corrections are shared randomly among all the targets to be constructed; besides, when several corrections concern a target, only the one with the largest module is chosen. In this way, we would like to imitate the actual behavior of a subject requested of obeying to several independent and inconsistent commands: probably the most imperative, here the largest value, will be followed.

4. Backpropagation: learning takes place, correcting weights in order to obtain guessed effects closer to the consequences of guessed actions, and guessed actions more consistent with guessed effects. Thus, we have two learning processes, both based upon the guesses of the elements of the opposite side of the network.

This double sided process of adaptation, with interaction among agents and long term learning introduced above, ensures the emergence of non trivial self–developed behavior, from the point of view of time paths of the values generated by the outcomes of the agents.

We can now explain in a formal way the acting and learning algorithm of CTs, introducing a generic effect E_1 arising from two actions, named A_1 and A_2. The target for the effect is:

$$\widehat{E}_1 = f(A_1, A_2) \tag{3.4}$$

where $f(\bullet)$ is a definition, linking actions to effects on an accounting basis.

Our aim here is to obtain an output E_1 (the guess made by the network) closer to $\widehat{E}_1$, which is the correct measure of the effect of actions A_1 and A_2. The error related to E_1 is:

$$e = \widehat{E}_1 - E_1$$

or, by convention in ANN development, one half of the square of $\widehat{E}_1 - E_1$. To minimize the error, we backpropagate it through network weights.

Our aim is now finding the actions, as outputs of our network, more consistent with the outputs produced by the effect side. So we have to correct A_1 and A_2 to made them closer to $\widehat{A}_1$ and $\widehat{A}_2$, which are actions consistent with the output E_1. We cannot figure out the targets for A_1 and A_2 separately. From (3.4) we have:

$$A_1 = g_1(\widehat{E}_1, A_2) \tag{3.5}$$

$$A_2 = g_2(\widehat{E}_1, A_1) \tag{3.6}$$

Choosing a random value τ_1 from a random uniform distribution whose support is the closed interval $[0, 1]$ and setting $\tau_2 = 1 - \tau_1$, from (3.5) and (3.6) we obtain:

$$\widehat{A}_1 = g_1(\widehat{E}_1 - e \cdot \tau_1, A_2) \tag{3.7}$$

$$\widehat{A}_2 = g_2(\widehat{E}_1 - e \cdot \tau_2, A_1) \tag{3.8}$$

Functions g_1 and g_2, being obtained from definitions that link actions to effects mainly on an accounting basis, usually have linear specifications; so equations (3.7) and (3.8) generally give solutions that are globally consistent. The errors to be minimized are:

$$a_1 = \widehat{A}_1 - A_1$$

$$a_2 = \widehat{A}_2 - A_2$$

Eqs. (3.7) and (3.8) would be unacceptable as inversions of true dynamic functions, but they are used here as a simplifying tool (mainly for the presence of random separation obtained by t_1 and t_2 values), always to generate time paths for variables, without a priori or external suggestions.

When the actions determine multiple effects, they are included in multiple definitions of effects. So, those actions will be affected by several corrections; as reported in point 3 above, only the largest absolute value is chosen.

Input and target variability, generated both in deterministic and random ways, is required to ensure the economic plausibility of the experiments, but is also necessary to ensure that the outputs and the targets of the ANN change. Lacking such variability, on the basis of initial random weights of the network and following CTs, in most cases all outputs would be frozen at about 0.5, with perfect but merely apparent learning results.

With the proper variability, we repeat for a given number of cycles (days) the four steps introduced describing Figure 3.4. The learning following the fourth step of each day gives a sort of local adaptation to the changes of the environment.

6.   THE SWARM BP–CT PACKAGE

We introduce here the bp–ct code as a package useful to develop and run ANNs in the Swarm framework. A complete "How to use bp–ct" explanation is included as a text file in the distribution of the package. Here we only outline the use of the program both with simple examples and with an economic application (in Section 7.).

At present the code runs with Swarm v.1.4.1 and it will be continuously adapted to the new releases of Swarm.

6.1   BP–CT AS BP, WITH EXTERNAL INPUTS AND TARGETS

The first example is related to the use of the program as a simple backpropagation tool. In the window reported in Figure 3.5 we point out: (i) the use of a unique agent–ANN (but the code can train and run in a parallel way any number of ANNs, with only memory and time limitations); (ii) the structure of the ANN (inputNodeNumber, hiddenNodeNumber, outputNodeNumber); (iii) the number of patterns in the Training Set and in the Verification Set; (iv) the Number of Epochs (an Epoch is here a complete learning cycle upon all the patterns, correcting the weights after the evaluation of the ANN outputs for each pattern).

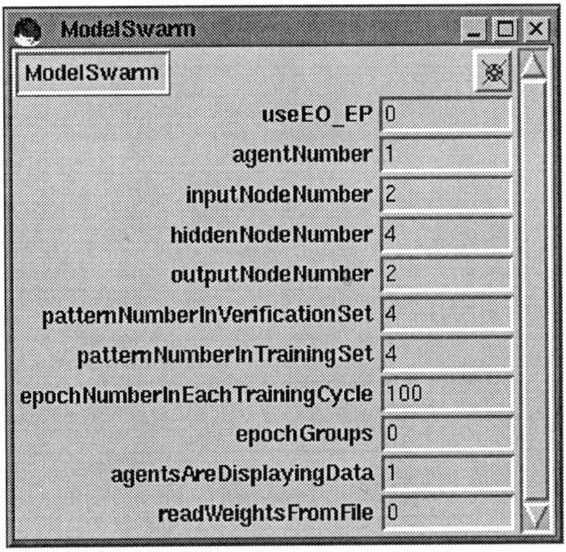

Figure 3.5   The control window of bp–ct in the external inputs and targets case

The patterns of this example represent a classic in the field of ANNs testing. It is based on the XOR logical function with $XOR(F, F) = F$; $XOR(T, F) = T$; $XOR(F, T) = T$; $XOR(T, T) = F$. In this case we can have only four patterns for the Training Set; the same patterns form the Verification Set (numerically, we will use 0 for F and 1 for T). We have here two outputs because our ANN simultaneously maps also the OR function on the input data.

Being positive the number of patterns pointed out for the Training and the Verification Set in the window of Figure 3.5, the program read the pattern data from two files (the name of the files is specified in the code and can be changed). After about 30 learning Epochs the XOR output of our ANN, as reported in Figure 3.6, matches perfectly the desired outputs (targets) of Figure 3.7.

6.2   BP–CT AS CT, WITH INTERNAL GENERATION OF INPUTS AND TARGETS

The second example is related to the use of the program with internal generation of inputs and targets, as a step toward the CT use. In the window reported in Figure 3.8 we point out the same choices of the previous example, except the point (iii) where we have the number of patterns in the Training Set equal to -1 and those in the Verification

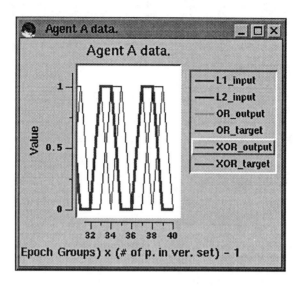

Figure 3.6   XOR outputs

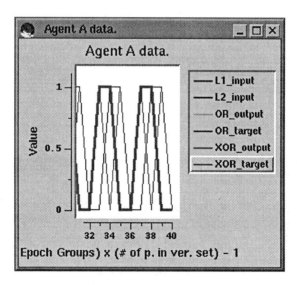

Figure 3.7   XOR targets

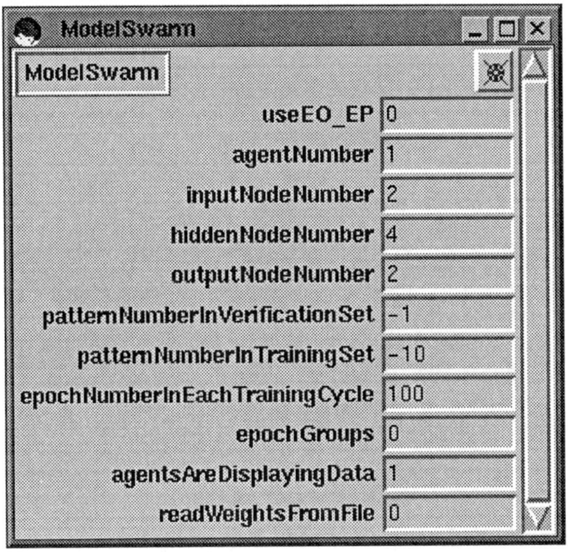

Figure 3.8 The control window of bp–ct in the internal inputs and targets case

Set equal to −10. A negative value has here the meaning of internal data generation: if negative, the patternNumberInTrainingSet variable can be only equal to −1; the negative value of the patternNumberInVerificationSet variable establishes the number of auto–generated patterns to be collected to form each training Epoch.

Also this example is founded on the XOR logical function: after about 30 learning Epochs the XOR output of our ANN, as reported in Figure 3.9, matches perfectly the desired outputs (targets) of Figure 3.10.

7. AN EXPERIMENT WITH THE CT SCHEME OF ACTIONS AND EFFECTS, TO OBTAIN A SPONTANEOUS HAYEKIAN MARKET

The main goal of the bp–ct project is that of using the code in the perspective of interacting agents, with internally generated inputs and targets, following the ERA scheme (Section 3.) and, above all, applying the rule structure described in the CT framework (Section 5.).

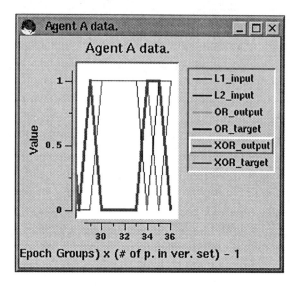

Figure 3.9   XOR outputs

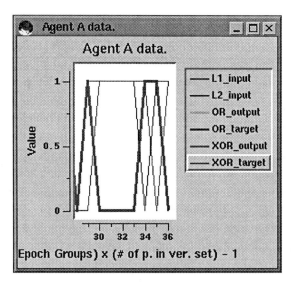

Figure 3.10   XOR targets

7.1 THE STRUCTURE OF THE EXPERIMENT

With CT we build an experimental framework with AAAs to test the consequences of the learning capabilities of the agents.

The experiment has the following structure (a detailed definition of the structure is reported in the code ct–hayek, which is the adaptation of bp–ct to the specific experiment).

1. The consumer agent has in input the variables: $Expenditure_0$, the expense of the previous period; $Requirement_0$, the requirement of the previous period; p_0, the price of the unique good, as proposed by the agent in the previous period; q_0, the agent buying proposal in the previous period.

2. The producer agent has in input the variables: $Revenue_0$, the revenue of the previous period; $ProductionStream_0$, the production stream requirement of the previous period; p_0, the price of the unique good, as proposed by the agent in the previous period; q_0, the agent selling proposal in the previous period.

3. The outputs of the ANN simulating the consumer agent and the related targets are: $actualP$, the guess about the exchange price (the target is simply the exchange price, true or latent, see below); $actualQ$, the guess about the exchanged quantity (the target is simply the exchanged quantity, may be 0); the $actualP$ and $actualQ$ values are effects in CT jargon, but they strictly depend by the action of another agent; being here not strategical to develop the agent capability of forecasting these values, they are not directly included in the cross targets to action; $Expenditure$, the guess about the expense in the current period (the target is obtained multiplying p and q); $Requirement$, the requirement in the current period (the target is $actualQ$); p and q, the price and the quantity proposed by the agent to exchange (the targets come from $Expenditure$ and $Requirement$ and so indirectly from $actualQ$).

4. The outputs of the ANN simulating the producer agent and the related targets are: $actualP$ and $actualQ$ (see above); $Revenue$, the guess about the revenue in the current period (the target is obtained multiplying p and q); p and q, the price and the quantity proposed by the agent to exchange (the targets come from $Revenue$ and $ProductionStream$ and so indirectly from $actualQ$).

5. We have 10 consumers and 10 producers; the production process is undefined; the producers are simply supposed to offer the quantity

that they are producing in each time unit; consumers and producers meet randomly each "day". The exchange is possible if the
producer proposed price is less or equal to the price proposed by
the consumer; the price used in the exchange is that proposed by
the producer and the quantity is the minimum between the consumer proposal and the producer proposal; if the exchange is not
possible the reference price (used in the determination of the mean
price of the day) is that of the consumer and the quantity is 0.

6. We introduce also external objectives (EOs) which are explained
   in detail in the distributed ct–hayek code. In the consumer case: if
   $useEO\_EP$ variable (see Figure 3.11) is set to 0 we have no EOs;
   if $useEO\_EP$ variable is set to 1, the effect Expenditure is trained
   with a lowering target; if $useEO\_EP$ variable is set to 2, the effect Requirement is trained with a constant target; if $useEO\_EP$
   variable is set to 3 both the previous EOs operate. The CT consequences are modification of the p guess, remembering that the
   EOs modifies the outputs of the effect side of the underlying ANN,
   but via CT also the action side; the modification of the guess about
   p facilitates or prevents the exchange measured by actualQ. In the
   producer case we act symmetrically, when $useEO\_EP$ is set to 1 or
   2 or 3, increasing the Revenue target and keeping constant the ProductionStream one; ProductionStream can be interpreted as the
   adequate production related to an existing fixed capital structure.

Following the distinction between short and long term learning introduced in Section 5., the experiment is run (i) with short term learning
(Figures 3.12, 3.15, 3.18 and 3.21), with agent adapting only to local
the local situation, (ii) with a light form of long term learning (Figures
96, 3.16, 3.19 and 3.22), where agent start developing the capability of
acting globally and (iii) finally (Figures 3.14, 3.17, 3.20 and 3.23) with
a complete form of long term learning.

The starting window of the ct–hayek code, with the no EOs and light
long term learning case, is reported in Figure 3.11, where we can see
the choice about EOs, the double choice of the agent number, the CT
selection with the negative numbers in the two pattern number boxes.

In the Hayek sense of individualism and economic order Hayek, 1949,
we are here dealing with agents behaving on a strictly individualistic
basis, without the over–simplification of an artificial auctioneer market.
A market with stable prices anyway emerges, with an empirical quasi–
equilibrium. Note that we explicitly exclude from our model any form
of prior description of this kind of equilibrium and that the agents have

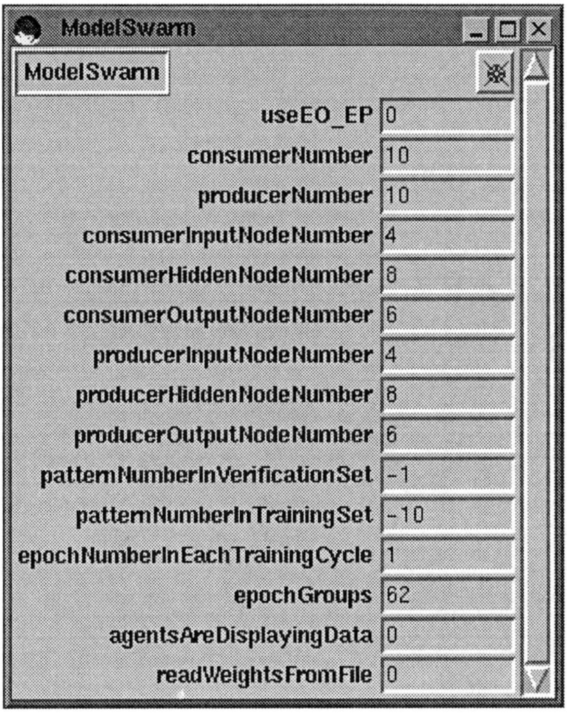

Figure 3.11   The control window of bp–ct as it appears in ct–hayek package

no knowledge about the mean price, which is only used by the observer to externally describe the experiment.

We have to read the lines of the graphics of the Figures from 3.12 to 3.23, as (bottom up): (i) mean quantity of the exchanges (divided by 10 for a scale necessity); (ii) Min price; (iii) mean price; (iv) Max price. Prices are obtained by the p variable described above.

7.2   EXPERIMENT RESULTS

A market spontaneous equilibrium emerges immediately in our first run of the model, with *useEO_EP* variable set to 0. We have a complex equilibrium situation: in the case of short term leaning, Figure 3.12, with a low price increase as a consequence of the internally generated (without EOs) values of *Requirement* and *ProductionStream*; in the case of light relearning, Figure 3.13, the complexity of the system increases, showing a few agents (the mean is always very close to the Max) leaving the general situation; the third case, the one with heavy relearning, reported

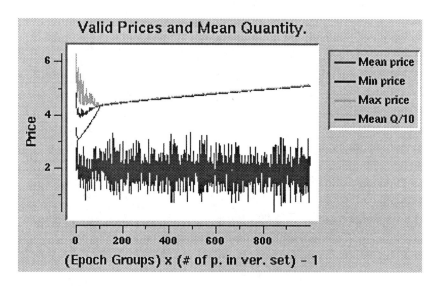

Figure 3.12   Short term learning, without EOs

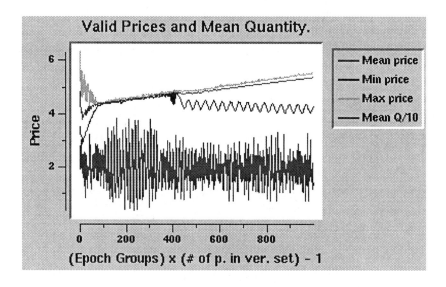

Figure 3.13   Light long term learning, without EOs

in Figure 3.14, we can see a robust equilibrium, with some individuals differentiating their behavior.

In the second run of the model, with *useEO_EP* variable set to 1, we have a perfectly calibrated model in the case of short term learning of Figure 3.15. The presence of long term learning introduces, both in Fig-

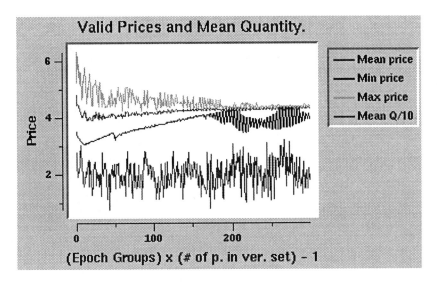

Figure 3.14 Long term learning, without EOs

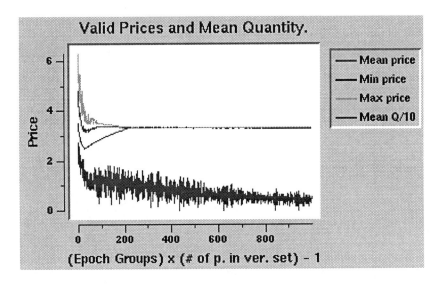

Figure 3.15 Short term learning, with EOs on Expenditure and Revenue

ure 3.16 and in Figure 3.17 a few cases of divergent behavior. Effectively the goal proposed, via EOs, to the agents have a poor economic sense if considered alone, being the suggestion of doing impossible things (to diminish expenditure and to raise revenue, without boundary conditions); the inconsistency of this situation emerges with the relearning process.

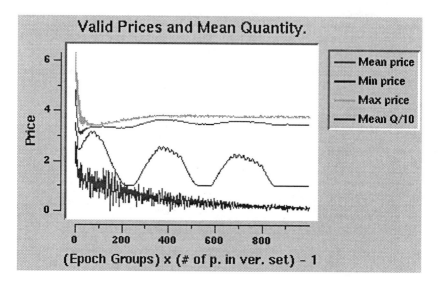

Figure 3.16   Light long term learning, with EOs on Expenditure and Revenue

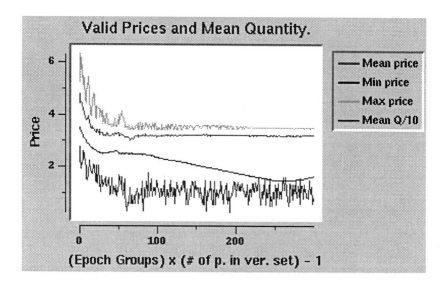

Figure 3.17   Long term learning, with EOs on Expenditure and Revenue

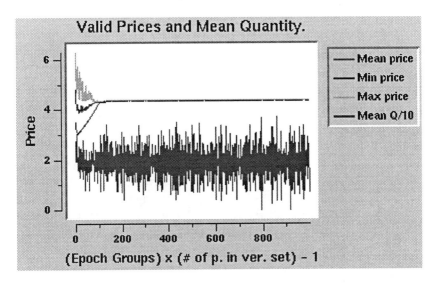

Figure 3.18 Short term learning, with EOs on Requirements and ProductionStream

The third run of the model, with *useEO_EP* variable set to 2, shows a stabilized situation in prices (not in quantities). The consequence of keeping requirements and production streams constant is represented by the equilibrium situation of Figure 3.18, 3.19 and 3.20, where prices stay near constant, but the quantities are heavily oscillating.

Finally, with *useEO_EP* variable set to 3, i.e. operating simultaneously to diminish expenditures, raise revenues, stabilize requirements and production streams, we have stabilized the market, with low oscillations in quantities, mainly when the agents are able to operate globally, after long term learning. This is true also without long term learning, in Figure 3.21, but becomes more evident with learning in Figure 3.22 and Figure 3.23. In Figure 3.22 we have also an interesting effect of stabilization of the market when learning takes effectively place, after an initial period of price diminution.

8. FUTURE IMPROVEMENTS

We report here some improvements to be included in the future versions of bp–ct.

We will introduce a probe to each agent, to allow the direct inspections of agent variables while the model is running. An important improvement will be that of the automation of the production of the CT formulas mainly on the basis of definitions of actions and effects (at present the formulas containing the CT rules are handwritten in the Interface code).

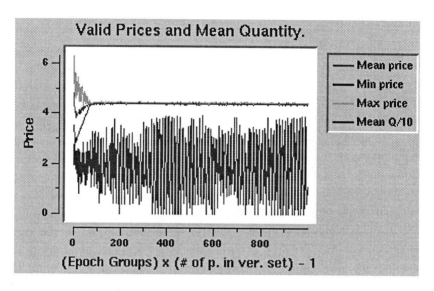

Figure 3.19   Light long term learning, with EOs on Requirements and Production-Stream

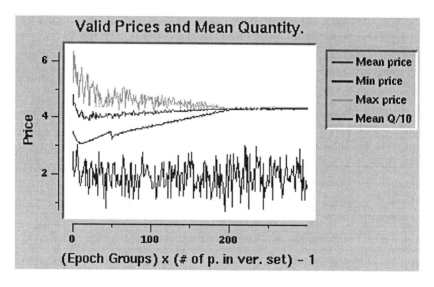

Figure 3.20   Long term learning, with EOs on Requirements and ProductionStream

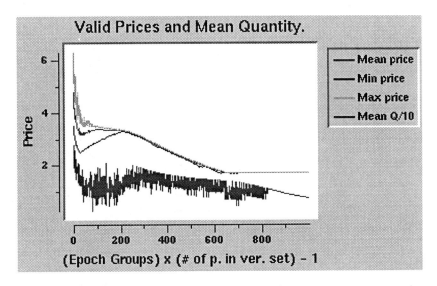

Figure 3.21 Short term learning, with EOs on Expenditure, Revenue, Requirements and ProductionStream

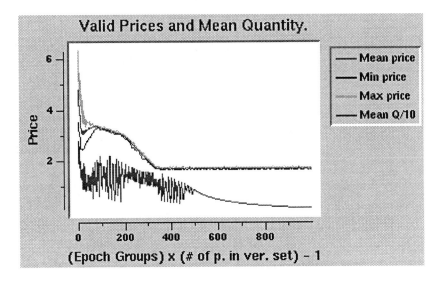

Figure 3.22 Light long term learning, with EOs on Expenditure, Revenue, Requirements and ProductionStream

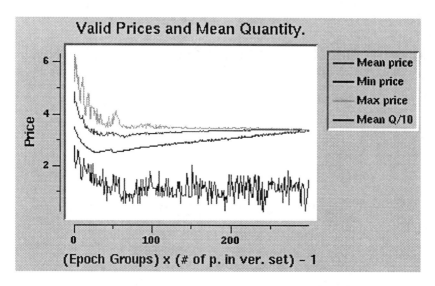

Figure 3.23 Long term learning, with EOs on Expenditure, Revenue, Requirements and ProductionStream

Finally we will operate to allow the automatic or quasi–automatic substitution of neural networks with classifier systems or with more general genetic algorithms.

We think that it would be useful to develop the GH of Section 5. also in other ways, to verify the reproducibility of our results in other contexts. We have to introduce algorithms capable of the same performances in order to reproduce short and long term learning, without the aid of ANN. Our algorithm must be able to modify its outputs in a smooth way, following cross–target suggestions about actions and guesses of action effects, to self–develop the behavioral skills of the acting and adapting phase. The algorithm – may be not the same – has also to develop a strong mapping ability between input and output (target) vectors, to produce the same behavioral results without further learning.

Acknowledgments

This research has been supported by grants from the MURST project "Intermediazione finanziaria, funzionamento dei mercati ed economia reale."

Notes

1. http://www.econ.iastate.edu/tesfatsi/sylalife.htm
2. http://www.econ.iastate.edu/tesfatsi/ace.htm

3. http://www.econ.iastate.edu/tesfatsi/getalife.htm

4. http://www.cea.uba.ar/aschu/complex.html

5. http://zia.hss.cmu.edu/econ/

6. http://hmt.com/cwr/ibm.html

7. http://www.lse.ac.uk/lse/complex/

References

Arthur, W.B. (1990). "A Learning Algorithm that Mimics Human Learning." *Santa Fe Institute Working Paper 90-026.* .

Beltratti, A., Margarita, S., Terna, P. (1996). *Neural Networks for Economic and Financial Modelling.* London: International Thomson Computer Press.

Conte, R., Hegselmann, R., Terna, P. (eds.) (1997). *Simulating Social Phenomena.* Berlin: Springer.

Epstein, M.E. and Axtell, R. (1996). *Growing Artificial Societies - Social Science from the Bottom Up.* Washington: Brookings Institution Press. Cambridge, MA: MIT Press.

Gilbert, N. and Terna, P. (1999). "How to build and use agent-based models in social science." *Mind & Society,* 1, forthcoming.

von Hayek, F.A. (1949). *Individualism and Economic Order.* London: Routledge.

Judd, K.L. (1996). "Computational Economics and Economic Theory: Substitutes or Complements?" ¡http://bucky.stanford.edu/¿.

Kirman, A. (1992). "Whom or What Does the Representative Agent Represent?" *Journal of Economic Perspectives,* 6, pp.126-39.

Rumelhart, D.E. and McClelland, J.L. (1986). *Parallel Distributed Processing. Explorations in the Microstructure of Cognition.* Cambridge, MA: The MIT Press.

Russel, S. and Norvig, P. (1986). *Artificial Intelligence. A Modern Approach.* Upper Saddle River, NJ: Prentice-Hall.

White, H. (1990). "Connectionist Nonparametric Regression: Multilayer Feedforward Networks Can Learn Arbitrary Mappings." *Neural Networks,* 5, pp. 535-550.

Chapter 4

ENDOGENOUS GROWTH WITH CYCLES IN A SWARM ECONOMY: FIGHTING TIME, SPACE, AND COMPLEXITY

Charlotte Bruun
Department of Economics, Politics and Public Administration
Aalborg University
9000 Aalborg Denmark
cbruun@socsci.auc.dk

Francesco Luna
Department of Economics
University of Venice Ca' Foscari
30120 Venezia Italy
fluna@unive.it

Abstract   The artificial economy proposed in this paper exhibits endogenous growth with cycles. Agents must fight time, space and complexity in order to obtain what they strive for: consumption and wealth. Constraints to growth originate from the demand side as well as the supply side, and from the real sphere as well as the monetary sphere. The real sphere of the economy is composed of a supply side (production units characterized as neural nets) and a demand side (with consumers signaling their demand in terms of XOR-instances). The monetary sphere is constructed as a pure credit system. Demand is a function of wealth and supply is demand-driven with certain complexity constraints. The resulting properties of the model dynamics were largely unexpected for the authors. A number of generalizations are also proposed.

1.   INTRODUCTION

Nobel Prize Laureate Robert Lucas maintains that the design and acquisition of new tools of analysis foster the advancement of scientific research. Not only do these tools permit the rigorous development of previously identified lines of thought, they also enhance the very emergence of original paths of research.

We believe that Swarm will both allow us to retrace an old line of research and break new ground in the study of the interaction of micro-behavior and macro-phenomena. In particular, the model we propose addresses a theme—growth with cycles—that was abandoned for quite some time and only recently revived. During that period, growth models, following Solow's approach, flourished and separated from business-cycle theory.

In this perspective, on the one hand, Swarm gives us the possibility to pursue some line of research that had been abandoned as not promising any longer. On the other hand, the original source of increasing returns to scale that we identify would not be easily substantiated at a micro-level without a computational support; similarly its effects on a macro scale could not be ascertained without a powerful object-oriented simulation platform like Swarm.

Section 2. introduces the model. We have built it combining our previous experience with agent-based modeling in diverse topics such as computable learning, the emergence of institutions, consumption theory and monetary theory. The mechanism that triggers growth is the creation of firms by innovative entrepreneurs that succeed in coordinating the efforts of heterogenous workers to satisfy the demand for a consumption good. The characteristics of the demand are unknown. The entrepreneur hires a certain number of workers and manages the induction effort of the organization. His reward is the right to the residual after he has paid wages.

There is no outside money in the system. A centralized institution updates the balance of each agent's checking account. The book-keeping activity includes a monthly check for bankruptcy. Losses are distributed across the board, with every agent bearing an equal share of the burden. Trade-cycles are the combined effect of income-distribution and activity fluctuations due to failures.

Section 3. presents some initial results. We believe the model flexible enough to be able to address a variety of issues that deserve a much more thorough investigation that could be offered in this limited format. Section 5., however, offers a sort of agenda of questions and topics the model could be employed to analyze. Among others we point at areas of interest such as the role of the public sector in smoothing cycles and fostering growth, the spontaneous emergence of industrial districts, financial markets and consumption, and labor market institutional arrangements and rigidities. Section 6. concludes.

2.   THE MODEL

We describe an artificial world geographically located on a torus and inhabited by economic actors which consume and earn a salary as self-employed "artisans", wages as hired employees, or profits as entrepreneurs. Initially, all actors are self-employed as individual production units. Firms emerge as the result of the induction process that each of the production units has to face to satisfy the consumer demand. Credit money is exchanged when a transaction occurs be it the purchase of a unit of consumption good or the monthly payment of wages. A centralized institution performs the book-keeping accounting and checks for bankruptcy. This section is divided into various subsections. In the first one we give an account of the schedule of events. In the second one we describe the behavior of the representative actor as production unit; then as consumer. Finally we give the details of the bankruptcy rule.

2.1   THE SCHEDULE OF EVENTS

The minimum unit of time in the model is a *day*. 20 days compose a *month*[1] A series of actions take place daily and some others occur monthly. Swarm controls actions by using a system of schedules:

```
dailySchedule = [Schedule createBegin: [self getZone]];
[dailySchedule setRepeatInterval: 1];
dailySchedule = [dailySchedule createEnd];
[dailySchedule at: 0 createActionForEach:
            consumerList message: M(signalDemand)];
```

The first line creates an object from the class **Schedule**. In the second line this object is told to act each period. The last line describes what sort of action the object **dailySchedule** is to perform. Every day each consumer decides whether to signal his willingness to purchase according to a rule that we will describe below.

```
monthlySchedule = [Schedule createBegin: [self getZone]];
[monthlySchedule setRepeatInterval: daysInMonth];
monthlySchedule = [monthlySchedule createEnd];
[monthlySchedule at: 0 createAction: modelActions];
```

Similarly, a monthly **Schedule** is created and is instructed to act once a month. In particular, every month (that is every daysInMonth periods) a well-defined sequence of actions is managed by the object modelActions:

```
[modelActions createActionForEach:
```

```
        entrepreneurList message: M(payWages)];
[modelActions createActionTo:  bankWorld message:
    M(checkBankruptcy)];
[modelActions createActionForEach: prodUnitList message:
    M(newLink)];
```

First, each entrepreneur pays her workers the agreed wages, then the
bank calculates the end-of-period balance sheet and enforces the bankruptcy rules on insolvent agents as described below. Finally, each production unit considers the possibility of enlarging its organization. It
is here that new firms are created and operating entrepreneurs decide
whether to increase the size of their firms.

2.2   FUNDAMENTAL METHODS

We describe now the most important routines (*methods* in the object-
oriented lingo) that dictate the behavior of our artificial actors.

2.2.1   Firms' Creation and Growth.   The production capability of each economic actor is represented by a *Production Unit*. We
model this prodUnit in terms of a single-layer network with two input
neurodes and one output neurode.

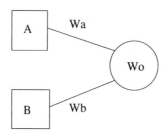

Figure 4.1 Single-layer two-input neural net. The letters A and B stand for the
values taken by the *variables* A and B

A specific location is assigned to each unit. As said above, the *world*
is represented by a two-dimensional torus. Hence, each location is univocally addressed by a pair of coordinates and is always surrounded by
exactly eight neighbours. Production units do not move. They try to
satisfy whatever demand is signaled to them by consumers who move
on the *grid*. The demand "function" will be described below. Here, it
is sufficient to say that no single actor can induce on its own the law
behind the demand signals.

Because of their *physical* cognitive and computational limitations, individual production units (self-employed artisans) are always bound to
make mistakes despite their on-going induction process captured by the

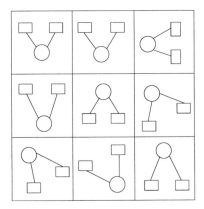

Figure 4.2   Each representative automaton is surrounded by eight structurallyequivalent neighbours

neural-net learning algorithm. They will not be able to react correctly to all the stimuli signaled by the consumers visiting their workshops. We see in this limitation of the inductive (or learning) capability of economic actors the trigger for the "natural propensity to truck and barter" as described by Adam Smith.

In our model[2] this *propensity* translates into the following specific behaviour. Each time a prodUnit does not manage to satisfy the demand signaled by a consumer, he interrogates each of his neighbour producers as of the reply they would have offered the customer had they received that particular request. Figure 4.2 depicts the typical neighborhood.

Whenever a neighbour gives the "correct answer", the confidence level attached to him increases[3]. An index of confidence in each one of the neighbours is established in this way and later updated after each mistake. When the confidence in a particular neighbour has grown beyond a certain threshold, the artisan will consider becoming an entrepreneur. That is, she will try to hire the labor of the neighbour. If she is successful, she will then be in charge of coordinating her own observation of the demand signals plus the elaboration (of the same signals) that her new worker has performed.

In terms of the neural network, what we have just described is one possible way to characterise a "constructive" algorithm. The original artisan's neural-net grows by adding one link to the output neurode of the hired neighbour's neural-net. For Example, Figure 4.3 represents a newborn organization linking the entrepreneur with her neighbour number 3. Naturally, this new and more complex organization will continue its inductive process making other mistakes in its evolution. This implies that the same hiring procedure may happen again until the organiza-

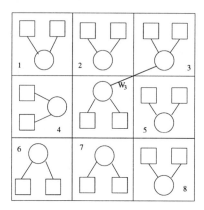

Figure 4.3   A new organization composed of the entrepreneur and one worker

tion reaches an *effective* configuration—it has learned how to respond correctly to all possible demand signals.

An effective firm can be composed of 2 up to 9 members. The advantage of being small is that fewer agents will share the product. The advantage of being large is that the *marketing* area is wider, i.e. there is a better chance of attracting randomly moving consumers. Effective firms are not eternal; they may be declared bankrupt, or they may be dissolved by mutation.

2.2.2   Demand Function.   Each time a consumer decides to express his willingness to buy (according to the wealth considerations described above), he signals his current consumption demand as one of four possible instances: {A, B}, {notA, B}, {A, notB}, {not A, notB} [4]. We assume that the consumer will purchase one unit of good whenever the reply he obtains (from the prodUnit he has signaled his demand to) satisfies the Exclusive-OR (XOR) Boolean function. This means that for {A, B} the consumer expects "False[5]"; for {A, notB} he expects "True"; for {notA, B}: "True"; and for {notA, notB}: "False[6]".

This function has been chosen as the simplest generator of a linearly non-separable problem. Production units, which we described as single-layer neural networks (see Figure 4.1), cannot, taken singularly, simulate a XOR function. All they can do is described by the function:

$$f(A, B) = W_0 + W_A A + W_B$$

Note that $f(A, B) = 0$ is the equation of a straight line dividing the space in points {A, B} for which $f(A, B) > 0$ (that is the Boolean function is "True") from points for which $f(A, B) < 0$ (the simulated Boolean function is "False"). Obviously, there is no way in which a straight line can separate positive from negative instances for the XOR function.

2.2.3   Money,Credit and Prices.

The XOR problems and the neural nets described above may be perceived as the real side of our artificial economy - a model that may be self-sufficient since we have a supply and a demand side. In order to replicate central aspects of real world economic systems we, however, believe that modeling the monetary sphere is just as important as modeling the real sphere. The monetary side of our economy is modeled as a pure credit system, and the two spheres are related by fixing the price of demand signals at unity.

The pure credit system has been chosen because of its simplicity - and its correspondence with reality[7]. We have chosen to operate with fixed prices because we do not find price adjustments to be central to the aspects of the real world we intend to model; although our modeling of a real and a monetary side would allow us to actually distinguish between relative and absolute price movements. Our model is not a model of exchanges of existing volumes of goods, but a model of the production of goods.

In a closed system with only credit money one cannot hide the fact that for someone to hold a monetary surplus somebody else must accept a deficit. How agents respond to surpluses and deficits is therefore crucial with respect to the macroproperties of our system. These are aspects of economic systems that are very hard to study without the use of agent-based simulation models.

Agents enter debt both in their capacity as producers and in their capacity as consumers. In order for production to take place there must be a consumption demand, and this requires consumers to be willing to enter debt before they have received any wage or profit. Once the money is spent it is returned to consumers as wages and profits - but of course there is no guarantee that the original spender gets back exactly what she spent.

2.2.4   Wage Setting.

When an artisan decides to become an entrepreneur, or when an entrepreneur who has not yet succeeded in forming an effective firm decides to hire one or more additional workers, she has to convince the chosen neighbour(s) to work for her. Each unit keeps record of the number of demand signals it has successfully replied to in the previous period X, and this volume is crucial to the wage bargaining.

Since the price of each unit of commodity sold is fixed to 1, we interpret X as the reservation wage that characterizes each individual and that depends on his own experience. Similarly, we assume that the would-be entrepreneur offers to pay precisely her own enterprise average rate of successes[8]. Hence, she will offer a wage equal to the number of successful replies to demand signals per member of the firm in the preceding period. This is a generous proposal since the entrepreneur offers the new worker a wage that approximates an equal share of the (expected) product.

If the wage offered by the entrepreneur or artisan is higher than or equal to[9] the candidate's X, he will accept the job offer. The wage paid W is then

$$W = X/N$$

Where N is the number of units, including the entrepreneur herself, working for the enterprise and X is the number of successful replies by the entrepreneur in the previous period.

If the wage offered is lower than the profit earned by the unit as an artisan, the potential worker will turn down the offer. In this case the entrepreneur or artisan may try to hire the same unit again after one month. In the meantime the potential worker may have had less luck in receiving and/or in replying to demand signals so that the candidate may now accept the very offer she had refused the previous period.

The last negotiated wage will be the wage of all workers employed by the entrepreneur. Thus the wage of a hired worker will increase and decrease with the successfulness of the entrepreneur. This is not the same as saying that wages are a fixed proportion of the product, since basing wage negotiation on the payoffs of the preceding period may result in positive as well as negative profits with entrepreneurs in the current period. Once a firm becomes effective, wages will be fixed at the level offered to the last hired worker. This wage is likely to leave a profit as a residual with the entrepreneurs, depending on her luck in attracting consumers.

2.2.5   Consumption Decision. Consumption demand is what drives the model since production units cannot start learning until they receive demand signals to be processed. Despite the important role played by consumption, we are merely interested in a relation between an agent's income, its monetary position and consumption with some correspondence to empirical data - not in the motivation for that consumption and its possible consistency with any rationality claims. The same priority may be found in Clower and Johnson, and we shall attempt to implement their empirical findings in our model.

Clower and Johnson (1976) suggest that agents attach utility to their wealth position as well as to their consumption. Saving is not a decision to consume tomorrow - it is a decision to increase wealth. Using the difference between actual wealth and desired wealth, consumption may be modelled as an adaptive process. From empirical evidence Clower and Johnson transform this principle into a macroeconomic consumption function of the following type:

$$c = hw^b$$

where w is wealth, h is a positive constant and b lies between zero and unity. In their empirical estimation, Clower and Johnson find that b lies between 0.35 and 0.40 in both the United States and the United Kingdom.

Since our model does not have any capital assets or any financial market except the credit system, we have had to modify the results of Clower and Johnson to make them fit our model. Since aggregate wealth in our model will always be zero, we must make sure that units consume out of a negative wealth. Without consumers being willing to become debtors in order to consume, our economy would never take-off. We have therefore redefined the consumption function:

$$c = \frac{h}{1 + e^{-w/b}}$$

where h and b are positive constants. In our base run we have set h to 10 and b to 25. For positive wealth holdings this gives us a consumption function which corresponds to the consumption function of Clower and Johnson except that consumption out of zero wealth will be higher. For negative wealth holdings our new consumption function assures that consumption will never become negative. We add a minimum consumption of 1 to our consumption decision. This may be interpreted as a subsistence minimum.

Besides deciding on how much consumption to demand every period, consumers must decide whether to move to another cell in order to stand a better chance of having its consumption demand satisfactorily fulfilled in the following period. The physical address of the consumer is fixed by the address of the accompanying production unit, but one may picture each consumer as having a shopping cart that can be pushed around the grid. If consumption demand in the current period has been satisfied by the production unit currently visited, consumers have no inclination to move. If, however, the production unit has not responded correctly to the demand, the consumer will move to a new production unit in the following period. The move is determined randomly. A mutation rate is added to the movement rule so that an agent may move randomly although it was situated on the cell of an effective firm, and thus received correct answers to all its consumption demands.

2.2.6   Bankruptcy Rule. In order to ensure an efficient allocation of resources in the long run, a bankruptcy rule has been imposed on our system. Until they reach the bankruptcy limit, agents have free access to credit. Without a boundary on debt, striving entrepreneurs may continue to hire more workers without ever managing to establish an effective firm. Such entrepreneurs may hinder the formation of effective firms in their neighbourhood, and in this way impose a limitation to growth.

It is of great importance to the stability of our system, how the losses inflicted by the bankruptcy rule are distributed among the remaining agents. Since the model does not contain any direct contracts between lender and borrower, we have chosen to let the system as a whole carry the burden of bankruptcies, i.e. the loss is equally distributed among all agents, creditors as well as debtors. The cost of the losses may thus be perceived as a lump sum cost of using the credit system. The equal distribution of losses lends more stability to the system, than a mechanism that assigns a few agent the whole burden of bankruptcy losses.

When a unit is declared bankrupt it is reinitialized; not only is the financial position of the agent set to zero; the neural net of the agent is randomly assigned new weights and all links are removed. The consumer cart of the agent is also randomly replaced.

3.   RESULTS

This model produces cycles around a growth path until a steady state is reached after approximately 500 periods (months). As illustrated in Figure 4.4, the cycles are independent of the seed given to the random generator. Changing the seed to the random generator only makes small changes in the cyclical path. We may therefore be confident that the cycles generated are a structural characteristics of our model.

3.1   IMPORTANCE OF SELECTED METHODS

In models as complex as the present one, it is hard to determine what produces a specific result; just as it is often hard to determine causalities in the real world. The advantage of using a simulation model rather than addressing the real world directly, is that we may modify the simulation model in order to check the importance of specific aspects of the model.

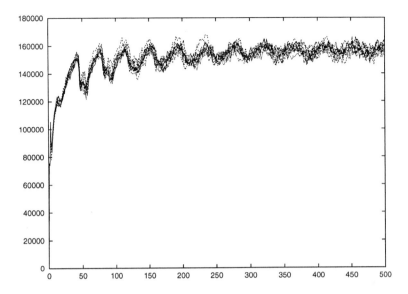

Figure 4.4 GDP with ten different random seeds.

In this section we shall impose such modifications to obtain an idea of what causes the observed macrobehaviour; growth with cycles.

3.1.1 **Firm Formation.** Although we have claimed that our model is demand driven, we must not forget the importance of the process of firm formation. Without firm formation production will fluctuate randomly around an average of just below 75.000 (see Figure 4.5). In recognizing the importance of firms we must remember that the same units produce and consume. Without entrepreneurs taking the risk of paying wages with no immediate profit in sight, there will be no workers consuming out of their wages, and no increase in demand to lift-off the level of production ¿from its initial level. By hiring a worker the entrepreneur induces another agent to increase its consumption, and by becoming more effective as a production unit, firm formation allows the economy as a whole to grow.

3.1.2 **Credit.** To understand why we get the cycles we must have a look at the credit side of our model. Comparing the cycles in the level of production to the cycles in the volume of credit (measured as the sum of positive money holdings), the close correlation between credit and production level becomes apparent (Figure 4.6).

The first period (0-40 months) with strong growing production is accompanied by an enormous growth in the volume of credit. No effective

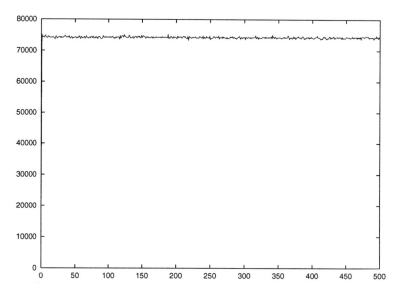

Figure 4.5   GDP with no firm formation

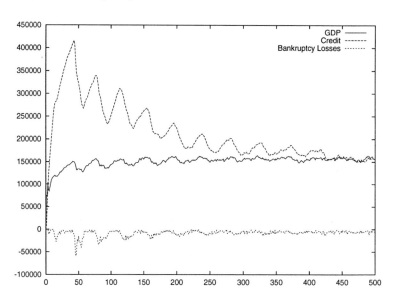

Figure 4.6   GDP, credit and losses due to bankruptcy

firms have yet been formed, and the costs of forming new firms is high. With a lot of agents striving to become entrepreneurs, the volume of credit is bound to explode. Entrepreneurs who have not yet succeeded in forming effective firms have to pay out wages, but they have no way of ensuring that income will follow expenses since consumers will only stay on their cell if they respond correctly. This situation cannot continue, and at some point ailing firms start to go bankrupt. Notice the high level of losses around the first turning point (Figure 4.6). Bankruptcies cause a fall in the level of production because other units must take the loss, but at some point they stop, and after the destruction of debt the level of production can grow again.

Credit is not only important to the cycles, but certainly also decisive with respect to the trend. Notice that as long as there is a growing trend in the level of production, there is a decreasing trend in the volume of credit. We shall return to this observation in the section on growth and inequality.

3.1.3   Bankruptcies.   The way bankruptcy-losses are distributed to the rest of the system turns out to be crucial to the cyclical pattern in the production level. Because losses due to bankruptcy are distributed to the other units, the bankruptcy of one unit may be the direct cause of the bankruptcy of other units. If, rather than distributing the loss equally to all units, we introduce a public sector who takes the bankruptcy losses on its shoulders, cycles disappear, and we get just the marginal decreasing growth path (Figure 4.7). Notice that in this case production reaches its steady state at a higher level (around 250.000 rather than 150.000). The cost of the higher level of production is a continous growth in government debt.

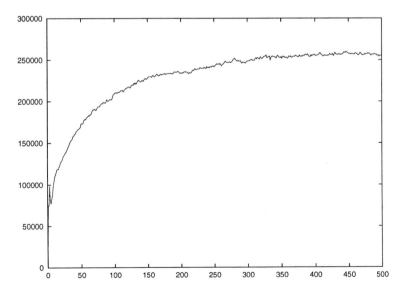

Figure 4.7   GDP with a public sector taking losses due to bankruptcies

3.1.4   Mutation. Two different mutation rates have been introduced; a mutation that makes consumers move to another cell although their consumption demand was successfully fulfilled, and a mutation that makes effective firms dissolve although they have not reached the bankruptcy limit. Innocuous as these mutation rates may appear, they turn out to be important for the results obtained.

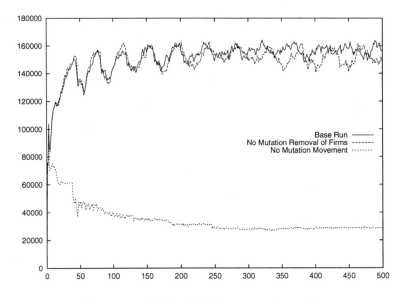

Figure 4.8 GDP with different mutaion rules.

If consumers never move once they have found an effective firm, consumers will concentrate on the first effective firms formed, and other production units do not stand a chance. Wealth will be very skewed (a Gini coefficient for the distribution of wealth around 0.8), and this depresses consumption demand to such an extent that production falls below the initial level.

The mutation removal of effective firms does not change the scenario much during the first 500 months, but after this period, the level of production falls without the mutation removal of effective firms. This mutation enables a continous reduction in the average firm size by removing firms at random. When new firms are formed, the striving entrepreneur will not have as many workers to choose from since an increasing number of production units are employed. This forces entrepreneurs into more efficient firm organization[10]. The removal of effective firms is necessary for growth to continue; not only because the declining average firm size allows higher wages and profits with a given number of customers, but also because there will be more attempts to form effective firms and these attempts have an expansionary effect.

3.1.5 Initial Distribution of Monetary Wealth. One might think that the initial growth in GDP as well as credit volume is only due to the fact that agents start of with zero monetary wealth, but this is actually not the case. As Fig. 4.9 shows, introducing an initial distribution of monetary wealth similar to the distribution after 1000 months, has surprisingly little impact on the behaviour of the model. It takes a very skewed initial distribution of wealth for it to have any impact on the growth path.

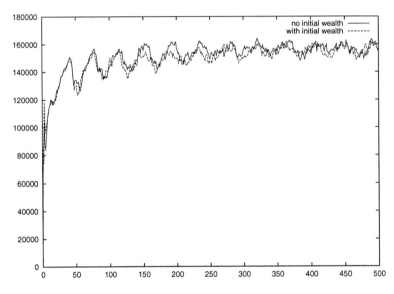

Figure 4.9 GDP with an initial distribution of wealth equal to the distribution after 1000 months in a simulation with zero initial wealth.

4. GROWTH AND INEQUALITY

An important advantage of using agent-based models is the ability to study dispersional effects as the relation between growth and inequality. In the following we have chosen to use the Gini coefficient for the distribution of monetary wealth as a measure of inequality [11]. Alternatively we might have chosen the Gini coefficient for income which displayes the same tendencies, but has weaker cycles. Another measure for inequality in our model is the volume of credit since credit is what bridges the gap between rich and poor.

4.1   THE KUZNETS CURVE

As Figure 4.10 shows, the model displays diverging results with respect to the relation between growth and inequality. In the short run there is a positive correlation whereas in the long run correlation is clearly negative. We interpret the long run correlation as a reproduction of the Kuznets curve since, on top of the negative correlation, the growth phenomenon depicted can be interpreted as caused by a technological paradigm shift. The original migration away from the agricultural countryside to the industrial city is equivalently depicted by the introduction of a new and more effective technology applied by a new generation of entrepreneurs. One could imagine one Kuznets curve being replaced by another by the introduction of a new technology, e.g. as demand signals of higher complexity are introduced. Since the movement in growth and the Gini coefficient is not very sensitive to the initial distribution of monetary wealth, introducing new demand signals with a higher pay off to be learned by firms, should be expected to cause a similar growth path on top of the path described here.

A large part of the most recent literature addressing the relation between growth and inequality finds evidence of a positive correlation between a fairly equal distribution of wealth and growth. Typically, these studies (Alesina and Rodrik 1994, Persson and Tabellini 1994) analyse the experience of a series of countries in the interval 1960-1985 regressing the average rate of growth (over the period) on various indexes of distribution (in)equality around the year 1960. Gini coefficient and land distribution for Alesina and Rodrik, income share of the middle class for Persson and Tabellini.

Aghion, Caroli, and Penalosa (1999) identify a series of theoretical explanations for why inequality should slow down growth in presence of agents heterogeneity and credit market imperfections. Inequality will have negative effects on investment opportunities, on borrowers' incentives and on macroeconomic volatility. On the same line, Todaro (1997) points at dissaving and unproductive investment by the rich, at too low level of human capital held by the poor, at the lower gains from trade in the consumption pattern of the poor and at the political unrest (or, as Jean-Paul Fitoussi would call it, at the lack of *social cohesion*) that unequal distribution of wealth would cause.

At the same time, however, our model seems also to suggest a possible explanation of why the Kuznets curve is not evident in empirical data. In Figure 4.10, for example, if an observer were to analyze the data for any short-term cycle, his conclusion would be that the Kuznets curve is a myth and that inequality and growth move in the same direction

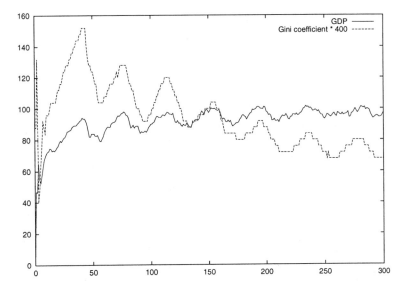

Figure 4.10 GDP and the Gini coefficient

according to the idea of the trade off between equality and efficiency in an economic system. The following section will also give us an idea of why the Kuznets curve is difficult to find in cross-sectional data.

4.2 EXPLORING THE CAUSAL LINK BETWEEN GROWTH AND INEQUALITY

One thing is finding a correlation between inequality and growth - another is to exploit the relationship in order to promote growth. Exploring the causal link between inequality and growth is particularly tricky in our model since we have opposite correlations in the short and in the long run. In this section we shall carry out two sets of experiments in order to explore the causal relationship between growth and inequality. First we shall see what happens if we introduce a redistribution of wealth to our model (i.e. a negative interest rate), next we shall se what happens if we manipulate the functional distribution of income.

4.2.1 Redistribution of Monetary Wealth.
Is it possible to promote growth by manipulating the distribution of monetary wealth? If we introduce a negative interest rate so that wealth is transferred from the rich to the poor we get no unambiguous answer since it involves both positive and negative effects.

If we move 2.5% of monetary wealth from creditors to debtors every period, we get a positive effect on GDP (GDP around 180.000 (Figure 4.11)), a Gini coefficient for income that is a little higher and a considerably higher Gini coefficient for wealth (Figure 4.12). If we increase the redisitribution to 10% we get a negative effect on GDP (GDP around 137.000) a considerably higher Gini coefficinet for income, whereas the Gini coefficient for wealth remains about the same. This illustrates that the effect of an unequal distribution of monetary wealth on the level of production is not monotonic.

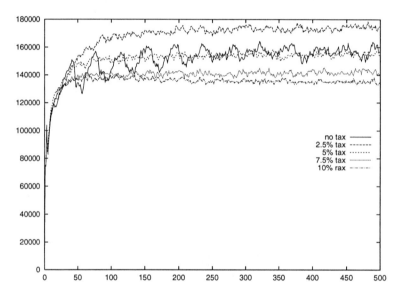

Figure 4.11 GDP with different redistribution rates (tax on wealth)

The positive effect on growth from a redistribution of wealth follows ¿from the fact that consumption is a marginally decreasing function of wealth. But why is there a negative impact as well? The most striking difference between the simulations with a redistribution of wealth and the simulations without such a redistribution is that the average firm size is much larger for the simulations with redistribution. The reason for this is that bankruptcies no longer remove the less efficient firms and, as discussed in section 3.1.4, efficiency in production, measured by average firm size, is important for growth. This effect constitutes a negative impact on growth from the redistribution of wealth. As redistribution is increased, the negative effect becomes stronger than the positive effect (Figure 4.11).

The effect of a tax on wealth to some extent merely replaces the redistribution through bankruptcy. Opposite to bankruptcies, however,

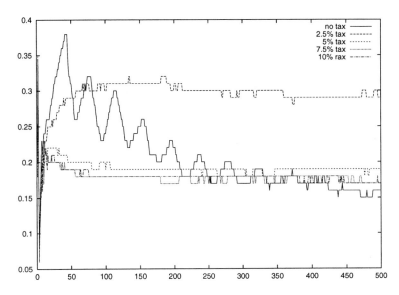

Figure 4.12 Gini coefficient for wealth with different redistribution rates (tax on wealth)

redistribution through taxation does not have the effect of removing the inefficient production units. Thus average firm size increases. All agents get involved with firms, and there is no underwood of striving entrepreneurs to expand credit and thus consumption. This result is quite Schumpetarian; business cycles are a necessary evil for cleaning up the business world - getting rid of the less efficient units.

4.2.2 Wage and Profit. Another way of manipulating inequality is by changing the wage negotiation algorithm, and thus affecting the functional distribution of income. For our base run we chose a very generous wage offer from entrepreneurs to their potential workers; an equal share of the expected production (see section 2.2.4). Once the steady state is reached this leaves workers as well as entrepreneurs with an average income just below 100. But what happens if entrepreneurs are less genereous, e.g. if they merely offer 25% of the expected number of successes per member of the firm? Surprisingly this does not change the average income of entrepreneurs or workers considerably. In the short run, however, there is an increase in income of both workers and entrepreneurs[12].

To understand why, it is important to remember that we are dealing with a macromodel where wage is not only a cost to entrepreneurs, but also the source of demand for the output produced. In the short run it may be a good strategy for entrepreneurs to offer low wages, but since consumption is not a linear function of wealth, it is bound to depress demand. This line of thought is confirmed if we look at the Gini coefficient(fig. 4.13) . At first the Gini coefficient is very high, i.e. wealth has a very skewed distribution, and the lower the wage offer the more skewed is the distribution. After a period with a high number of bankruptcies (50-250), wealth gets redistributed to such an extend that the experiment with most inequable wage offer, ends up with the lowest Gini coefficient.

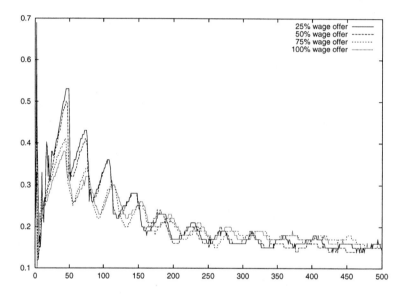

Figure 4.13   The Gini Coefficient with different wage offers

Figure 4.14 reveals the cause of the high number of bankruptcies. Not only do many workers go bankrupt due to the poor wage - entrepreneurs also have a harder time forming effective firms because more potential workers will turn down the job offer due to the poor pay. Once the steady state is reached the wage will not differ much between the different wage-offer regimes because workers will only accept the poorer percentual offer after the entrepreneur has had a period of luck, and thus will offer a fair wage in absolute terms.

It appears that in the longer run, the wage-setting mechanism is not central to the distribution of monetary wealth in our model. Counter-intuitively, the poorest wage offer gives the lowest Gini coefficient and thus the most equal distribution.

4.2.3   From Growth to Equality or From Equality to Growth?.

Both our attempts of affecting growth by manipulating inequality failed.

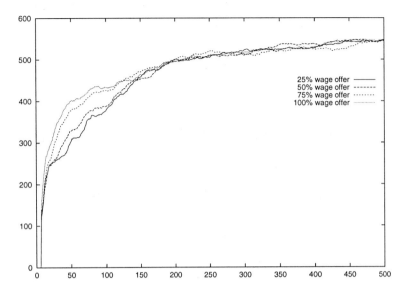

Figure 4.14   Number of effective firms with different wage offers

This makes us ask, whether the causality of the relationship goes from growth to equality rather than from equality to growth. Since the marginal propensity to consume out of wealth is decreasing, increasing inequality means a smaller demand and thus a smaller level of production. However, growth only takes place when artisans become striving entrepreneur and enter debt in order to pay wages. This debt increases inequality measured as the Gini coefficient for monetary wealth. This is what generates our positive short term correlation between growth and inequality. The debt, on the other hand, is used for paying wages to agents that were formerly poorly paid artisans. Eventually these artisans will decrease their debt, and begin to consume more. The striving entrepreneurs will succeed in their venture and begin to make a profit, or they will be declared bankrupt. In both cases the Gini coefficient will decrease.

Thus, in the short run, causality primarily goes from growth to inequality, but in the long run it is the causality from equality to growth that matters. This causality works through the demand side and is due to the decreasing marginal propensity to consume. Because of the complexity of the relationship, it appears risky to base any policy measures (or non-measures) directed towards growth on the relation.

5.   RESEARCH AGENDA

We believe that the model presented is flexible enough to address a large series of issues with only minor changes in the code. However, because of the limited space at our disposal, we can only hint at such topics that are in our research agenda.

5.1   PUBLIC SECTOR AND GROWTH

We plan to expand our model to include explicitly a public sector, a government whose role is that of collecting taxes and paying transfers. The purpose of the exercise is to see whether—as expected for a model with decreasing marginal propensity to consume—income redistribution can foster sustained growth and, more significant for such a system, whether such an arrangement can decrease the amplitude of the business cycle, smoothing consumption dynamics.

With respect to Figure 4.7, it might be possible to address the following question. Assume that the government stabilizes its debt once the economy is at some per capita GDP level higher than the "natural" one. Is the system going into a recession? In other terms is there an "optimal" level of public debt $\neq 0$?

With such a model it will also be possible to identify the form of taxation which is more appropriate to this goal and which imposes the minimum level of distortion to the system. We plan on experimenting with lumpsum taxes, proportional and progressive taxation on income and/or wealth. The model will obviously allow us to introduce indirect taxes such as the sale tax. Furthermore, we will be able to evaluate what form of transfers serves better the stability of the system. Again, should transfer be of the lump-sum kind, or rather be proportional to income levels below some poverty line? Or is perhaps wealth the relevant variable to target?

A related question regards the "Kuznets curve." Can the curve be explained with a particular behaviour on part of the government, or is it a phenomenon that reflects some deeper regularity? These are questions that have been recently addressed in the literature. Various econometric techniques have been employed to identify such regularities and to link them with explicit policy measures implemented by different countries. (Barro 1999, Quah 1997 etc.). Is the Kuznets curve obtained with the current specification robust to the introduction of a government? What can be inferred with respect to the economic policies pursued?

5.2 FIRM SIZE DISTRIBUTION

There exists a striking regularity that encompasses natural as well as social science phenomena. The observed statistical size distribution of different entities such as the urban agglomeration in a country, the radio and light emissions from galaxies, oil field reserves in the world, daily USD-Mark exchange rate variation seem all to fit a power law[13]. In particular, the size distribution of firms in the US in the sixties is one such regularity documented by Ijiri and Simon (1977). Even more surprising is the fact that the same distribution appears to be relevant for economic system and industrial structures very different ¿from the one observed by Simon. For example, Luna and Volpe (1999) record the same regularity for enterprises in the Italian North East, which is famous for its small-medium family-run firms: an economic structure very much different from the US of the 60's.

Paul Krugman recently stated that the understanding of such stylized fact would probably further our knowledge of economics in a substantial way. Clearly, one way to investigate the issue is precisely through the construction of artificial experiments that may suggest hypotheses to be tested later. One such exercise has been proposed by Axtell (1999) who concentrates his attention on the relation between increasing returns to scale and the increasing incentive to shirk for workers belonging to growing enterprises. Surprisingly enough, the size distribution of the firms in this artificial society strictly resembles the one of real firms, exhibiting the power-law distribution.

Our model can be employed to suggest a different process behind the same phenomenon. The size of a firm can be calculated in various ways: the number of employees, profits or sales. In our case, the observable measure will be sales, represented by the number of customers served per period. Increasing returns are not imposed *ad hoc*, rather they are due to the on-going inductive activities performed by entrepreneurs, furthermore, we do not have a shirking mechanism available to workers, but consumption decisions based on income and bankruptcy may play an equivalent role.

5.3 FINANCIAL MARKETS AND CONSUMPTION

Empirical studies reveal, as mentioned above, that wealth position is a significant determinant of consumption. This is not necessarily a confirmation of the permanent income hypothesis, but may just as well be a rejection of the rational economic man hypothesis.

Independently of this discussion it is important to model wealth as it is perceived by economic agents. In our current model this is not a problem since the only financial asset modelled is credit money. In the real world financial markets do, however, continuously reevaluate assets, and although agents do not trade their assets they may change the value they assign to them with changes in the "mood" of financial markets. This is important to the consumption decision since consumption out of a given income and a given nominal wealth may shift due to a shift in financial markets.

To capture such effects, we need to model some kind of capital assets that is traded on a financial market. Agent-based models are strong tools for modelling herd behaviour and other phenomena that may be observed on financial markets. The strength of our proposed approach, is that we can study the impact of the financial market on real economic activity.

5.4   DEMAND-DRIVEN GROWTH IN THE LONG LONG RUN

In the current version of our model growth evaporates after about 250 months. This is not surprising since our consumption function is a short run function and production is demand-driven. When consumption is determined as a decreasing function of wealth, one has implicitly set a limit to growth.

A part of the growth in our model is caused by the increased effectiveness of firms. There is, however, also an implicit limit to growth generated by increased effectiveness. Once a firm has learned to respond correctly to the XOR problem, it cannot increase its productivity any further.

One way of generating permanent growth would be to let the nature of the demand signals change, i.e. through demand-driven technological progress. If new demand structures emerge with a bigger payoff than the XOR problem, this could force the economy into a new growth phase. Our hypothesis is that this would result in a new "Kuznets curve", i.e. an upwards jump in the Gini coefficient followed by a continuous fall.

5.5   THE EMERGENCE OF INDUSTRIAL DISTRICTS

Another issue that can be addressed by our model is the endogenous emergence of industrial districts intended as the clustering of industrial activities concentrated in a small geographical area. To do that it will be necessary to give each consumer some sort of vision[14] that will let him know in which direction, in a limited radius from his current position, a successful firm—or an above-average concentration of exchanges—is located. He then will start moving in that direction, addressing his consumption demand to the various producers met on the way. It is easy to expect that production units close to the original successful enterprise will receive the demand signals from these traveling consumers. They will have a larger set of signals from which to learn how to deal with the demand, reaching perhaps the construction of new successful enterprises.

Obviously, this process would capture only one aspect that may explain the emergence of industrial districts, namely, the size of the market driven by a geographical demand concentration. Other issues such as the spill-over of technological know-how may require some other more sophisticated mechanisms. However, as long as these processes depend on the interaction of economic actors, it will certainly be possible to introduce them in our setting exploiting the modularity offered by the object-oriented structure of the program.

5.6 LABOR MARKET RIGIDITIES

Finally, the wage setting mechanism used in this version of the model can be modified to study the effects of minimum wage and other labor market rigidities for the growth of the economy. In particular, it may be interesting to determine what is the effect on growth of the introduction of some "union" which fixes a generally enforced minimum wage. Such mechanism certainly would render bankruptcy more likely for enterprises, but, simultaneously, it would increase the purchasing power of workers. Could this implicit redistribution more than offset the negative impact on bankruptcy?

6. CONCLUSION

Studying macroeconomic phenomena from agent-based models requires quite a complex structure. In its simplest form such a model needs a market for consumption goods, a market for labour and a clearing mechanism for debt. Once the framework is specified, it may be employed for tackling a multitude of issues. Besides answering our initial questions on growth and cycles, we have therefore sketched a number of problems for which we believe our model will be useful.

Concerning growth we found that our model does not produce continuous growth, but has a marginal decreasing growth rate. This is not surprising since consumption demand does not evolve. This sets a limit not only to demand but also to the learning ability of firms. Once a certain level is reached, productivity cannot increase.

What is more surprising is the existence and regularity of cycles. Due to the bankruptcy rule, the attempts from the underwood of artisans to establish effective firms, are syncronized so that cycles are produced. Upper and lower turning point can, however, not be predicted from a study of the model, and we may therefore think of the cycles as an emergent property of our system.

Another important result is the decreasing Gini coefficient in the long run. As the economy grows, wealth becomes more and more evenly distributed, although, in the short run, growth and inequality move together. The volume of debt sets a limit to growth, and the tendency to a more unequal distribution of wealth, which may be observed in the short term behaviour of the model, needs to be suppressed for long term growth to take place.

Notes

1. Clearly this is a parameter which can be modified at the beginning of the simulation thanks to a "probe", without having to re-compile the program.

2. For a more detailed description of this aspect of the model see Luna (1999).

3. In reality one can assume that an unsatisfied customer is likely to visit a neighbouring shop. In case the customer buys the good, the initial salesman can observe the purchase. The process we have chosen has the advantage of speeding up the final emergence of an organization.

4. Intuitively we can think of A and B as two observable characteristics like *Gender* and *Age*. There are four combinations of: (Male/Female) (Minor/Adult).

5. That is, he will complete the exchange if he receives the reply "False".

6. In the example described above, if a male shows up in a toy shop, the dealer may propose a doll only if the customer is an adult, whereas for a young customer a doll may be appropriate if that customer is a girl.

7. However, we have not tried to model the credit system as to make it function as a real-world system with outside money.

8. This hypothesis is rather reasonable. The would-be entrepreneur considers her own experience as normal. Hence, she believes that one extra unit of production and marketing can at least lead to average revenues equivalent to the average revenue of the current firm's composition.

9. Assuming risk aversion on the part of the worker.

10. This conclusion is confirmed by the fact that forcing all effective firms to be of the most efficient structure (one entrepreneur, one worker) has a similar, but stronger, effect on growth.

11. We have had to modify the original definition of the Gini coefficient since our system has no net wealth. Since the Gini coefficient operates with the distribution of a positive volume of wealth, we add a positive constant to all holdings of monetary wealth to ensure that they are positive.

12. What is recorded in the simulation is the result of the implicit selection process. Since workers can refuse any offer which is lower than their reservation wage, no successful organization can emerge until some entrepreneur has been "lucky enough" so that the 25% of her expected revenues is high enough to "buy" some workers.

13. or some connected distribution such as the stretched exponential. See Laherrere and Sornette (1998). We thank Robert Axtell for giving us this reference.

14. Axtell and Epstein (1996) is the classic reference and inspiration for this excercise.

References

P. Aghion, E. Caroli, and C. Garcia-Penalosa: 1999 "Inequality and Economic Growth: The Perspective of the New Growth Theories", University College London, Mimeo.

A. Alesina and D. Rodrik: 1994 "DIstributive Politics and Economic Growth", Quarterly Journal of Economics, 109, pp. 465-490.

R. Axtell: 1999 "The Emergence of Firms in a Population of Agents: Local Increasing Returns, Unstable Nash Equilibria, and Power Law Size Distributions", Center on Social and Economic Dynamics, Brookings Institution Discussion paper

R.J.Barro: 1999 'Inequality, Growth and Investment., Harvard University Mimeo.

R. W. Clower and M. B. Johnson.: 1976 'Income, Wealth, and the Theory of Consumption., pp. 76–129

J.M. Epstein and R. Axtell: 1996 'Growing Artificial Societies.', Brookings Institution Press and MIT Press. Cambridge, Massachusetts.

Y. Ijiri and H.Simon: 1977 'Skew distributions and the sizes of business firms.', North Holland Press, Amsterdam.

S. Kuznets. : 1955 "Economic Growth and Income Inequality", American Economic Review, 45:1 pp.1-28.

F. Luna: 1999 "The Emergence of the Firm as a complex problem solver", Taiwan Journal of Political Economy, forthcoming.

F. Luna and M. Volpe: 1999 "Firm-Size, Transition, and Convergence", Department of Economics, Mimeo, Università di Venezia.

T. Persson and G. Tabellini: 1994 "Is Inequality Harmful for Growth?", American Economic Review, 84, pp. 600-621.

D.T.Quah: 1997 "Empirics for Growth and Distribution Stratification, polarization and convergence clubs", CEPR Discussion Paper No. 1586.

M. Todaro: 1997 "Economic Development", Longman, London.

Chapter 5

IMITATIVE BEHAVIOUR IN TAX EVASION

Luigi Mittone
Department of Economics - University Of Trento - Italy

Paolo Patelli
CEEL, Department of Economics - University Of Trento - Italy

1. INTRODUCTION

Tax evasion is a topic widely explored by the microeconomic literature, both from the theoretical and the experimental perspective. The theoretical approach to tax evasion started with the seminal paper by Allingham and Sandmo (1972), which treated it within the expected utility maximisation frame a la Von Neumann Morgenstern. The experimental approach includes a large number of works, mainly devoted to the verification of theoretical results and to the discussion of behavioural assumptions.

Allingham and Sandmo's model soon attracted criticisms on either theoretical or empirical grounds. The most important theoretical shortcoming of the model is that the evaluation of the influence of an increase in the tax rate is indeterminate because two effects of opposite sign operate: a positive income effect and a negative substitution effect. This shortcoming was dealt with by Yitzhaki (1974), who modified the assumptions of Allingham and Sandmo's model by relating the sanction to unpaid taxes and not to undeclared income. Yitzhaki also showed that if the hypothesis of decreasing risk-aversion is retained, declared income changes more slowly than taxable income. This means that individuals with higher incomes tend to evade to a proportionally lesser extent.

The modifications proposed by Yitzhaki did not satisfy many of the criticisms brought against Allingham's and Sandmo's model, and the conclusion that rich people should evade less than the poor people increased criticisms even further. Therefore, most of the weaknesses remained unsolved, in spite of the changes introduced by Yitzhaki and by other authors (e.g. Srivansan, 1973).

From our point of view the most interesting part of this discussion are the criticisms based on analysis of the role played by psychological motives in taxpayer's choices. The implicit assumption derived from the neo-classical architecture of the models used both by Allingham-Sandmo and by Yitzhaki is that the decision to evade is part of a utilitarian budget, and is therefore determined by the taxpayer's preferences structure. As is well known, the neo-classical approach does not investigate preferences, but takes them as given. This explicit disregard by microeconomic theory of the mental mechanisms that shape agents' preferences, together with the assumption of optimising behaviour, have been widely criticised, mainly on empirical grounds, with reference to numerous specific aspects and assumptions of the theory. Taxpayer theory is no exception to this general critique based on psychological, motivational and empirical considerations.

Most of the criticisms brought against the neo-classical approach to tax evasion are based on empirical evidence. Numerous experiments, in fact, have shown that taxpayers engage in a peculiar decision process, in which the results differ from those obtained if the same decision problem is framed differently. Significant examples of this phenomenon are provided by Baldry (1985, 1986) and more recently by Mittone (1999). Baldry shows that moral factors play a significant role in determining taxpayers' behaviour, while Mittone reports that changes in the experimental environment - a pure tax payment context versus an experimental design that includes some form of moral constraints to tax evasion - produce notable modifications in taxpayer choices. The results from these experiments broadly show that when a subject perceives the experimental environment as if it were a real tax payment environment, s/he tends to pay more taxes than s/he would do in an more abstract context. Furthermore, this phenomenon seemed to be related to the social relationships that tie the experimental subjects together.

Of the theoretical approaches that treat this apparent inconsistency we shall only cite studies that come closest to the model described here. The first is by Cowell and Gordon (1988) and is a model that relates the decision to pay taxes to the production of a public good. The second and third studies are respectively by Gordon (1989) and by Myles and Naylor (1996) and both belong to the so-called social customs literature (Akerlof, 1980; Naylor, 1990). Gordon's model introduces a psychological cost linearly related to the decision to evade, while Myles and Naylor's model starts from the model by Gordon, trying to eliminate the major flaw which, according to these authors, weakened its results. This flaw was Gordon's assumption of a direct (linear) relationship between the psychological cost of the decision to evade and the amount of money evaded. To remove this hypothesis Myles and Naylor suggest to incorporate the social cost that the tax payer pays when s/he decides to evade into the standard model of tax evasion. This cost depends on the loss of her/his status of "honest citizen" and is therefore independent of the amount of money evaded.

The Myles and Naylor model (p. 52) defines the utility level of an agent that receives an income Y taxed by a tax rate of t and decides to pay the whole tax due as follows:

$$U^{NE} = U(Y[1-t]) + bR(1-\mu) + c \tag{5.1}$$

with $b \geq 0$ and $c \geq 0$. The element $bR(1-\mu)$ can be defined as the utility that the tax payer receives to conform with the group of those who pay taxes, where $1-\mu$ is the proportion of honest taxpayers in the total population. Parameter c represents the increase in the utility level obtained by following the social norm. By contrast, when the tax payer decides to evade, her/his utility is computed as follows:

$$U^E = \max_{\{I\}}\{[1-p]U(Y-tI) + pU(Y-tI-ft[E])\} \tag{5.2}$$

where I is the declared income, $E = Y - I$ is the amount of money evaded, p is the probability to be audited and f is the fine to pay if found guilty of tax evasion.

In this paper we carry out a dynamic simulation, starting from a model which closely resembles Myles and Naylor's. We integrate the model in two ways: first, we follow Cowell and Gordon's analysis by introducing a public good, and we then hypothesize the existence of taxpayers who modify their behaviour by adapting to the environment. In other words, we want to model a fiscal system that must cope with different kinds of taxpayers and must finance the production of a public good. In particular, we define three different kinds of agents:

- the honest taxpayer;
- the imitative taxpayer;
- the perfect freerider.

All three types of agent follow the same utility maximisation logic but their utility functions differ. We shall describe these differences in the following section.

The environment is influenced by some given parameters, while its dynamic structure is generated by the agents' behaviour and vice versa. This means that the environment is constituted by the behaviours adopted by the different populations of taxpayers, while at the same time the agents modify their behaviours in accordance with the environment itself. We can test what happen to the environment and to the agents population by changing the following parameters:

- composition of the starting population of taxpayers;

- the probability of fiscal audit;

- the value attributed to the public good by taxpayers;

- total amount of the public good financed.

The hypothesis to test is described in more detail in the following section.

2.   THE MODEL

As mentioned, the simulation model is based on a set of agents making decisions independently and interacting with each other through the environment. These decisions are based on the signals that each agent receives from the environment and which depend on the characteristics of the agent him/herself. The aggregate behaviour of the agents is a function of the initial environmental conditions. The computer simulation enables exploration of the space of the initial parameters, and allows the modelling of agents characterized by decision functions (behaviours) able to evolve, given that otherwise they would not be amenable to analytical description. It should be pointed out that although for the sake of convenience we use the terms "agent" or "taxpayer" (here to be taken as synonymous), what we are in fact talking about are forms of reaction to the introduction of a tax, or more precisely taxpaying behaviours.

The environment is the space which encompasses the decisions of the n agents involved in the simulation and the source of the information required to make decisions relative to subsequent behaviours. Once the initial structure of the population has been defined, the simulation can be used to study the dynamics of the various types of taxpayer. The experimenter first establishes the characteristics of the agents and then analyses their dynamics. The term "dynamic adaptation" denotes the ability of the agents to modify their behaviour on the basis of past experience. In other words, it is possible to describe a certain number of initial scenarios which represent different historical moments of a given population of taxpayers, and to analyse their evolution over time. What does not evolve is the preference structure of the taxpayers who are able to adapt their choices - that is, modify their behaviour - but are not able to comply with "tastes" other than those of the group (category) to which they belong.

Put otherwise, the entire initial population is characterized by agents who share the same decision-making algorithm, i.e. the set of rules that guide their behaviour, but are, at the same time, heterogeneous with respect to their utility functions. A genetic algorithm causes the population to evolve by eliminating weak agents and reproducing the stronger ones. The purpose is to verify under what conditions groups of agents with homogeneous utility functions prevail over others and induce the system, the population of taxpayers, to converge on a shared behavioural paradigm.

The simulation model makes it possible to reproduce a fiscal context in which taxpayers base their decisions (to pay taxes, not to pay them, or to pay them only in part) both on the examination of the decisions made by the tax authorities and on the assessment of the behaviour of other taxpayers. Compared with the traditional theoretical set-up, the principal novel feature of the model proposed here is its evolutionary view of taxpayer behaviour. Actually, as we have already pointed out, the realization that taxpaying decisions are not taken in a sort of social vacuum is not new to the theoretical literature on tax evasion. However, our simulation model fosters the analysis of tax evasion to be extended from the calculation of individual utility to the broader sphere of its repercussions on the composition of the population of taxpayers. Whilst traditional models do not deal with the dynamics of the taxpayer population and do not examine the interactions among taxpayers with different preference structures, the model used here allows these dynamic mechanisms of reciprocal influence to be investigated, at least in part.

A further aspect that we intend to explore with this model is the effects exerted on the population of taxpayers by the auditing policies implemented by the tax authorities. Put more precisely, the aim is to assess the effects on the process of selection by the types of taxpayer generated by control strategies which concentrate on that part of the population declaring the lower incomes (and therefore those paying the lowest amount of taxes).

2.1   THE ENVIRONMENT

In the model, agents receive the following information from the environment:

- the tax rate that the agent must pay at time t;

- the average amount of tax that the population has paid at time $t - 1$;

- the fine that the agent will have to pay if discovered evading tax.

Agents undertake two actions: they pay taxes to the state, and they consume the public good. The environment performs the twofold function of (i) collecting, mediating and transmitting information to taxpayers, and (ii) simulating the state with respect to its enforcement of tax control procedures and its production and distribution of public goods.

For the sake of simplicity, the model hypothesizes the existence of one single public good. The production function is linear. The quantity of public good produced at time t, using inputs relative to time $t - 1$, is made available at time $t + 1$ jointly with any amount of the public good not consumed at time t. The only production factor employed by the public sector is capital, which is assumed to be equal to the tax yield at time t.

2.2   THE AGENTS

The agents used in the model can be regarded as static. Each agent, in fact, is endowed with a decision-making "engine" (the logic of utility maximization) and with a utility function that do not change over time. This definition does not imply that the agent does not behave adaptively; rather, it states that the agent decides on the basis of the same set of rules in all the periods of the simulation. Put more precisely, an agent has two distinctive features: a mechanism of behaviour selection (decision-making algorithm) and a utility function.

The decision-making algorithm used is the traditional model of reinforced learning. The choice of the behaviour to adopt is based on probability, and the probabilities associated with the options available are updated on the basis of past experience (Bower & Hillgard, 1981). In the model in question an agent has three possible choices: pay more tax than paid previously, pay the same amount as previously, or pay less than previously. We denote these three choices with respectively W_g, W_e e W_l. At the beginning of the simulation the agents randomly choose the amount of tax to pay. Associated with W_g is probability P_g, with W_e probability P_e and with W_l probability $(1 - P_g - P_e)$ and $P_g + P_e \leq 1$.

Let us suppose that at time t the agent has decided to pay the same amount of tax, i.e. s/he has opted for choice W_e. The agent will know the outcome of his/her decision - that is, s/he can calculate the utility obtained from this choice, which we denote with $U(t)$. This utility is compared against that relative to the previous instant: if $U(t) > U(t-1)$, then the choice has had a good outcome. Conversely, if $U(t) < U(t-1)$, then the outcome is negative. The information obtained on the outcome of the decision is used to update the choice probability.

If $P_e(t)$ is the probability associated with choice W_e at time t, in the case of a positive outcome it is calculated as follows:

$$P_e(t) = (1 - \alpha)P_e(t - 1) + \alpha \qquad (5.3)$$

In the case of a negative outcome:

$$P_e(t) = (1 - \alpha)P_e(t - 1). \qquad (5.4)$$

The probabilities associated with the other choices are updated as a consequence:

$$U(t) \geq U(t - 1) \quad \begin{cases} P_g(t) & = (1 - \alpha)P_g(t - 1) \\ P_l(t) & = (1 - \alpha)P_l(t - 1) \end{cases} \qquad (5.5)$$

$$U(t) < U(t - 1) \quad \begin{cases} P_g(t) & = (1 - \alpha)P_g(t - 1) + \alpha/2 \\ P_l(t) & = (1 - \alpha)P_l(t - 1) + \alpha/2 \end{cases} \qquad (5.6)$$

The parameter α represents the learning rate, or the intensity with which agents update the probabilities associated with the choices. The utility function is the second important element in the characterization of the agent. The differentiation among the agents' utility functions explains their differing behaviour and the different dynamics of the populations. The following utility functions are used:

1. Honest Agent. The agent labelled "honest" obtains an increase in utility if s/he belongs to a group which pays its taxes in the following manner:

$$U_o = U(Y(1 - a)) + U(G) + bR(1 - \mu) \qquad (5.7)$$

where a is the amount that s/he intends to pay, Y is income, G the portion of the public good that s/he can consume, and $R(1 - \mu)$ is the utility that s/he obtains if s/he does not evade given the proportion $(1 - \mu)$ of honest taxpayers in the population.

2. Imitative Agent: The imitative agent receives a "extragratifica-tion" because s/he pays an amount close to that paid by the average of the population, according to the following relation:

$$U_i = U(Y(1 - a)) + U(G) + U\left(1 - \frac{|a - \langle a \rangle|}{a^*}\right) \qquad (5.8)$$

where a is the amount that s/he intends to pay, Y is income, G the portion of the public good that s/he can consume, $\langle a \rangle$ is the average amount paid by the population, and a^* the amount that s/he has to pay.

3. Free Rider Agent: the more this agent succeeds in his/her opportunistic behaviour, the more his/her utility increases, according to the following equation:

$$U_f = U(Y(1-a)) + U(G) + U\left(\frac{a - \langle a \rangle}{a^*}\right) \qquad (5.9)$$

where a is the amount that s/he intends to pay, Y is income, G the portion of the public good that s/he can consume, $\langle a \rangle$ is the average amount paid by the population, and a^* the amount that s/he has to pay.

At each stage of the simulation, the agents choose the amount that they intend to pay and communicate it to the environment. Once the environment has gathered the taxes paid by the agents, the tax authority carries out random audits, computes the average rate, the size of the group of non-evaders, and the quantity of the public good that it is able to produce. This information is then transmitted to the agents, who are thus able to calculate the utility of their last decision and to update the probabilities associated with choices. Each round of the fiscal audit involves a constant number k of agents. These agents are extracted by means of the following strategies:

- through use of a uniform distribution: all agents have the same probability of being selected for audit.

- audits are concentrated in the lower tail of the distribution of agents constructed according to contribution. The probability of being audited by the tax authorities is higher when the average contribution of the group is lower.

If an agent is audited and is found to have evaded, s/he will have to pay a fine proportional to the amount evaded. If a^* is the amount to pay, and a is the amount paid, then the fine M is:

$$M = m\, Y(a^* - a)$$

, with $m \geq 1$ being the severity of the sanction. Every n steps, the genetic procedure (Holland, 1992) is performed in order to select a new population of taxpayers, taking account of the probability distribution based on the agents' fitness values. This procedure divides into two phases:

1. Construction of the "roulette wheel" with sectors proportional to fitness, in the following steps:

   - calculation of the fitness value $eval(v_i)$ for each agent v_i: $(i = 1, \ldots, pop\_size)$.
   - computation of the total fitness of the population $F = \sum_{i=1}^{pop\_size} eval(v_i)$.
   - calculation of the probability of selection p_i for each agent v_i: $p_i = eval(v_i)/F$.
   - calculation of the cumulated probability q_i for each agent v_i: $q_i = \sum_{j=1}^{i} p_j$.

2. Section process based on *pop_size* extractions with the "roulette wheel". The steps in this phase are the following:

   - generation of a random number r within the interval $[0 \ldots 1]$
   - if $r < q_1$ select the first agent (v_1) , otherwise select the *i*th agent v_i $(2 \leq i \leq pop\_size)$ such that $q_{i-1} < r \leq q_i$.

Obviously some agents may be selected more than once. The selection procedure based on the genetic algorithm can be interpreted from the economic point of view as a mechanism discriminating among choice behaviour rules rather than one which selects agents. It is assumed, that is to say, that taxpayers seek to adapt their choices to the limit of the zero utility balance, and then 'die' when the balance becomes negative. It should be borne in mind, in fact, that what we have called agents, or taxpayers, are nothing but choice models subordinate, as said, to the logic of utility maximization. In this sense it is not the taxpayers that die but styles of tax payment, which are abandoned as they prove themselves unable to maximize utility. The use of a genetic algorithm to select behaviours allows simulation of the survival of taxpaying styles in the memory of taxpayers, who may decide to reactivate them after a certain number of periods.

3. COMMENTS TO THE SIMULATION

The first test has been made using only imitative agents. At the beginning of the simulation each agent is randomly assigned the tax that s/he should have paid. A uniform probability distribution U defined in the interval $[0, tax]$–where *tax* is the tax due–has been employed in the simulation. Even the parameter ε has been defined using a uniform distribution U' defined as $[0, \frac{tax}{n}]$ with $n = 2, 4, 8, 10$.

One can notice that:

1. If n is small, then ε is very large. This means that only agents "located" far from the average will decide to pay a tax equal to the average tax paid by the population. The agents close to the average will mantain unchanged their choices and the variance is very small.

2. If n is large, then ε will be small, therefore there will be a greater number of agents choosing to pay the average tax from the beginning and the variance increases.

   We shall come back on the results obtained from a the simulation carried out only with imitative agents in the following points.

3.1   NO FISCAL AUDITS, NO SELECTION

Modifying the initial population's composition, i.e. introducing the honest and the freerider agents, we have a more complete picture. In this section some graphs synthesize the results obtained carrying out simulations with different initial compositions of the population in a context without fiscal audit and without selection. Although the starting environment chosen, without fiscal audits and without selection, is very simple, it allows us to analyse the evolution of the "pure" choices in a sort of primitive society.

Looking at fig. 5.1 one can notice that around the 500th round all three groups choose the same behavioural strategy, i.e. reduce near zero the amount of tax paid. The group that converges more rapidly towards the low fiscal contribution behaviour (around the 90th round) is obviously that of the freeriders and, remembering that the utility level of the honest agents is influenced by the amount of public good financed through the fiscal yield, it is reasonable to expect that the speedness of convergence of the three groups will be influenced by the percentage of freeriders in the population. This means that the low contribution given by freeriders to the fiscal revenue of the state reduces the utility that honest agents can obtain from the public good, pushing them towards progressively lower levels of tax payments and at the same time attracting the imitative group in the same direction.

To substantiate this intuition we run a simulation modifying the initial composition of the population. Figure 5.2 records the results of such a simulation made with 200 honest agents, 100 imitatives and zero freeriders. As expected the convergence towards a stable and common behaviour at this time comes later, near the 600th round, this means that the equilibrium is reached after 75% of the total rounds, while in the simulation with freeriders the same result is reached already after 62.5% of the total rounds. It is worth noticing that the role played by the imitative agents in the two simulations is identical, given that the imitative group reaches the steady behaviour in both cases between round 400 and round 500.

The weakness of the role played by the imitative agents is even more clearly shown in fig. 5.3 where we report the results from a simulation carried out using 200 honest agents, 100 freeriders and zero imitative. With this composition of the population the convergence towards the steady behavior is reached approximately in the same number of rounds required by the first simulation, i.e. with the same number of agents for each group. The reason of the irrelevance of the imitative agents in determining the speed of convergence is that the form chosen for the utility functions of these agents push them towards a behaviour which is the nearest possible to the average and therefore can be considered as a sort of "neutral" behaviour.

On the other hand, it is worth noticing that carrying out simulations only with honest or imitative agents (respectively fig. 5.4 and fig. 5.5) the imitative agents reach a stable behaviour, faster than the honest agents. This quite reasonable result is due to the form of the utility function of the honest agents, that in absence of controls and selection push each of them to behave in a perfectly identical manner towards the stable behaviour, following a relatively slow process. Conversely each imitative agent is continuosly trying to approximate the average tax paid and therefore the process that push them towards the steady style of low tax payment is faster, because is reiforced by the engine powered by the extragratification that they receive when imitate the others.

3.2   FISCAL AUDITS, NO SELECTION

Introducing the fiscal audits the results of the simulations change enormously. Fig. 5.6 records the results of a simulation carried out using the same composition of agents of fig. 5.1 but introducing an uniform fiscal auditing. This time there is not a convergence towards a common and stable style of fiscal contribution, each group follows a specific pattern of behaviour. Furthermore the more rounds pass, the more radical become the differences between the three groups. More precisely, the tendence to increase the difference between the groups seemed to have a stop between round 600 and round 700 and a slow inversion after round 780, i.e. at the end of the simulation. The group that pay more taxes is obviously the honest one, while the group that pay the lowest amount of money is the freeriders one.

Carrying out simulations with different compositions of the initial population do not change the story, the introduction of uniform fiscal

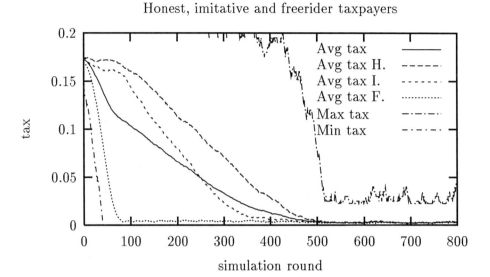

Figure 5.1 Simulation with n.100 honest (H.), 100 imitative (I.) and 100 freerider (F.) taxpayers. No tax auditing, no selection.

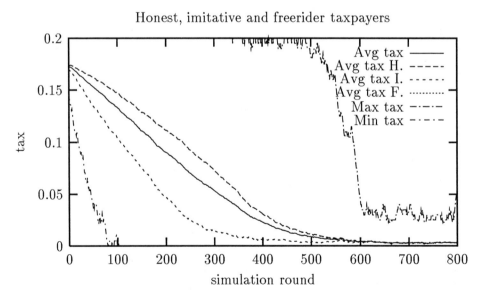

Figure 5.2 Simulation with n.200 honest (H.), 100 imitative (I.) and 0 freerider (F.) taxpayers. No tax auditing, no selection.

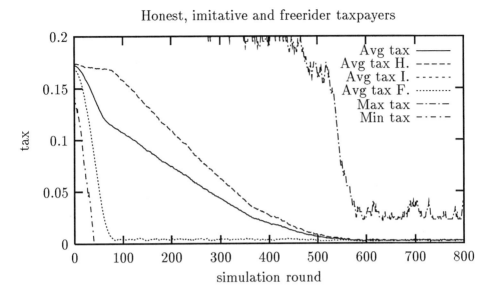

Figure 5.3 Simulation with n.200 honest (H.), 0 imitative (I.) and 100 freerider (F.) taxpayers. No tax auditing, no selection.

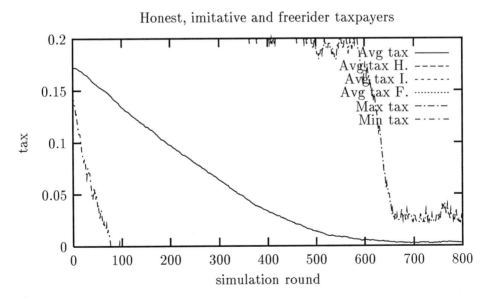

Figure 5.4 Simulation with n.300 honest (H.), 0 imitative (I.) and 0 freerider (F.) taxpayers. No tax auditing, no selection.

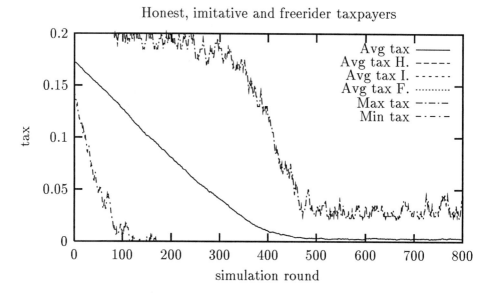

Figure 5.5 Simulation with n.0 honest (H.), 300 imitative (I.) and 0 freerider (F.) taxpayers. No tax auditing, no selection.

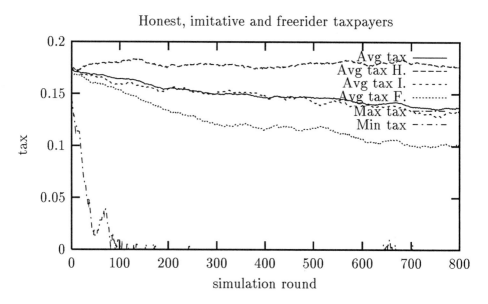

Figure 5.6 Simulation with n.100 honest (H.), 100 imitative (I.) and 100 freerider (F.) taxpayers. **Uniform auditing**, no selection.

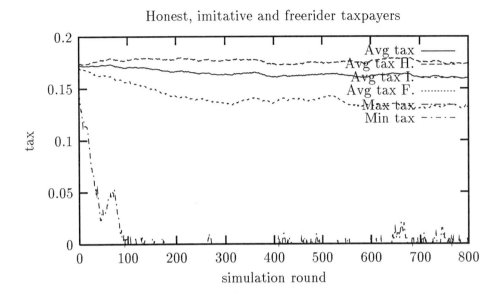

Figure 5.7 Simulation with n.200 honest (H.), 100 imitative (I.) and 0 freerider (F.) taxpayers. **Uniform auditing**, no selection.

audits always produce well separate styles of fiscal contribution independently from the weigth . To see an example of this phenomenon we report in fig. 5.7 the results of a simulation carried out with 200 honest agents, 100 imitative and zero freeriders. As in fig. 5.6, the honest agents pay the higher amount of taxes while the imitative always pay as close as possible to the average. The only but easily foreseeable difference with the result of the previous simulation is that the average amount of tax paid by the entire population is higher than it was when there were freeriders.

3.3   NO FISCAL AUDITS, GENETIC SELECTION

The results obtained from the simulations carried out introducing a selection of the agents based on a genetic algorithm are much more interesting than those discussed until now. Once more, we started with a population made by groups of the same size. Fig. 5.8 and fig. 5.9 show respectively the evolution of the agents behaviours and the trend of each group. Comparing fig. 5.8 with fig. 5.1, i.e. with a world without selection, one can notice that in both cases the agents' behaviours converge towards the same steady style of tax payment (pay a very low amount of tax) and approximately in the same number of rounds. The interesting point is that in the world with selection this result is obtained with a population made only by pure imitative agents. In fact looking at fig. 5.9 it is easy to see that after round 240 only imitative agents survive, while both the honest and the freeriders ones die (notice that the honest survive a bit longer than the freeriders).

Furthermore, it is worth noticing that if we compare the results shown in fig. 5.8 with those of fig. 5.5 the total amount of tax paid during the whole simulation by the imitative agents in absence of selection is higher than the correspondent amount paid in an environment with selection. This difference is produced during the first 240 rounds and is due to the interaction of the imitative agents with the agents of the other groups.

Running a simulation with an initial population made of 200 honest taxpayers, 100 imitative and zero freeriders do not change in a noticeable way the results. The only difference with the results obtained using a starting population with groups of the same size is that the honest agents die later (commenting the results of fig. 5.9 we have seen that no honest taxpayers survive after round 240, with a starting population made by 200 honest and 100 imitative; the honest totally disappear at round 280). The steady behaviour of tax payment is the same for both the simulations and is reached near round 500.

More interesting are the graphs shown in figs. 5.10 and 5.11, which report the results from a simulation carried out with a starting population made by 200 honest taxpayers, zero imitative and 100 freeriders. The first lesson that emerges from the analysis of the graphs is that the steady style of tax payment is reached later in the world without imitative agents. Comparing fig. 5.8 with fig. 5.10 one in fact notices that the usual low tax payment style is reached about 100 rounds later in the simulation run without the imitative agents. The slowest convergence is exclusively due to the higher percentage of honest taxpayers (200) on

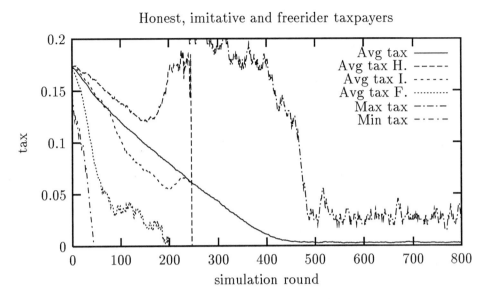

Figure 5.8 Simulation with n.100 honest (H.), 100 imitative (I.) and 100 freerider (F.) taxpayers. no auditing, **selection**.

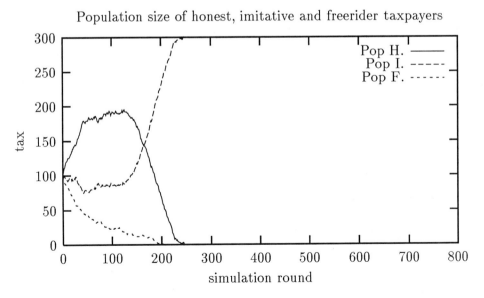

Figure 5.9 Simulation with n.100 honest (H.), 100 imitative (I.) and 100 freerider (F.) taxpayers. no auditing, **selection**.

the whole population and confirm the "neutrality" of the role played by the imitative agents in reaching the equilibrium.

The second interesting phenomenon emerged from the simulation without imitative agents is that both the initial groups of agents, the honest taxpayers and the freeriders, survive. Looking at fig. 5.11 one can notice that the freeriders group, after an initial quite dramatical reduction, tends to re-emerge (near round 300) and progressively increase its weigth on the total population. The honest agents group mirrors the evolution but the two groups never reach a convergence because, between round 600 and round 700, the trends change once more and the freeriders start to die. We do not know if this result is in some way influenced by the initial higher weight of the honest taxpayers on the total population, but surely there is a close relationship between the trend of the freeriders group and their average style of tax payment. Comparing fig. 5.10 with fig. 5.11 one can in fact notice that the initial fall of the freeriders population coincide with a strong reduction of the level of the average tax paid by this group. After round 180 the taxes paid by the freeriders have a strong increase and correspondingly their number starts to increase. In a similar way between round 600 and 700, i.e. when the freeriders adopt a stable style of tax payment which is almost identical to the one followed by the honest agents, their group starts once more to decrease.

The reason for this phenomenon is probably due to the fact that when the honest taxpayers stabilise their style of tax payment on the minimum level, the freeriders lose any possibility to obtain extragratification from their opportunistic behaviours. On the contrary the honest agents continue to receive their extragratification because in their case the extra-monetary reward depends on the percentage of honest taxpayers on the population.

3.4   UNIFORM TAX AUDITING AND SELECTION

The fourth group of simulations have been carried out by introducing uniform tax audits and by maintaining the genetic selection. The results of the simulation with 100 honest taxpayers, 100 imitative and 100 freeriders are reported in figs. 5.12 and 5.13. The introduction of fiscal audits changes both the kind of steady style of tax payment and the result of the genetic selection. The amount of the average tax paid is much higher than the one obtained in the simulation without tax audits and the group that survive at the end of the simulation is the honest taxpayers one.

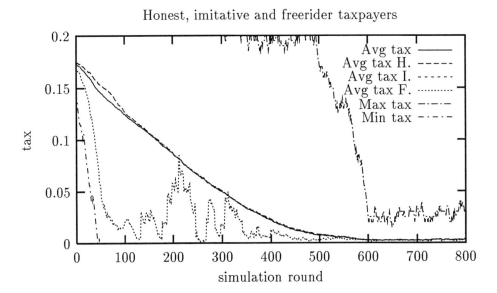

Figure 5.10   Simulation with n.200 honest (H.), 0 imitative (I.) and 100 freerider (F.) taxpayers. No auditing, **selection**.

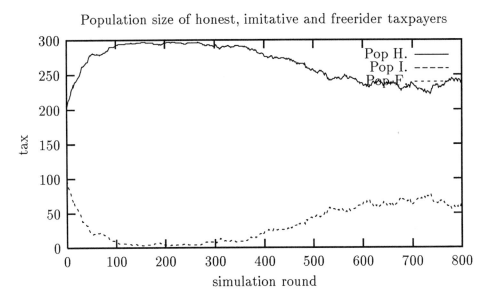

Figure 5.11   Simulation with n.200 honest (H.), 0 imitative (I.) and 100 freerider (F.) taxpayers. No auditing, **selection**.

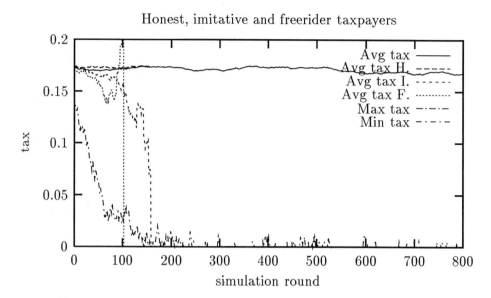

Figure 5.12 Simulation with n.100 honest (H.), 100 imitative (I.) and 100 freerider (F.) taxpayers. **Auditing and selection.**

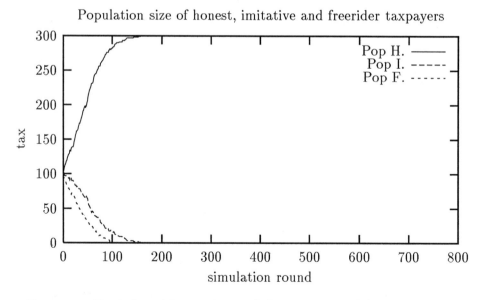

Figure 5.13 Simulation with n.100 honest (H.), 100 imitative (I.) and 100 freerider (F.) taxpayers. **Auditing and selection.**

It is also worth noticing that the selection device does not increase the speed of convergence towards the steady style of tax payment and the total amount of the tax revenue cumulated during the simulation. To check this consideration it is useful to look at fig. 5.14 which shows the results of two simulations: the first one has been run without selection, with uniform tax auditing and with a population made only by honest taxpayers, the second simulation is the same of figs. 5.12 and 5.13 but the trends reported are only those of the average tax paid respectively by the whole population and by the honest agents.

Looking at fig. 5.14 it is quite clear that the simulation without selection seemed to produce only a very slightly better result, in terms of reduction of evasion. Furthermore, we cannot be sure that this minimum increase of the level of the average tax paid was only due to the absence of selection, or is related to the different composition of the initial populations.

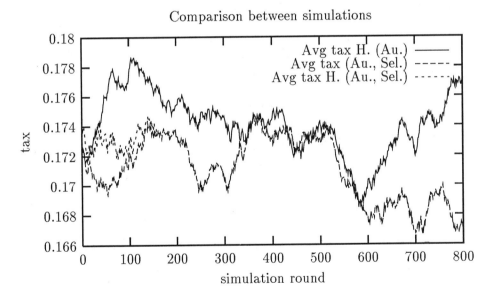

Figure 5.14 Comparison between two simulation: a) with 300 honest (H.), uniform auditing (Au.), no selection; b) 100 Honest, 100 Imitative, 100 Freeriders, selection (Sel.) and uniform auditing.

Running the simulations with different compositions of the initial populations does not add important pieces of information, the only consideration that can be made is that the imitative agents tend to survive somewhat longer than the freeriders do.

3.5   LOWER TAIL TAX AUDITING AND SELECTION

The last group of simulations have been carried out by introducing tax audits concentrated on the lower tail of the distribution of tax contribution. The first simulation (fig. 5.15) is without genetic selection while the second simulation (figs. 5.16 and 5.17) includes selection. All the simulations have been carried out using only the usual balanced starting population, i.e. with 100 honest taxpayers, 100 imitative and 100 freeriders. These simulations allow to compare the effects produced by different systems of fiscal auditing.

Comparing fig. 5.15 with the results previously obtained from the simulation run with uniform tax auditing (fig. 5.6) the most important difference is that the tail auditing produces a convergence of the behaviours of the taxpayers towards a common level of contribution, while in the case of uniform tax auditing each typology of taxpayers follows a specific pattern of behaviour. The stable level of average tax paied produced by the tail tax auditing is only a bit higher than the corresponding level observed in the case of absence of tax auditing. The tail tax auditing can therefore be considered as a weak deterrence against tax evasion, at least when is modelled in the way here chosen.

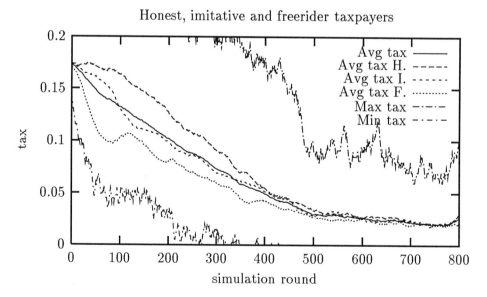

Figure 5.15 Simulation with n.100 honest (H.), 100 imitative (I.) and 100 freerider (F.) taxpayers. **Tail auditing.**

When selection is introduced the results look very similar to those already observed in the case of selection without tax auditing. Comparing fig. 5.16 with fig. 5.8 and fig. 5.17 with fig. 5.9 one can notice two main differences:

1. the speed of reduction of the population of honest taxpayers, and the mirror like increase of the population of imitative agents, is lower when the tail tax auditing is applied than in absence of fiscal controls;

2. the steady average amount of tax paied is lower in absence of fiscal auditing.

The positive performance of the imitative taxpayers is due to the nature of their extra-gratification, that push them towards a style of tax payment which is the nearest possible to the average amount of tax paid by the whole population. This behaviour in the long run is very successful because prevents them from the fiscal audits and at the same time ensures relatively high levels of net income. On the other hand is worth noticing that the population of imitative agents starts to increase after a quite dramatical initial reduction that takes them very near to a total estinction between round 100 and round 200. The imitative population at the beginning of the simulation extract an higher utility by following the freeriders style of payment and this choice take them very near to the destiny of the freeriders that, in fact, die before round 200. On the other hand as the tail tax auditing starts to penalize the freeriders the level of the average tax paied by the whole population progressively increases, and therefore the imitative begin to be attracted towards the honest taxpayers style of tax contribution and contemporaneously towards a demographic increase.

Finally is worth noticing that the tail tax auditing here designed is so weak that a simulation run with 150 freeriders, 50 imitative and 100 honest taxpayers has produced not only a survival of the freeriders but, in the very long run (after 400 rounds), a progressive increase of their population.

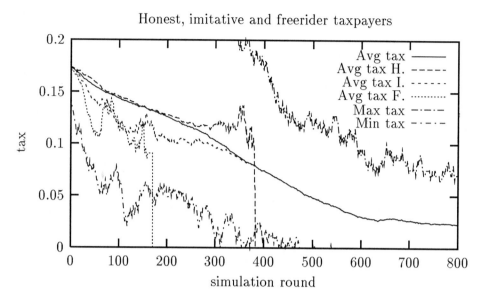

Figure 5.16 Simulation with n.100 honest (H.), 100 imitative (I.) and 100 freerider (F.) taxpayers. **Tail auditing and selection.**

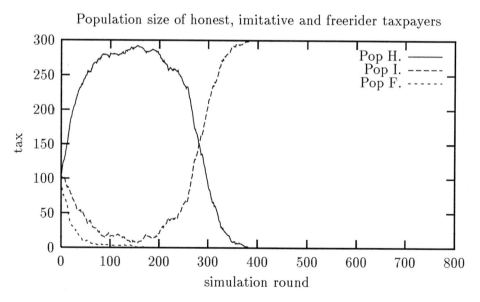

Figure 5.17 Simulation with n.100 honest (H.), 100 imitative (I.) and 100 freerider (F.) taxpayers. **Tail auditing and selection.**

4.   CONCLUSIONS

The main economic interpretation of the results just discussed is that in a world without a fiscal authority, or with a fiscal authority so weak as to be perceived by the taxpayers as totally ineffective, a behaviour oriented towards the almost total evasion prevails. The existence within the population of a group of honest people that attribute a sort of moral importance to the tax payment is not enough by itself to change the final result. Furthemore, the role played by the interaction among taxpayers is particularly crucial in pushing the system towards a convergence to low levels of tax payments in absence of fiscal audits, while it seemed less important when the fiscal audits are introduced . This means that in absence of fiscal audits the honest ones stay honest until their number is reasonably high, if the prevailing attitude of the whole population is to progressively reduce the amount of money paid, then also honest agents start to follow this trend. On the other hand, in a world with fiscal audits each typology of agents tend to behave following its own specific style and the interaction is almost unperceivable.

Paradoxically, imitative agents, as have been designed here, have a weaker influence than the honest taxpayers in the interaction among agents. Furthermore, neither the introduction of a process of genetic selection of the agents nor the use of different systems of fiscal audit change in a significant way the story. The most important change produced by genetic selection, both with or without fiscal audit, is that at the end of the simulation only one kind of agent survive. Given the form of the utility functions we employed, it is not surprisingly that without tax audits the selection produces only imitative agents, while with fiscal inspections only the honest taxpayers survive.

This last consideration allows us to make an interesting connection with a special form of imitation that is very common in Italy, i.e. the tax payment style of the small retailers. In Italy, the majority of the owners of small shops belong to a strong national association that operates as a sort of information device, keeping updated the associates about the average tax paid by each typology of shop. In this way the retailers can declare an income as near as possible to the average, weakening the effectiveness of the fiscal audits, which are concentrated on the low tail of the income declarations. The Italian small retailers example is very similar to the case described by the simulation with selection and without tax audits, because the Italian fiscal audit system is so weak in detecting this form of tax evasion (evasion near the average) to be almost totally ineffective. From this perspective the only survival of the imitative taxpayers in the simulation here discussed can be interpreted, with all the obvious limits of the tool adopted, as a very worrying lesson for the Italian fiscal authorities.

References

Ackerlof, G. A., 1980, *A theory of social custom of which unemployement not be one consequence*, Quaterly Journal of Economics, 95, 749-795.

Allingham, M. G. and Sandmo, A., 1972, *Income Tax Evasion: A Theoretical Analysis*, Journal of Public Economics, 1, 323-338.

Baldry, J. C., 1985, *Income Tax Evasion and the Tax Schedule: some Experimental Results*, Public Finance, 42, 357-383.

Baldry, J. C., 1986, *Tax evasion is not a gamble: a report on two experiments*, Economic Letters, 22, 333-335.

Bower, G. H., and Hilgard, E. R., 1981, *Theory of learning*. Prentice-Hall, Englewood Cliffs, NJ.

Cowell, F. A. and Gordon, J. P. F., 1988, *Unwillingness to pay*, Journal of Public Economics, 36, 305-321.

Gordon, J. P. F. 1989, *Individual morality and reputation costs as deterrents to tax evasion*, European Economic Review, 33, 797-805.

Holland, J. H., 1992, *Adaptation in Natural and Artificial Systems*. MIT Press, Cambridge MA, 2nd edition.

Mittone, L., 1999, Psychological constraints on tax evasion: an experimental approach, PhD thesis, University of Bristol (GB).

Myles, G. D. and Naylor R. A., 1996, *A model of tax evasion with group conformity and social customs*, European Journal of Political Economy, 12, 49-66.

Naylor, R. A., 1990, *A social custom model of collective action*, European Journal of Political Economy, 6, 201-216.

Srinivasan, T. L., 1973 *Tax Evasion: A Model*, Journal of Public Economics, 2, 37-54.

Yitzhaki, S., 1974, *A note on Income Tax evasion: A Theoretical Analysis*, Jornal of Public Economics, 3, 201-202.

Chapter 6

AN EXPERIMENTAL APPROACH TO THE STUDY OF BANKING INTERMEDIATION: THE BANKNET SIMULATOR

Massimo Daniele Sapienza*

Universita' di Roma Tor Vergata

sapienza@economia.uniroma2.it

Abstract   We propose a restatement of a simulating model based on artificial agents (BankNet), designed to incorporate some relevant stylized facts (transaction costs, economies of scale, bounded rationalityrationality, heterogeneity and strategical interaction) in a financial network where operations of deposit and credit continually take place. BankNet develops, cycle after cycle, a non-intentional credit system in an absolutely decentralized way, excluding any form of conjecturable constructive programmes. The continuing interaction among the agents is the evolutive engine, which, "from the bottom-up" makes it possible for the system to evolve over time through a selecting mechanism.

Keywords: Graph-Based Modeling, Financial Intermediation, Transaction Costs, Asymmetric Information, Borrow Link, Invest Link, Financial Network, Financial System Entropy, Banking Crisis

1.   ECONOMICS AND FINANCIAL INTERMEDIATION

Capital markets aren't the most important source of funding for firms[1]. The activity of financial intermediaries and in particular of banks is of primary importance to describe the structure of financial systems, also

---

*I am really grateful to Professor Pietro Terna for his constant help during the elaboration of this work. I'd like to thank Wolfang De Martino and Alessio Fancetta for their accurate work on the text. Many thanks to Alessandro Perrone who read a draft version of the document and provided his great skill and care in preparing the final LaTeX version of this document

in presence of securitization and globalization, which should tendentially reduce the role of the banking sector in determining the equilibrium of the financial systems.

Setting aside an accurate analysis of different schools' contributions, which is beyond the scope of this essays, we shall try to illustrate briefly in this first section the most important arguments proposed by economic research to explain the existence of an institutional context similar to the one typical of the Western economies.

The credit market has been studied mainly as a market for intertemporal exchange. The main reason of these exchanges is the fact that individuals aren't indifferent about their distribution of consumption and leisure over time. The notion of "time preference", which comes from the classical analysis of Fisher (1930), has made it possible to study the credit market in an analytical way. Transactions between "surplus" units and "deficit" ones can be viewed as a mechanism to match flows of desired and realized income in every period. The presence of a credit market should be an incentive toward an efficient allocation of resources. It allows to discriminate between a plurality of investment opportunities and, in this way, it determines the real equilibrium of the system. At this stage of the analysis we can think of a direct financial circuit as showed in figure 6.1

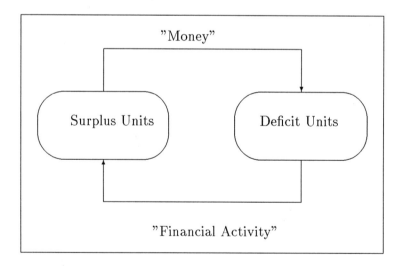

Figure 6.1   Direct Finance

The presence of financial intermediation could be represented by a scheme as in figure 6.2. Figure 6.2 shows the presence of actors between surplus units and deficit ones, realizing an indirect financial circuit.[2]

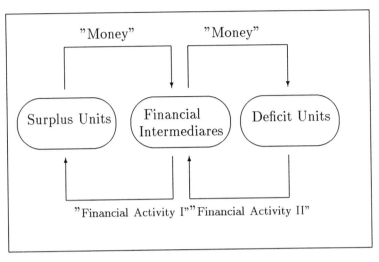

Figure 6.2 Indirect Finance

This essay focuses on the explanation of the reason why the second scheme dominates the first one in the real world and on the identification of the forces which push toward this second ideal model.

In abstract terms the presence of intermediaries is a disadvantage, because the chain of transactions between demander and supplier of funds is lengthened consequently leading to greater transaction costs in the economic system, ceteris paribus. The presence of intermediaries between demand and supply has to be explained in terms of benefits of intermediation compared to costs of transaction. Using Coase's (1937) traditional analysis, we can think that the firm emerges alternatively to the market when some processes are feasible in a more efficient way through hierarchical procedures rather than through the price system. The firm is now viewed as a coordination system which allows to internalize transactions, thus making feasible exchanges that in a pure market economy would not be feasible.

"Money in a Theory of Finance" by Gurley and Shaw (1960) is one of the most important work for financial intermediation theory. The analysis of the two authors starts from the consideration of the agents' subjective propensity to negotiate, making a distinction between risk and liquidity propensity. The exchange could not occur, even without any information problems, if the financial instruments and market's organization are not adequate to reconcile the divergent agents preferences. In market economies based on the use of money, the volume of desired financial transactions tend to be greater than the volume of feasible transactions using the circuit of direct finance. In other terms, it means that the volume of directly realizable transactions under the conditions hypothesized is not sufficient to satisfy the total number of potential transactions: thus we can argue that direct finance puts the system in a situation of "incomplete market".

Gurley's and Shaw's analysis of the role of intermediation show that primary bonds issued by firms (funds demander) are transformed into derived financial activities that embody the requirements of the final investors (funds supplier). Therefore financial intermediation may be assimilated to a technology for the production of transportation services, intended to reduce the problems that come from the differences in preferences toward liquidity among agents. Unlike direct finance which doesn't use a sufficient degree of risk's diversification for supplier and demander, the banking activity would transform illiquid activities into liquid loans. In Gurley's and Shaw's opinion, financial intermediation is useful when the indivisibility problems and the no convexity affects the transaction's technology[3] limiting the possibility of risk diversification realizable with direct financing operations. The liquidity function is for this approach one of the most important characteristic of the banking activity.

A second and more modern approach to banking intermediation[4] considers intermediaries as institutions set to avoid the problems of imperfect and asymmetric information[5]. In this vision, the problem of asymmetric information finds a solution in the capacity of the intermediary to obtain, to elaborate and to evaluate information for the agent.

The screening pre-contractual activity of investment opportunities selection, is an important moment of banking activity to explain the existence of financial intermediaries. In absence of an adequate screening activity, adverse selection reduces the average credit operation probability of success if the intermediaries don't use credit rationing solutions. A market solution to the problem of adverse selection is private production of information. Given the existence of the free rider problem we can observe examples of private information production business on the main financial market worldwide that are not fully sufficient to solve the problem. The government regulation is also a partial solution of informational asymmetries.

The huge role of banking intermediaries in the management of nowadays monetary economies, shows without any doubt that the two solutions described above are not sufficient to solve the difficulties on the ground.

The banking system has developed an experience in the information production which enables it to lower costs and to obtain in a more efficient way the huge amount of information necessary to discriminate among the projects to finance. Directly interposing themselves between supplier and demander and assuming a relevant role in the exchanging process, the intermediaries are able to solve the free rider problem. They internalize in a single productive function the information- acquisition phase and the realization of profits by borrowing funds, using private loans instead of standardized market bonds. Bilateral loans are not in general available on marketplace, and, in this way, consequently, the information, that comes out of them, is not usable by the potential competitors of the banking firm. Banks maintain an advantage that justifies the existence of positive profits and explain why expensive operations of screening and monitoring are realized.

The monitoring activity, unlike the screening one, is a set of post-contractual verification operations required to obtain a good result from the financing transaction in presence of incomplete contracts. Diamond (1984) proposed an example of the effectiveness of the intermediation on the reduction of agency costs for external financing in an environment with moral hazard conditions, through verification. The monitoring activity[6] should be interpreted in a wide sense, considering any form of information collection on the financed agent, his investment perspectives and his strategy. The information collected is useful to punish deviating behaviors. For Diamond the monitoring activity shows natural economies of scale, because an intermediary would be able to control a firm with the same effectiveness of a group of shareholders, thus economizing on costs. Moreover, if the intermediary has a well diversified portfolio, its relationships with funds suppliers are not exposed to moral hazard, because the expected return is nearly risk free and financing operations, at fixed interest rate, are fully feasible.

One last aspect useful to explain the existence of banking firms can be linked to the idea of customer relationship. The previous concept can be clarified thinking of the intermediation process as a mechanism to stimulate in a long term commitments assumptions. In absence of complete contracts, the agreements among the counterparts are not just open to the constraint that derives from the distribution of information, surmountable with the monitoring activity. If long term commitments are not feasible using contracts, then financial intermediation represents an alternative mechanism with its intense relation between bank and firm. Even in presence of a certain degree of competition between intermediaries in an intermediate phase, the informational advantage, built on past transactions gives the bank the the opportunity to defeat the rivals.

The simulation based on artificial agents, which we have designed, tries to illustrate some of the phenomena briefly described in this first section. Adopting an experimental approach we have tried to verify the propositions about the importance of economies of scale and focalization (experience) in portfolio diversification and in transaction costs. Moreover we have tested the importance of the screening and monitoring activity to explain the existence of financial intermediation in a context with heterogeneous agents (while in traditional models the assumption of a representative agent is fundamental), interacting in an environment with imperfect information where phenomena of bounded rationality rationality are observable.

The intellectual charm of a similar operation comes from the non deductive approach to modeling, trying to enlighten the passage between scheme 1 of direct finance and scheme 2 of indirect finance. BankNet is useful because it provides a new vision on problems studied deeply by economic theory during the past years, but it is also interesting to explore fields not fully studied at this moment. For instance, our knowledge of the strategical interactions among intermediaries under imperfect information is really far from being fully satisfying. Studying the competitive dynamics inside the simulators could be useful to analyze this aspect, once the study of the emergence of banking has been exhausted.

2.   BANKNET

In this section we will illustrate the simulating model based on artificial agents (BankNet) and the implementations, designed on it to incorporate some of the stylized facts described in the previous section: transaction costs, economies of scale, bounded rationalityrationality, heterogeneity and strategical interaction.

BankNet has been developed by Manor Askenazy as an example of graph-based model in Swarm without any particular interest in the economic relevance of the results.[7] The implementation realized in a second phase during our work is a trial to conduct the structured software, prepared by Askenazy into an experiment of Artificial Life interesting for Economics. We made a sequence of substantial changes to illustrate a set of aspects of reality, enlightened by the theoretical research.

Our goal, is to show the emergence of banking activity from the interaction of a series of financial transactions between heterogeneous economic agents. This goal is finally reached varying the action scheme of the artificial actors and some of their characteristics. We use the graphical potential given by the Askenazy's original framework, which enables the user to interpret the experiment in a direct and effective way.

The core idea of the BankNet experiment is that economic agents work in a financial network where operations of deposit and credit continually take place, in an environment characterized by great variance of the optimal capital and of cash flows for each agent (heterogeneity), imperfect information, which leads to positive transaction costs and limited exchanging opportunities.

To express the concept of limited transactional capability, which characterizes the imperfect information environment, a network structure has been chosen, so that each agent is part of a well defined relational network. The traditional neoclassical abstraction of perfectly multilateral negotiation, based on the Walrasian hypothesis of centralized auction markets, is in this way excluded. With this choice we represent the time - space dispersion of the operators which frequently makes centralized transactions unfeasible.

Each agent has a limited set[8] of links that relate it with other artificial operators. Links are divided into two categories: borrow links, that represent the communication channels to send loan request for matching available capital with its optimal level ; Invest links that describe the channels for deposit relation. With the operation of deposit each agent has the possibility to entrust to other agents the cash flows generated in every cycle of the productive process, here considered as exogenous, waiting for a personal use of these resources. The investments that pass through investment links are similar to deposit operations of surplus units. The borrow operations, which go through borrow links, represent the resources demanded by units in deficit. The Financial Network composed of the entire set of borrow and invest links defines the development opportunities, the functioning and the limitations of this "in silico" system.

In the experiment, a series of parameters described in table 6.1, are freely changeable by the user.

Each agent receives every year an income[9] derived from activities not described in the simulator, and exclusively devoted to financial transactions. For the sake of simplicity we made the choice of a partial-equilibrium modeling of the economic system. Income varies randomly, cycle after cycle under a uniform distribution[10] on an interval, from zero to two. The mean income is a parameter exogenous under the control of the experimenter as illustrated in table 6.1.

We now describe the actions made by the agents and their order over time.

At the initial stage, all the agents have the same capabilities. We will try to show how a process of specialization and division of labor could take place creating a sequence of multilateral relations. These relations accomplish with an indirect circuit what in the initial circuit was obtained thanks to a set of diversified and fragmented direct transactions.

Table 6.1 "Model's Parameters"

Population:	Number of Agents operating during the experiment
Average Income:	Agent's Average income
ProbIop:	Agent's Probability to get an IOP during a cycle (investment Opportunity)
ProbIopSuccess:	Probability of a successful credit operation. The supplier of funds will be paid back only with a success
IopMultiplier:	Multiplier associated to a successful investment. It represents the interest rate earned by the financier
ProbEncounter:	Probability of an encounter among two agents during every cycle
Initial Transaction Costs:	Common initial level of transaction costs. These costs are mainly related to the negotiation phase and to the redaction of the contractual agreements

Examining the time schedule of the model we can observe that every cycle is divided into four fundamental steps named: "Encounter", "Deposit", "IOP" and "Financing".

At first we suppose that each agent starts with looking for counterparts, after having observed the realization of his income. Costs of information, transport and selection limit the relational capability: it is

Schedule			
Encounter	Deposit	IOP	Financing
I	II	III	IV

Table 6.2   Time schedule of the model

not possible to obtain contacts beyond a certain threshold fixed in the model.

An agent may contact another operator, chosen randomly[11], in every cycle with probability ProbEncounter. When one agent meets another one, it can decide to move its borrow or invest links from their previous positions, considering the new information acquired. New information enables the agent to estimate, in an adaptive manner, the profitability of the new encounter through the ROI[12] of the previous period, revealed during the encounter.

To decide whether to move or not his borrow link, the agent needs to estimate the financing capacity of the encountered agent. This estimate is obtained evaluating the amount of capital that the financing agent would have been able to give in the previous period, if, in that occasion, he had received an additional request of funds.

In the "Deposit" phase, each operator trusts his income to the agent connected by his invest link, as in reality units in surplus invest their own cash flow in external activities to maximize their intertemporal utility. The agent, who receives funds from a depositing unit, uses the amount of resources received in the same period of the deposit operation [13]. Depositing, the agent delegates the fund's management, relying on the capacity of another agent to generate returns sufficient to repay the contracted debt.

The third moment is named "IOP" in the temporal line of the model. At this stage each agent may try to augment his available funds, sending credit requests to the other components of the financial network. In every period, with probability ProbIop, an agent will run into a new opportunity of Investment (IOP), which requires larger funds than those available to the agent. If the agent is interested in financing the IOP, he can use the credit channels, looking for money through the borrow link, which connects him to other agents. For the financed agent the IOP is an impulse to go to the financial market and ask for credit. The probability of success (ProbIopSuccess) is directly observable.

For the unit that supplies funds, an Iop represents the occasion to invest capital in an external firm, with the goal of obtaining a positive flow of interest on loans (Loan*IopMultiplier)[14] with probability ProbIopSucces.

Finally, the financing operation takes place. Any time an agent receives a funding request he has to evaluate whether to supply or not the resource to the external demanding unit. The present version of BankNet doesn't describe explicitly this process. The borrow link should be looked at as an open credit line freely usable by the agent connected. In other words the operations of evaluation are not directly on stage in the simulator because it is assumed that credit-evaluation operations have occurred at the time when the credit relation starts. This is probably the major weakness of this example of artificial life. To analyze the procedures of credit analysis Beltratti, Margarita and Terna (1996) developed a simulation founded on the use of neural networks. The use of this kind of tools is supported by epistemological motivations and by the massive diffusion in the banking practice worldwide of virtual systems for credit analysis based on artificial intelligence similar to the ones employed in the essays quoted above. The next version of BankNet should internalize similar well tested connessionist devices for selecting the financing requests.

Focusing on the present characteristics of the simulator we have to describe the borrowing phases: an agent receiving a plurality of loan requests will share his capital in equal parts among the agents demanding for funds. This strategy reaches the goal of minimizing the variance of the expected returns. While in the original specification, it was assumed that profits from the financial operation were consumed before the end of the period, so excluding the phenomenon of capital accumulation, this factor is introduced in the present version because it is important to determine economies of scale and for his role of canvenant in asymmetric information contexts.

In the fourth period it is possible to observe the results of the IOP realized. Each agent may calculate the economic result of the period on the basis of return flows coming from credits and losses of capital deriving from faulted credit operations. Two innovations have been introduced in this particular phase. First of all, transaction costs assume an explicit role in determining the final result. Second, experience is a relevant variable to evaluate the probability of success of a financing operation. Both factors show the role of economies of scale in the intermediation activity in the spirit of Gurley and Shaw. The second factor underpins also how in a world with asymmetric information, the intermediaries having a more intensive activity of monitoring and screening may reduce the moral hazard and adverse selection problem, raising consequently the probability of success of a financial operation[15].

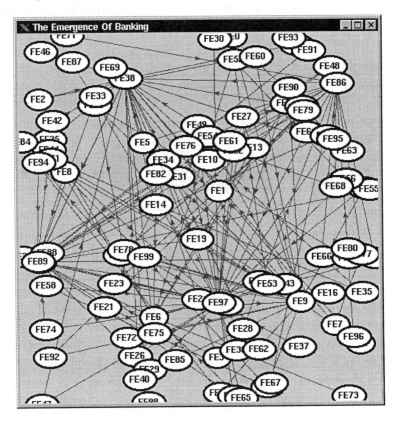

Figure 6.3 "The Financial Network'

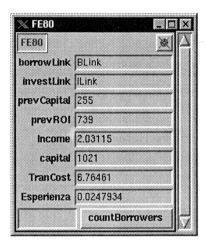

Figure 6.4 'BankNet Probes'

3.   THE EMERGENCE OF BANKING

Using the simulating device described in the previous section we can finally devote our attention to some experiments for testing the most accredited theoretical propositions. Choosing a set of initial values[16] it is possible to "start" the artificial life in the financial network, observing, cycle after cycle, the repetition of the operations described above.

In the beginning, each agent borrows and lends with the other operators in the system, as we can imagine in a primitive society where every agent tries to reallocate his resources to match them efficiently with his needs.

No institution exists in this phase and the efficiency of the transaction is only derived from the random encounters among individuals that cannot use information channels powerful enough to conclude multilateral transactions. Each agent, as we stressed, does not make his decision using a maximization scheme. Rather, he uses simple rules of thumb to decide where, when and with whom he is to conclude a financial transaction. The heterogeneity among individuals is guaranteed not only by the difference in their income, but also by the randomness of their encounters. Encountering good or bad debtors, having the possibility to deposit resources with agents with heterogeneous ROI, determine the level of transaction costs and the capability to select investments (Experience) for each individual. In the model it is present a great path dependence that relates deeply the individual's action with his personal history and with that of the entire system.

Using the instruments of analysis provided in the simulation, it is possible to observe the emergence of banking institutions. These are not introduced a-priori by the programmer, but they are derived by the dynamic interaction among agents which leads to an interesting phenomenon of chaos reduction (entropy) in the system, related to the specialization of work. As a consequence of the specialization of work, a few units collect the deposits from the population and lend resources as in the modern capitalistic economies.

In its implemented version, BankNet enables the user to observe the creation of contemporary economies' key institutions. The artificial world simulates reality. It develops a non intentional credit system in an absolutely decentralized way, excluding any form of conjecturable constructive programmes. The process which realizes this specialization is described with an accuracy difficult to realize by an analytical model that has to face important difficulties to represent chaotic movements and disequilibrium dynamics as in BankNet.

We need to stress how the selection mechanism does not work in the strictly deterministic way, which comes from the hypothesis of perfect information and of representative maximizing individuals. Even if "efficient" agents[17] are in general "rewarded", expanding their financial activity, the system does not identify the most efficient ones by far. In the first phases of the experiment an interesting phenomenon is observable. It is the existence of successful individuals that are absolutely not the best in the population, even though they all belong to the upper middle class of the efficiency distribution. Figure 6.5 shows the fast decrease, cycle after cycle, of the number of "active banks", that is the number of agents that, receive deposits and lend loans.

Even if initially all the individuals perform credit and deposit operations after a certain number of repetitions the quantity of intermediaries is sensibly reduced. As is possible to observe in figure 6.6, after six hundred cycles "the banks" are consistently less than twenty, that is just one fifth of the initial amount. After almost two thousand cycles, the system reaches its level of stationary equilibrium with just six active financial operators. After having reached this equilibrium point the graph of figure 6.5 stops its fluctuations in absence of exogenous shocks, that are reproducible varying the parameters of the simulation.

Figure 6.6 shows the entropy of the financial network during the experiment. We can observe how, with the proceeding of the experiments and the progression of the division of labor the value of the entropy declines constantly, both for financing and deposit operation.

As soon as the banking institution emerges, the "disorder" of the system is reduced for the stabilizing and regulating effect of the banking

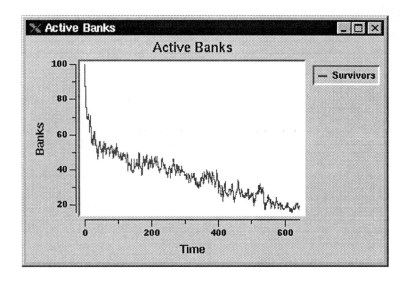

Figure 6.5 'Active Banks'

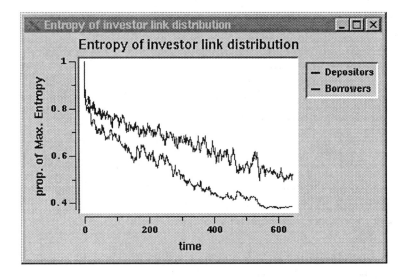

Figure 6.6 ' System Entropy'

firm. The financial network generates spontaneously behavioral rules sufficient to govern complexity more efficiently, thus reducing environmental disorder, also in presence of bounded rational agents. Furthermore, in the case of limited computational capability of the agents–which leads to the adoptions of rules of thumb instead of the sophisticated schemes of maximizing interaction–and of imperfect information, the individual units may coordinate themselves in time to solve the problem of credit allocation, or to approximate a solution.

Observing through the probe the characteristics of every operator, the phenomena of transaction cost reduction and of financing capacity growth is relevant in all agents. The emerging institutional structure allows many evolutive opportunities that expand the financial capital circulating in the system, and increase the agents' average ROI and their probability to obtain a loan.

If at the beginning each individual was in a situation close to that of a primitive or high medieval man who was forced to work in autarchic conditions , in an economy of self consume, after less than one thousand cycles the scenario is completely revolutionized. For every activity it is possible to find amounts of capital many times large than at time zero, using credit lines enforced through time. For a fund supplier, the opportunities of investment get much larger and easier to exploit thanks to the acquired experience in monitoring and screening the intermidiaries' activity. The growth in experience increases the mean probability of success of the credit operations provided by the bank agents.

At the beginning of the selection process not all of the emerging intermediaries are the most efficient of the population. However the exchanges make possible an improvement in the evolutive selection process, which makes the system really efficient in the medium - long term. The stationary state intermediaries are the agents that operate with the lowest transaction cost, that have the greatest experience coefficient, and that generate the largest ROI.

Using BankNet it is possible to analyze not only the evolutive process which helps intermediaries emerge, but also credit market's trends, once that the banks have emerged. According to what we said in the first section, the simulator is useful not only to show the emergence of the intermediation phenomenon, but also to provide interesting points for the study of the performance and the strategy of banks.

Varying the individuals' mean income and the average propensity to use the credit channel for financing entrepreneurial activities (ProbIop), and the probability of success of these activities (ProbIopSuccess) we can analyze a large sequence of phenomenona. For instance, the recessive phases of the economic cycle, are representable with a decrease in the level of the mean income, deriving from exogenous shocks (we can think of real causes such as the oil crises), or with a reduction in the propensity to assume debts coming from negative expectations about the future results of the economic activity, and finally with an increase in the banking sufferance's, reflected in a decrease of ProbIopSuccess. Obviously expansionary phases of the cycle are analyzable with changes of opposite sign in the variables indicated above.

One of the most surprising conclusions of this kind of experiments is about the relation between the frequency of loaning requests of the agents and the speed, of banking intermediaries emergence required by the process, and the number of these ones. Counterintuitively, great run-ups in the number of active banks are observable when the credit propensity of the population goes down. It should appear paradoxical that, with a smaller request of financing activity, the number of agents, ready to provide financial services, multiplies. However, if we consider that a fall in the ProbIop generates a substantial decrement in the effort towards the division of labor, which is the fundamental engine of the emergence of banking mechanism, we can clearly understand how the phenomenon observed is perfectly coherent with the economic logic. It is a sort of return to the origins of the system which does not maintain its institutions forever once it has developed them, but it adapts institutions to the demand of the environment where agents operate.

An increase in the initial level of transaction costs or in the imperfections of the information available (a lower ProbEncounter) generates, as is intuitive, an acceleration in the selecting process and leads to a faster emergence of the intermediaries. However, it is important that the steady state number of banks is not much different in the benchmark experiment for any values of these two parameters. This fact seems to suggest that the structure of the economies of scale in the transaction costs and in the information process are more important than the initial conditions of the system. While the initial conditions appear relevant in determining the shape and speed of the adjustment path, the structure of the economies of scale should determine almost univocally the long term characteristics of the financial system.

A separate analysis is required for ProbIopSuccess. If we examine the perverse case of economies in a deep state of recession[18] (figure 6.7), like the one experienced during the great Depression, the success probability of the investments is particularly low. In this case we can observe the emergence of the phenomenon of bank-runs, which hits pathologically the financial system, causing the sharp interruption of the dynamic path of adjustment and sensibly reducing the degree of specialization.

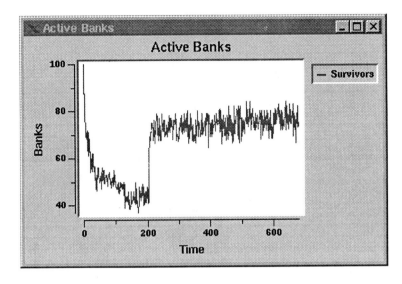

Figure 6.7 'Banking Crisis'

4.   CONCLUSIONS

In this brief essay we tried to pursue two main goals: illustrating a research method and exploring a fundamental aspect of financial economics.

We choose a syncretic way to express simultaneously these two aspects to enlighten qualities and limitations of the artificial life project applied to the economic science. The implementation of a simulator like BankNet allows to show the full potential of experiments with artificial agents in the study of economic problems.

In the model, the existence of banking intermediation is displayed in presence of bounded rationalityrationality, highly imperfect information and high transaction costs. The non coordinated agents choose on the basis of simple rules of thumb and unintentionally create institutions useful to reduce the complexity of the environment. The perspective is dynamic, and the adjustment processes are in great evidence. This aspect is more effective than in the traditional analytical models of differential equations employed in orthodox dynamic analysis. The continuing interaction among the agents is the evolutive engine which, "from the bottom-up" makes it possible for the system to evolve over time through a selection mechanism.

The analysis can fairly go beyond the simple identification of the evolutive path of the banking institutions. It is possible to observe the strategical behavior of the agents when they have to face a wide range of exogenous shocks.

BankNet's future version will try to introduce in the model neural networks functions, or similar devices, provided by the study on artificial intelligence. Similar implementations would be useful to represent, in a more interesting way, the learning processes of the agents, thus greatly improving the esplicative power of the experiment.

Examining the results obtained, we can conclude that artificial experiments are a good research tool for dynamic, non linear and stochastic environments. As was usefully applied to the study of banking intermediation, this approachcan be extended in many other fields. It could be considered an alternative to the traditional deductive - analytical method, combined with econometric empirical testing.

The artificial life program is a device provided to lead economic science along lines different from the canonical paradigm. As in the experimental economics approach, which designs experiments using real agents, there is the goal of making economic analysis using test and experiments "in vitro", focusing at the same time on a set of elements of reality systematically underrepresented in the literature. As we underlined in the second section, there are obviously great differences between the experiments performed with real and artificial agents. However, we would like to use the concluding part of this work to stress the fact that these two research areas should not to be considered rival and antagonistic, rather they should develop along a dimension of complementary and continuous exchange.

Notes

1. For U.S. firms its share is just of 2.1% between 1970 and 1985

2. Between the two schemes presented in the text, it should be necessary to add the direct and assisted scheme, to represent the great variety of organizational forms empirically observable. This last scheme of exchange is operative when the agents of the demand and supply side are direct counterparts, but they don't negotiate with autonomy, because they are assisted in a lot of different ways by financial operators. Without the work of this operators, not merely technical, the meeting between the counterparts could not be realized

3. As transaction cost we mean the set of costs that the agent has to pay to make and manage the exchange : in a context with no zero transaction costs the feasibility of the exchange should be evaluated, having in mind these factors that modify the desirability of the operations for the counterparts. As we will underline during the essay, speaking of the implementation of this aspect on BankNet, in the second paragraph, also the volume of resources exchanged is relevant if we assume the existence of scale economies.

4. In the simulation we will not use the insights that come from a third theoretical position, even if it is interesting. For this reason in this introductive paragraph we don't talk about the works on the choice of external financing by firms as a device of signaling. Fama (1985), Stiglitz and Weiss (1988).

5. Heffernan (1996) indicates four kinds of information costs : Research, Verification, Monitoring and Enforcement Costs

6. Similarly to what said about adverse selection, it is possible to identify a free rider problem also for monitoring. If in the first case it was caused by the concurrence among intermediaries on financial markets, in this case it is more correct to think of the presence of a plurality of stockholders for each bonds issue. Each creditor would be incentivated to try to take upon the other the economic burden of verification activity

7. Askenazy in the presentation paper declared in the initial *caveat* that his work should not be considered as a contribution to economic science

8. In the present version of BankNet the number of links is limited to two (a borrow and an invest link), but it is probably a too restrictive assumption. To modify this assumption would be desirable, also considering the empirical evidence which shows, with a certain importance the phenomenon of credit fractioning among a plurality of financiers. To modify this aspect of the simulation it will be necessary to change the simple behavioral rule, described in the paragraph, e,ployed by the agents to choose how to direct their links. We don't work in this area, because we have in mind a future implementation of the model based on neural networks, more interesting for their capability to reproduce learning behavior in selection problems, than the simple deterministic rules employed in this version. In the conclusive section this project will be presented with more emphasis and in much detail.

9. It would be more correct to speak of a financial flow in excess of its consumption needs, but being all the non financial activities out of the goals of the simulation, to make things simpler we prefer to speak of the measure as income, in consideration of the fact that consumption choices should not modify the conclusions of the experiment.

10. The original scheme, even if it incorporated this element of heterogeneity, attributed the same income to all the agents in the system. In the present version of BankNet the income varies from an agent to another one and, cycle after cycle. It could be interesting in the future to analyze the effects of the introduction of income distributions different from the uniform case chosen for simplicity in the simulation (we can think for instance to a Pareto distribution or other similar better approximations of the reality).

11. The encounters are established through a uniform probability distribution.

12. We maintained the original nomenclature by Askenazy, even if in the model this variable measures X the amount of returns realized in the previous period rather than a rate of profitability

13. The modeling of complex multiperiod structures of investment and financing has been omitted because it would not be probably a real advantage for the experiment in excess of the costs deriving from the difficulties related to such structures

14. The financial transaction is modeled in the following way: with probability ProbIopSuccess the supplier will receive Loan*IopMultiplier-transaction costs ; where Loan is the amount lent. With probability 1-ProbIopSuccess the agent will receive 0. The transaction costs are decreasing in the number of the credit operations performed because it is assumed that the operators acquire through experience the capability to negotiate in a standardized manner. The transaction costs are (2*TranCostIni)N*-(10*TranCostIni)/Capital. N* is the number of credit operation successfully executed. The possibility to vary the interest rate is unfortunately not available inside the present contraction scheme. Consequently, it is not possible to match different risk profiles with different levels of the interest rates. In other words, we are supposing that the Iop are all of the same riskyness and that they all pay an identical interest rate (IopMultiplier). It is evident how a similar structure is not interesting for studying phenomena like credit rationing or adverse selection. A set of modifications will be required on the present model to represent the heterogeneity in the investment opportunities. Once these modifications are implemented, the negotiation scheme between supplier and demander would become crucial. Different bargaining power of the counterparts may result in different solutions with direct effects not only on the level of the interest rate, but, more in general, with indirect effects on the system. For modeling this kind of relations the use of connessionist tools of artificial intelligence should be an important advance, as noted also in the text and in the footnote 10. Beltratti, Margarita and Terna (1996) provide a good example of neural network modeling of banking activity.

15. The result of a credit operation is determined in the following way: if the realization of a random variable uniformly distributed in the interval [0,1] less a quantity named "experience factor" is minor than ProbIopSuccess than the investment is "good" and the supplier of funds

16. The values utilized in the simulation examined in the text are: Population 100; Mean Income 100; ProbIop 0,7; ProbIopSucces 0,8; IopMultiplier 1,1; ProbEncounter 1 ; TranCostIni 5. The values have been chosen relying on a general criterion of plausibility. Obviously a sequence of tests has been performed with different starting values to test if the results obtained depend crucially on a particular set of initial conditions. All the tests we ran, led to similar results as the ones presented in the text. Ample space will be devoted in the section to the analysis of the found exceptions. The number of agents is limited by the hardware resources available ; working with high level workstations it will be possible to run experiments with a larger number of agents.

17. The efficiency terms, we are referring to are: the level of transaction cost, the experience coefficient, the generated ROI and the credit capacity.

18. The figure clearly records the effect of the shock which has been introduced by varying the parameter ProbIopSuccess from the original value 0,8 to the really small 0,1. In this way it is possible to depict an economic crisis that generates the default of a great part of the activities financed by banks.

References

Askenazy M. (1996), "Some notes on the BankNet model", Santa Fe Institute

Baltensperger E. (1980), "Alternative approaches to the theory of the Banking Firm", in Journal of Monetary Economics, vol. 6

Beltratti A., Margarita S., Terna P., (1996), "Neural Networks for Economic and Financial Modelling", London, ITCP

Coase R. H. (1937), "The Nature of the Firm", in Economica, n. 4, pp. 386-405

Diamond D.W. (1984), "Financial intermediation and delegated monitoring", in Review of Economic Studies, n. 51, pp. 393-414

Fama E. (1985), "What's different about Banks?", in Journal of Economics, n. 15, pp. 29-39

Fisher I. (1930), "The theory of interest", New York, MacMillan

Gurley, Shaw (1960), "Money in a theory of finance", Washington, The Brooking Institution Press

Epstein M.E., Axtell R. (1996), "Growing Artificial Societies - Social science from the bottom up", Washington : Brooking Institution Press, Cambridge (MA) : MIT Press

Heffernan S. (1996),"Modern banking in theory and in practice", London, John Wiley and sons

Minar M., Burkhart R., Langton C., Askenazy M. (1996), "The Swarm simulation system : a toolkit for building multi - agent simulations", Santa Fe Institute

Santomero A. (1984), "Modeling the banking firm", in Journal of Money Credit and Banking, vol. 16

Stiglitz J.E., Weiss A. (1981), "Credit rating in market with imperfect information", in American Economic Review, vol 71, June, pp. 393-410

Stiglitz J.E., Weiss A. (1988), "Banks as social accounts and screening devices for the allocation of credit", in National Bureau of Economic Research Working Paper n. 2710

Terna P. (1998), "Simulation tools for social scientists : building agent based models with Swarm", in Journal of Artificial Societies and Social Simulation, vol.1, n. 2,
< http//www.soc.surrey.ac.uk/JASSS/1/2/4.html>

Chapter 7

NUMERICAL MODELING, NOISE TRADERS, AND THE SWARM SIMULATION SYSTEM

Timothy E. Jares
University of North Florida
jares@unf.edu

Abstract
This paper investigates the long-run effects of noise traders in an artificial financial market in which risky asset returns are endogenously determined. "Noise traders" are agents irrationally trading on noise as if it were information. Some researchers have argued that traders following seemingly irrational strategies can have little influence on financial markets because they will tend to buy high and sell low on average. Eventually, their wealth and market influence will be lost.

However, complete noise trader elimination as traditionally hypothesized is not found. Model analysis strongly suggests that noise traders can affect prices in the long run. The effects of market configuration changes on various market characteristics (e.g., trading volume and risky asset returns) are also assessed. A curious result from our simulations is that increased volume is observed in our base (homogeneous) market when traders can buy/sell on margin.

1. INTRODUCTION

There is a large literature that suggests financial markets are too volatile. Several hypotheses are given to explain this volatility. One strand of literature related to excessive volatility is based on the existence of "noise traders".[1] Rational traders are supposed to trade for one of four basic reasons: 1) to re-balance their portfolio, 2) to consume, 3) to hedge, or 4) to exploit inconsistencies between asset fundamentals and prices. Those trading for reasons other than these basic ones are termed noise traders. Trueman (1988) and Dow and Gorton (1994) have also pointed out that since investors cannot easily identify "informed" portfolio managers, all rational portfolio managers have incentives to trade on noise. Finally, DeLong, Shleifer, Summers, and Waldmann (1990) have suggested sophisticated investors may temporarily follow positive feedback strategies even though they know prices do not reflect fundamentals.

Regardless of the behavioral motivation, it is commonly argued that traders following irrational (noise trading) strategies can have little influence on financial markets. The basis of this traditional argument, as given by Friedman (1953), is that following such irrational strategies will cause the noise traders to buy high and sell low on average. Eventually, he argues, they will lose their wealth. In other words, even if noise traders' actions do result in too much volatility, their influence, and accordingly the excess volatility, should not persist. Ultimately, the elimination of noise traders is dependent on the severity of the hypothesized financial punishment; and, how that punishment impacts the noise traders' rate of exit from the market. Of course, even if noise traders buy and sell at inopportune times, they may not actually lose money. They could simply do worse than sophisticated fundamental traders or those that buy-and-hold. Shleifer and Summers (1990) point out that noise traders might not disappear if they are more aggressive and thus, bear more risk than other traders. Bearing more risk should lead to higher expected returns; but, because of the increased risk, the higher returns do not necessarily translate into greater long run wealth.

For noise traders to have a negligible impact on market prices they cannot persistently represent a significant portion of the market. The traditional argument does not claim noise traders will never represent a significant portion of the market; it does say they cannot retain their large share while following irrational strategies. In a statement weaker than Friedman's, Figlewski (1978) suggested it might take a very long time for irrational investors to lose their wealth; but, nonetheless, they will eventually disappear.

Counter to the positions offered by Friedman and Figlewski, DeLong, et al. (1987, 1989, 1990, 1991, 1993) have analytically described conditions in which noise traders may persist and even come to dominate financial markets. In their early work, the authors address noise trader risk and their expected returns when they can have an impact on prices. In subsequent work, they assess the long-run survival of noise traders in financial markets in the context of a model where all agents are price takers. The authors suggest that the next logical step in this literature is to develop a *tractable* model in which noise traders can affect prices and in which survival and dominance issues can be analyzed.

2. PURPOSE OF THE STUDY

In order for noise trader risk to be meaningful, we have noted that noise traders must possess wealth sufficient to affect market prices. Moreover, they, and the strategies they follow, must financially survive over time. The main thrust of this research is to address noise traders' survival and possible long-term impacts on the market as suggested by DeLong, et al.

If noise traders fail to survive in financial markets, they clearly will not impact prices. Survival issues are most easily addressed. If a noise trader, or a relatively homogenous group of noise traders, represent an insignificant proportion of aggregate initial wealth, then an analytical or simulated model in which asset prices are exogenous is sufficient to address the question of trader elimination.[2]

A model in which asset prices are determined exogenously, however, has nothing to say about noise trader elimination if their wealth is significant in the beginning. If noise traders initially dominate the market, can they maintain or improve their position? Moreover, such a model has nothing to say about how these traders may affect the market should their wealth become significant. Can noise traders come to control or dominate the market? To address these types of questions, we utilize the Swarm Simulation System to develop a model in which asset prices evolve endogenously. In this model we study the survival prospects of noise traders, as well as dominance issues, under various conditions.

Previously we noted that it is commonly believed that financial markets are too volatile. One purpose of our research is to introduce common sources of volatility (e.g., heterogeneity in beliefs, liquidity needs, noise, etc.) to our dynamic market and measure the relative importance of these sources. Since these factors add risk to the market, we assess the degree to which each is priced. Various market parameters are modified enabling us to assess the sensitivity of our results to these changes. We also analyze how changes in these parameters affect trader survival.

3. MARKET ARCHITECTURE

3.1 INTRODUCTION

Simulated models were inspired by DeLong, et al. (1987, 1990, 1991, 1993), Dow and Gorton (1994), and Black (1986). Some traders exhibit standard rational behavior, while others make systematic, stochastic mistakes as suggested by the work of Kahneman, Slovic, and Tversky (1982), Thaler (1991) and others. The primary random, exogenous influence in the market is the stochastic cash flow from the risky asset.[3]

Risky asset returns are obviously influenced by this process, but the returns are also directly affected by the evolution of the risky asset price process. This provides an interesting venue to address questions of survival and the influence of various trading strategies in financial markets.

3.2   MARKET DESCRIPTION

Multi-agent simulation models are a relatively new research method. The rapidly decreasing prices and rapidly increasing computing power that is available has contributed to the growth of simulation and numerical modeling. The methodology and technical advances offer the opportunity to examine more complex models than were ever thought possible.

The model (a single swarm) implemented is a simple market with several classes of traders (e.g., fundamental and noise), a market statistician, and a market maker. Various parameter settings influence the market behavior. Only two classes of assets are traded on this market – a risky and a riskless asset.[4] The riskless asset pays a fixed coupon payment, and its price is fixed at unity. The risky asset pays a stochastic dividend. Figure 1 depicts this model graphically.

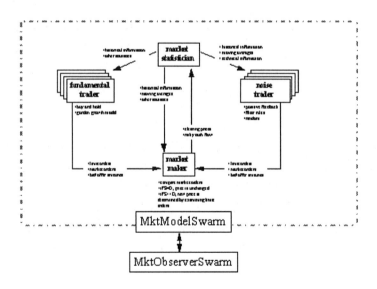

Figure 7.1   Artificial Stock Market

Though the artificial market has several sources of risk, there is only one risky asset. Thus, no opportunity for risk reduction via diversification is available. The stochastic risky asset cash flow, which is exogenous to the model, is the primary source of risk. This risk is present in all model configuration s.

Other sources of risk are only present under some model configurations. Although all of these sources of risk are exogenous to the model, they lead to endogenous price risk since traders participating in the market simulation determine the risky asset price. Liquidity needs, for example, precipitate trades that would not otherwise have occurred. Noise, which is added in two ways, also provides a meaningful source of risk in several market configurations. Some traders forecast the risky asset cash flow with error. Noise is also added to the market by modeling traders with "irrational" views of either risky asset cash flow or the risky asset price. Because these traders are irrational, or noise traders, this noise is also exogenous to the model. Nevertheless, the presence of the noise traders provides significant, endogenous price risk. To reiterate, the importance of all of these risks is that they are all unavoidable through diversification. Since these risks are unavoidable, it follows that compensation in the form of higher average returns should be present.

3.3   MARKET DESIGN

As is the case in real markets, our market is event-driven. For example, in order for a "trading event" to occur, traders must first determine trading strategies - or at least perceived values. In our simple market a sequence of five basic event types is indefinitely repeated in each trading period. To simulate quarterly dividend distributions an additional event, dividend distribution, occurs every ninety trading periods. Upon initialization, the following schedule of events is established over our "swarm":[5]

1. The market maker distributes interest payments proportionate to each trader's holdings. Traders with negative holdings are required to pay interest proportionate to their short position. The non-stochastic, riskless asset cash flow is determined at model initialization.

2. The market maker scans for (bankrupt) traders with non-positive overall wealth. The "bankrupt" traders are then forced to liquidate their risky asset positions (long or short) at the (to be determined) market clearing price.[6]

3. The next major event in the market simulation is to instruct each trader to perform its major task. Though these instructions are submitted serially, the effect is for each trader to determine an

optimal portfolio composition and trading strategy for the current period. Each trader is allowed to submit either market or limit (bid or offer) orders for a specified number of shares to the market clearing mechanism. Traders opting to submit limit orders may submit a series of orders to more completely define their demand schedule.

4. Once all traders have submitted their orders for the risky asset, the market maker clears the market by matching the market and limit orders.

5. The market statistician compiles various statistics and updates the historical database.

6. The fundamental price of the risky asset is calculated.

7. Every ninetieth trading period, a dividend distribution event is inserted as the first event. Following this event all other events as discussed above are executed. The periodic cash flow (dividends) are determined and distributed to the traders proportionate to their holdings. Traders with negative holdings of the risky asset are required to pay dividends proportionate to their short positions. The risky asset cash flow is determined by the ARMA(1,1) process $X_t = \rho X_{t-1} + u_t - \lambda u_{t-1}$, [7] where X_t is the risky cash flow to be distributed this periods, X_0 is set to $0.10, \rho = (1+\text{risky cash flow growth rate}, \lambda$ is 0.75, and u_t is independently and identically distributed $u_t \tilde{} N(0, 0.0009)$.[8].

3.4   TRADER BEHAVIOR

The behavior we model is a starting point for the simulation and is not an emergent phenomenon (endogenous); however, market behavior and prices are endogenous. Fundamental traders base their strategies on the unbiased expected cash flow to be derived from owning the risky and riskless assets. Noise trader strategies possess an irrational component. For instance, they may have biased expected cash flow forecasts because they follow simple, but incorrect rules-of-thumb.

All traders are endowed with researcher-determined risky and riskless asset holdings. All traders have real net liquidity needs determined by a normal random number generator. Since our simulations are in nominal terms, the liquidity needs are "grossed up" by the riskless rate in an attempt to ensure that liquidity needs remain proportionately meaningful with respect to overall wealth. The mean and variance of the random number distribution are controlled by the researcher.

The following is a description of one market participant's strategy. Other modeled strategies are described in Jares (1998). This strategy is fundamental because the trader actually calculates a fundamental price using the well-known constant growth model and a forecast of next period's cash flow. The Fundamental Trader submits a demand schedule at prices above, at, and below the perceived valuation. Of course, when the risky asset is "fairly" priced the expected return is equal to the required return for this type of trader and when it is over (under) priced the expected return is below (above) the required return. The Fundamental Trader class algorithm is:

1. Check net liquidity needs and pay (deposit) from/to cash holdings.

2. Check total wealth and risky/riskless wealth distribution.

3. Make a rational forecast of the risky cash flow. This trader only re-estimates the risky cash flow forecast after the realization of a new risky cash flow. Since this is the only "true" information the trader acquires during the simulation, it is the only factor that should change the risky cash flow forecast. If X_t is generated by the stochastic process described above, the optimal (rational) predictor of X_{t+1} becomes $\hat{X}_{t+1} = \rho \hat{X}_t + (\rho - \lambda) X_t$, which is simply the weighted average of the last risky cash flow and its forecast value (Kmenta (1986)).

4. Use discounted cash flow methods to determine the present value of expected risky cash flows. The required return on the risky asset for all tests is 10%.[9]

5. Determine risky and riskless asset expected returns. The trader determines prices at which he/she is willing to buy/sell the asset. Expected risky asset return is based on the prior clearing price and the price points in this trader's demand schedule. The demand schedule price points include the actual risky asset valuation and prices 0.5%, 1% and 2% above and below that valuation. Expected returns for each price point are calculated assuming a clearing price consistent with the trader's risky asset valuation. Hence, expected returns will be greatest when prices are furthest from the perceived fundamental value.

6. Get risky return variance from the market statistician.

7. Choose optimal portfolio allocation between risky and riskless assets. Since the trader has determined a series of acceptable bids

and offers for the risky asset, he/she will determine multiple "optimal" portfolio allocations. Traders do not know the price that will clear the market; thus their allocation problem must be solved for the price at which they anticipate market clearing given their transaction request. Because traders assume prices will move toward their perceived valuation, their shares demanded will increase commensurate with the expected returns. Traders have constant absolute risk aversion utility functions. Assuming the utility functions are three times continuously differentiable, an approximation via tailor-series expansion is possible. It is straightforward, then, to derive the optimal portfolio allocation formula $y = \frac{Er - r_f}{A \times Var(r)}$, where Er is the expected risky return, r_f is the risk free return, A is the coefficient of absolute risk aversion, and $Var(r)$ is the variance of the risky return.[10]

8. In determining the number of shares to pair with his/her bid or offer, the trader will compare the optimal number of risky units with those currently held. If the optimal number exceeds (is less than) those currently in his/her portfolio, then the difference becomes the number of shares he/she desires to purchase (sell).

3.5   MARKET CLEARING MECHANISM

3.5.1   Clearing Price.   The clearing price[11] in our market is that price which maximizes volume for the period (i.e., the intersection of the supply and demand curves). As the demand and supply curves are not continuous, it is possible for maximum volume to occur at more than one price. The lowest price satisfying the maximum turnover condition is chosen to clear the market. All traders' requests are satisfied at a uniform clearing price. In the event that the market sides are not equally long, the traders on the short side of the market will be equally rationed. When a clearing price cannot be determined, the reported market price will be an average of the highest bid and the lowest offer. A volume of zero will also be reported.

3.5.2   Trading Restrictions.   We enforce two (researcher-adjustable) trading restrictions. To help prevent poor traders from going bankrupt, we do not allow traders to purchase the risky asset when their wealth falls below a certain percentage of initial wealth. In the event a trader becomes bankrupt (non-positive wealth), the market maker forces the bankrupt trader to liquidate risky asset positions.

Short selling is restricted in a manner similar to the margin requirements in real financial markets and can be eliminated if desired. For instance, if the short margin factor is set at 50%, a trader must have one dollar in the riskless asset for every two dollars of the risky asset sold short. The market maker can decrease a trader's order to a level not in violation of short selling restrictions. Prospective purchasers of the risky asset have analogous restrictions. They may short (borrow) at the riskless rate in order to fund risky purchases. The maximum risky purchase is a function of the long margin factor, current risky asset holdings, and overall wealth.

4. DISCUSSION OF RESULTS

Preceding sections have described several potential sources of additional risk in our market. Though it is interesting to assess the effects of each individual parameter, it is also very important to understand how the parameter changes interact. Hence, Jares (1998) devises fifty-four combinations of the most interesting market parameters. Matched-pairs analysis is performed so that the marginal impact of each variation can be assessed.

The matched-pairs analysis is somewhat limiting since it only provides a comparison of various statistics that are based on averages over an entire simulation run. Parameter effects of such items as average return and volume can be observed; but, because these are arithmetic averages, it is difficult to determine if these effects were prominent throughout the simulation or isolated to a particular time segment. Graphical analysis is also used to study the model. This enables observation of price, volume, and wealth evolution throughout a simulation run. Market prices are compared to (known) fundamental prices and volume characteristics are studied under various conditions. Key results from Jares (1998) are reviewed in this section.

4.1 HOMOGENOUS TRADERS

It is not entirely surprising that volume increases with short selling and/or margin buying. Heterogeneous traders are able to take positions that, due to wealth constraints, they previously could not. A curious result from our simulations is that we observed an increase in volume in our base (homogeneous) market when we allowed margin buying and short selling. All traders in this market have exactly the same perception of the risky asset cash flow, and accordingly, the risky asset value; so why do we observe an increase in volume? The answer to this question can be found by more closely examining the market clearing mechanism. Essentially, the reason volume increases with margin buying/selling is because trades that could not have occurred before can now take place. The resulting volume is a function of the submitted demand/supply schedules, the market-clearing mechanism, and the exogenous liquidity needs experienced by the traders. Liquidity-need realizations affect trader portfolio compositions. Because trader beliefs are homogenous, submitted demand/supply schedules will have identical price points. Nevertheless, portfolio re-balancing motivates traders to calculate different share levels at those price points. When a relatively high volume of shares is offered for sale due to liquidity needs, traders on the purchasing side of the market may buy more than intended or expected due to the "bargain" price. Prior to the allowance of margin, those traders may not have had the resources to purchase as many shares.

4.2   LIQUIDITY

Not surprisingly, risky asset returns were positively correlated with noise and liquidity needs. In terms of economic significance, liquidity-need-based risk was compensated more when external noise was the least. Models with greater amounts of noise exhibited less sensitivity to changes in liquidity needs. This could imply that the liquidity-based price risk was uncorrelated with the noise-based price risk. It could also suggest that either the liquidity needs or the noise hastened the departure of some traders from the simulation, thereby removing some of these risks.

4.3   FORECASTING ERRORS (NOISE)

Noise in the form of risky cash flow forecasting errors led to increases of up to 7.8% in average annual returns. More remarkable were the increased returns observed when noise traders were added. Compared to the returns from models in which traders were homogenous, we observed increases of up to 32%. The price risk was extremely significant in these markets and was priced as such. The existence of a single risky asset precluded diversification, thus the only way to completely avoid these risks was to simply hold the riskless asset. Nevertheless, if these risks could be eliminated or reduced in some way, the returns should have decreased.

4.4   SHORT SELLING AND MARGIN BUYING

Evidence of lower returns and the corresponding risk reduction was found in the results on the effects of short selling and margin buying. When these activities were allowed in our market, average annual returns significantly decreased. The changes were minimal in models with lower noise levels. However, in a noisy model we observed up to a 25% decrease in average annual returns when margin buying was allowed and a 31% decrease when short selling was allowed. Short selling and margin buying provide traders with the means to attenuate price risk in our market by reducing some of the sources of that price risk. Specifically, these tools enable traders to more swiftly eliminate other traders who are the ultimate source of the risk. This is not to say that the traders eliminated are necessarily the noise traders. Figures 2-6 illustrate the effects of short selling and margin buying on price and wealth evolution. These simulations are based upon exactly the same risky asset cash flow sequence; the only variations are with regard to market parameter changes that allow short selling and margin buying. The more significant price variation in Figure 2 illustrates the presence of a greater degree of price risk.

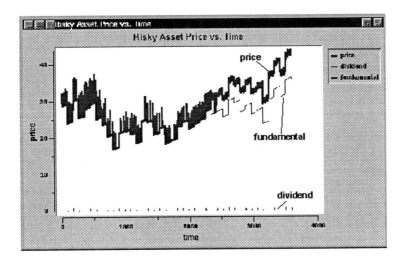

Figure 7.2 Price Evolution with No Short Selling or Margin Buying

Figure 3 shows the source of this risk is from the persistent effects of the Optimistic and Pessimistic Trader classes. Figure 5 shows a very rapid elimination of the Trend Chaser class and a subsequent elimination of the Pessimistic Trader class. Only the Trend Chaser class was eliminated in Figure 3. In addition, Figure 6 indicates that short selling and margin buying quickly lowers trading volume. Large volumes of intra-class trade occur later in the simulation between traders within the wealthy Optimistic trader class.

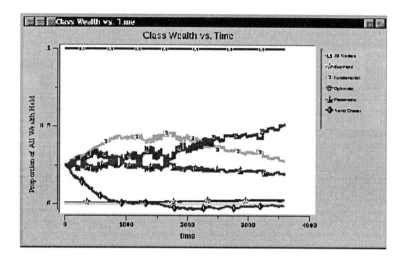

Figure 7.3   Wealth Evolution with No Short Selling or Margin Buying

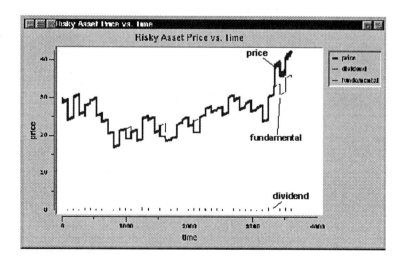

Figure 7.4   Price Evolution with Short Selling and Margin Buying

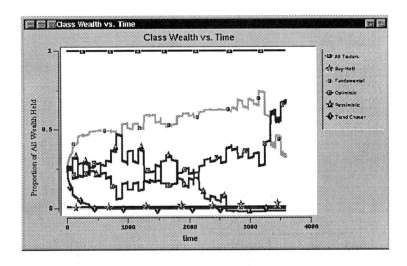

Figure 7.5   Wealth Evolution with Short Selling and Margin Buying

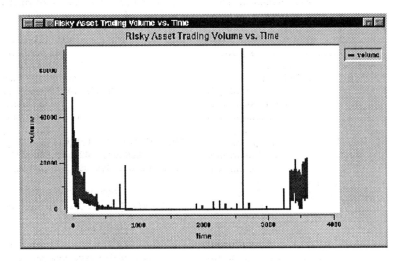

Figure 7.6   Trading Volume Evolution with Short Selling and Margin Buying

4.5   MARKET DOMINANCE (NOISE)

In contrast to the assertions of Friedman, Figlewski, or Fama (1965), ex ante, it is not a certainty that the "best forecaster", the Fundamental Trader class, will accumulate the largest amount of wealth and that market prices will reflect fundamentals. Recall that the Fundamental Trader class asset-valuation strategy is based on a correct view of the risky asset cash flow generation process. Nevertheless, under noisy market configurations the Fundamental Trader class never ultimately dominated the market. Upon reflection, this is understandable. The Pessimistic Trader and Optimistic Trader classes (i.e., noise traders) have very persistent, correlated beliefs.[12] Since each of these classes was provided equivalent endowments and since their beliefs were never consistent with fundamentals, it should not be surprising that eventually one of these classes dominated. If risky asset cash flows evolved such that initial realizations were relatively low, the Pessimistic Trader class was able to eliminate other traders early in the simulation. Although in the long run risky asset cash flows did not evolve in the way the Pessimistic Trader class expected, their views on risky asset prices were self-fulfilling when they eliminated the other traders. Figures 7 and 8 illustrate a case in which the Pessimistic Trader Class dominates.

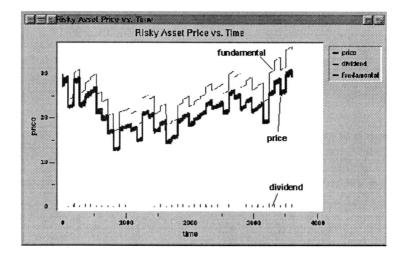

Figure 7.7   Price Evolution with Low Cash Flow Realization

Since the risky asset provided a larger average return than the riskless asset and since the risky asset never went to zero in fundamental value in our experiments, it is also not surprising that the Optimistic Trader class, and its positive forecasting bias, dominated in most cases. If

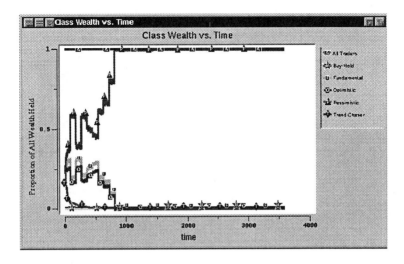

Figure 7.8   Wealth Evolution with Low Cash Flow Realization

they were able to survive "down" sequences in risky cash flows and market prices, they were eventually rewarded with higher cash flows and sufficient wealth to drive prices to or above fundamental value. This is illustrated in Figures 9 and 10.

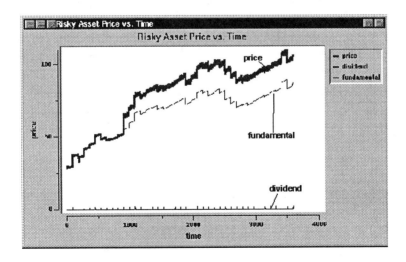

Figure 7.9   Price Evolution with High Cash Flow Realization

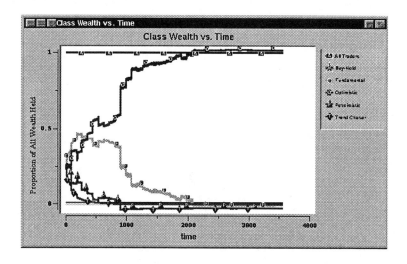

Figure 7.10   Wealth Evolution with High Cash Flow Realization

4.6   UNBIASED FORECAST ERRORS VS. CORRECT FORECASTS

We are unlikely to find classes of traders in the "real world" proportionately as large as any of the classes modeled thus far. Also, "real classes" are not likely to have beliefs as highly correlated and as consistently different from fundamentals, as either the Optimistic Trader or Pessimistic Trader classes. To examine the survival and dominance of a class of noise traders with uncorrelated beliefs, Jares (1998) provides a graphical analysis of model comprised of Fundamental and Erroneous Fundamental traders. Some of the noise traders, the Erroneous Fundamental Trader class in this example, were optimistic and others were pessimistic at various times during the test. In the aggregate, Erroneous Fundamental Trader class wealth trended to zero in most test cases. In the majority of these cases, however, the trend to zero took nearly 3600 trading periods. Overall, Erroneous Fundamental Trader class wealth approached zero; nevertheless, Figures 12 and 14 depicting aggregate class wealth show Erroneous Fundamental traders success is dependent on market configuration. Figure 12 shows a test case in which the Erroneous Fundamental Trader class wealth did not approach zero. When no short selling was allowed, for example, the Erroneous Fundamental Trader class actually did better through 3600 trading periods than the "more sophisticated" Fundamental Trader class. Given an identical risky asset cash flow sequence, Figures 13 and 14 show what happens short selling is allowed. It is clear from these experiments that the market configuration *does matter*.

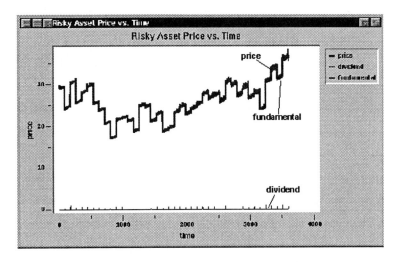

Figure 7.11   Price Evolution with No Short Selling or Margin Buying

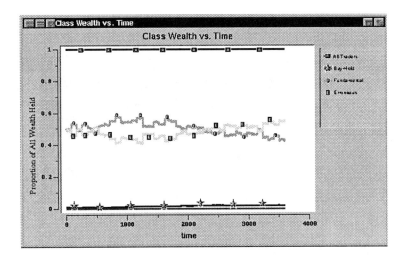

Figure 7.12   Wealth Evolution with No Short Selling or Margin Buying

4.7   SUMMARY AND DISCUSSION

Our tests suggest that the ability to short sell risky assets provides traders with the greatest ability to impact markets. The level of trading volume significantly increased when short selling was allowed, al-

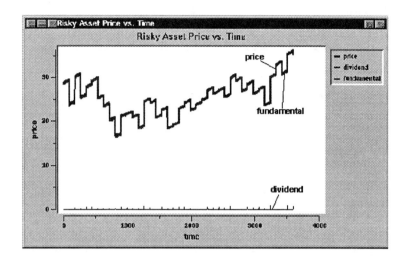

Figure 7.13   Price Evolution with Short Selling

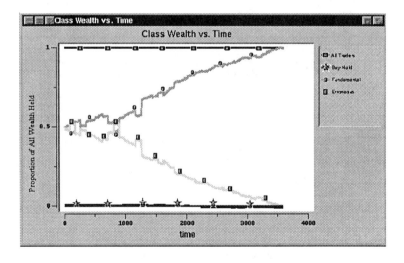

Figure 7.14   Wealth Evolution with Short Selling

though convergence to a much lower level of volume was generally very rapid. The convergence to a steady state in prices was also generally quite rapid. In some experiments prices actually converged to a steady state below fundamental value. This is because the Pessimistic Trader class was able to accumulate all of the market wealth. In other cases the Optimistic Trader class was able to accumulate all of the market wealth quite rapidly. In these cases the result was a steady state market price above the fundamental value. Market prices persistently different from fundamental values were the result of the biased forecasting errors of the Pessimistic Trader and Optimistic Trader classes. In the more noisy model configurationsconfiguration, several test cases resulted in a convergence to fundamental value for a significant number of trading periods. Nevertheless, all tests eventually led to market prices above or below fundamental value.

In our market there is an asymmetry between short sellers and traders that purchase shares of the risky asset on margin that does not exist in the real world. In the real world, traders must "borrow" shares in order to sell them short. In our market traders are not required to borrow shares in order to sell them short. In effect, traders that short sell "create" shares of the risky asset. Hence, the number of shares traded in our market can, and did, actually exceed the actual number of shares existing in the market. Traders that perceive a significant overvaluation in the risky asset can "create" as many shares as they deem necessary (within the wealth and margin restrictions) to increase the supply of risky shares available and subsequently drive prices down. On the other hand, traders perceiving an underpricing of the risky asset are limited to accumulating the number of shares outstanding and by their riskless holdings.

5.   CONCLUSION

Although it depends on a variety of factors, our results strongly suggest that noise traders *can* affect prices in the long run. If a sufficient proportion of the population has and continues to have similar beliefs, they can dominate the market and significantly influence prices. When traders can short sell the risky asset, the level of wealth necessary to significantly influence prices decreases. In markets where noise trader beliefs are not highly correlated, fundamental traders are able to dominate under most market configurations. Noise traders are systematically eliminated, prices converge to fundamental values, and volume converges to zero.

Notes

1. Black (1986) defines "noise traders" as those trading on noise as if it were information. He suggests that informed (or fundamental) traders can never be sure if they are trading on information and not noise. If the information motivating their trade is already discounted in the asset price, then the informed traders are actually trading on noise.

2. See Jares (1998) for a numerically modeled approach or DeLong, et al. (1991) for an analytical approach to these issues.

3. Trader forecasting errors and liquidity needs are also exogenous to the model. Liquidity needs are *net* consumption/income realizations.

4. In all of our experiments we offer the investor a choice between a single risky and a single riskless asset. We argue this is a reasonable simplification. One could view a unit of the risky asset as a unit of the market portfolio; and, the well-known capital asset pricing model (CAPM) suggests each investor hold the same market portfolio.

5. A more detailed description of the schedule and events is contained in Jares (1998).

6. Liquidity realizations are net income and consumption needs; hence, they may be positive. Traders cannot participate in further trading unless their wealth becomes sufficiently positive. Wealth may become positive in the event of positive liquidity-need realizations. It is also possible that the risky asset liquidations occur at favorable prices.

7. We choose this process because, while any given cash flow may be negative, a rational forecast of the negative periodic cash flow is highly unlikely. We choose parameters to minimize the likelihood of a negative forecast. This representation is consistent with earnings realizations and forecasts in actual markets. It is certainly possible to have negative earnings in any given period. However, it is not plausible to have indefinite negative earnings. In this model our forecast may be termed a "permanent earnings forecast" (Marsh and Merton (1986)) analogous to Friedman's permanent income hypothesis.

8. The risky cash flow growth rate ρ and u_t are researched-adjustable parameters

9. The required return will be the same for all traders in the simulations. However, since forecasts will vary among traders, the value they assign to the risky asset will vary.

10. This formula is appropriate when:

   1. Traders have constant absolute risk aversion utility and risky asset returns are normally distributed. (see e.g., DeLong, et al. (1987))

   2. Traders have quadratic utility functions.

   3. Utility functions, assumed to be three times continuously differentiable, are approximated via tailor-series expansion.

11. See Jares (1998) for additional detail.

12. The Pessimistic Trader class asset valuation strategy is based upon a correct view of the risky asset cash flow; but, this class of trader consistently under-estimates the risky asset cash flow and, accordingly, the risky asset value. Similarly, the Optimistic Trader class consistently overestimates the risky asset cash flow and value.

References

Black, Fischer, 1986, Noise, *Journal of Finance* 41, 529-543.

DeLong, J. Bradford, Andrei Shleifer, Lawrence H. Summers, and Robert J. Waldmann, 1993, Noise Trader Risk in Financial Markets, no. 2, in Richard Thaler, ed.: *Advances in Behavioral Finance* (Russell Sage Foundation, New York, NY)

DeLong, J. Bradford, Andrei Shleifer, Lawrence H. Summers, and Robert J. Waldmann, 1991, The Survival of Noise Traders in Financial Markets, *Journal of Business* 64:13.

DeLong, J. Bradford, 1990, Positive Feedback Strategies and Destabilizing Rational Speculation, *Journal of Finance* 45.

DeLong, J. Bradford, Andrei Shleifer, Lawrence H. Summers, and Robert J. Waldmann, 1989, The Size and Incidence of the Losses from Noise Trading, *Journal of Finance* 44:3, 681-696.

DeLong, J. Bradford, 1987, The Economic Consequences of Noise Traders, *Working Paper Series No. 218*, Center for Research in Security Prices, Graduate School of Business, University of Chicago.

Dow, James and Gary Gorton, 1994, Noise Trading, Delegated Portfolio Management, and Economic Welfare, *NBER Working Paper No. 4858*, National Bureau of Economic Research.

Fama, E. F., 1965, The behavior of stock market prices, *Journal of Business* 38, 34-105.

Friedman, Milton, 1953, The case for flexible exchange rates, in Milton Friedman (Ed.) *Essays in Positive Economics*, University Press of Chicago Press, Chicago, IL.

Figlewski, Stephen, 1978, Market "Efficiency" in a Market with Heterogeneous Information, *Journal of Political Economy* 86:4, 581-597.

Jares, Timothy E., 1998, *The Survival and Consequences of Noise Traders in Financial Markets: A Numerical Modeling Approach*, Ph.D. Thesis, University of Nebraska-Lincoln.

Kahneman, Daniel, Paul Slovic, and Amos Tversky, 1982, *Judgment Under Uncertainty: Heuristics and Biases*, Cambridge: Cambridge University Press.

Kmenta, Jan, 1986, *Elements of Econometrics*, University of Michigan Press, Ann Arbor, Michigan.

Marsh, Terry A. and Robert C. Merton, 1986, Dividend Variability and Variance Bounds Tests for the Rationality of Stock Market Prices, *American Economic Review* 76:3, 483-503.

Rieck, Christian, 1994, Evolutionary Simulation of Asset Trading Strategies, in *Many-Agent Simulation and Artificial Life*, E. Hillebrand and J. Stender (eds.), (IOS Press)

Schleifer, Andrei, and Lawrence Summers, 1990, *The Noise Trader Approach to Finance*, Journal of Economic Perspectives 4:2, 19-33.

Summers, L. H., 1993, Does the Stock Market Rationally Reflect Fundamental Values?, no. 6, in Richard Thaler, ed.: *Advances in Behavioral Finance* (Russell Sage Foundation, New York, NY)

Thaler, Richard, 1993, in Richard Thaler, ed.: Advances in Behavioral Finance (Russell Sage Foundation, New York, NY)

Thaler, Richard, 1991, *Quasi rational economics* (Russell Sage Foundation, New York, NY)

Trueman, Brett, 1988, A Theory of Noise Trading in Securities Markets, *Journal of Finance* 53:1, 83-95.

Chapter 8

NONLINEAR STOCHASTIC DYNAMICS FOR SUPPLY COUNTERFEITING IN MONOPOLISTIC MARKETS

Marco CORAZZA

Department of Applied Mathematics
University of Venice "Ca' Foscari"
30123 Venice, Italy
corazza@unive.it

Alessandro PERRONE

Department of Economics
University of Venice "Ca' Foscari"
30120 Venice, Italy
alex@unive.it

Abstract   Counterfeiting is a well known world wide phenomenon afflicting several real economies. Notwithstanding the importance of this topic, there are not many works on this topic in the literature; moreover, they mainly deal with counterfeiting with models developed in a static time frame. In this paper we propose, by means of a system of first order nonlinear and stochastic difference equations, a discrete time dynamical model for a monopolistic market characterized by the presence of a supply counterfeiter. More precisely, we determine some theoretical results peculiar to such a dynamics, and relevant to the solution of the model and to its asymptotic behaviour. Nevertheless, because of the presence of nonlinearities and stochastics, these results cannot fully characterize the proposed dynamical system; so, in order to fill this deficiency, we also carry out a numerical investigation by a Swarm based code.

Keywords: Supply counterfeiting, monopolistic market, discrete time dynamical system, nonlinearities, stochastics, market dynamical evolution, asymptotic market state, numerical analysis, Swarm.

1.   INTRODUCTION

Counterfeiting is a well known world wide phenomenon afflicting, in its various forms, several real economies. The increasing significance of its impact on many markets has been recently emphasized by some authoritative international Organizations, like, for instance, the U.S. International Trade Commission [1984] and the Comité Colbert [1992]. Notwithstanding the importance of this topic, there are not many works about it in the literature; mainly, these works deal with counterfeiting employing economic models developed in a static time environment, as, for instance, in Bamossy *et al.* [1986], Higgins *et al.* [1986], Grossman *et al.* [1988a and 1988b], Rowley *et al.* [1991] and Mossetto [1992 and 1998], and only a few authors propose quantitative dynamics for such a phenomenon, like, for instance, Corazza *et al.* [1996, 1998a and 1998b].

The latter works consider, by means of a system of first order linear difference equations, the dynamical behaviour of a monopolistic market characterized by the presence of a supply counterfeiter; the closed form solution of this system specifies the asymptotic equilibrium state of this market. In this paper we propose a generalization, among the possible ones, of this economic model by introducing, in the starting system, some nonlinearities and some stochastics. Notice that, in general, coping with such a generalized dynamics becomes technically quite more difficult than coping with the basic linear and deterministic one; in fact, the time evolution of the system might have "bad" mathematical properties (like, for instance, nowhere differentiability), and its solution might not exist in a closed form. Because of that, in the following we investigate the features of the considered model by using both an analytical approach and a numerical one.

The remainder of the paper is organized as follows. In section **2** we describe qualitatively the dynamical relationships existing among the economic agents, i.e. the monopolist, the consumers and the supply counterfeiter, acting in the market; in sections **3** to **5** we detail the economic agents' behaviours; in section **6** we propose our nonlinear and stochastic dynamical model, and its main analytical properties; in section **7** to **8** we present both the frame and the results obtained thanks to numerical investigations of the specified dynamics, and in section **9** we give some concluding remarks.

2.   ECONOMIC AGENTS' DYNAMICAL BEHAVIOURS

The economic agents dynamically interacting in the considered supply counterfeited monopolistic market are the "classical" ones, i.e. the monopolist, the consumers, and a new one, i.e. the supply counterfeiter. In this market the supply counterfeiter counterfeits the goods or the services produced by the monopolist in order to sell them as originals to the consumers. More on details, the dynamical relationships existing among such economic agents may be logically described, in a discrete time frame, as follows:

Step 1 – At time $t = t_0 := 0$ the supply counterfeiter starts to counterfeit the goods or the services produced by the monopolist and sells them as originals to the consumers. In particular, she/he satisfies a fraction of the part of the consumers' demand which is, tipically, not satisfied by the monopolist.

Step 2 – Usually, comsumers are unacquainted with the monopolist cost structure and, consequently, they do not know the quantity of goods or services produced by her/him. Moreover, we assume that the consumers are not able to distinguish the original products from the counterfeited ones. Because of both these causes, at time $t = t_0$ they act like in a normal monopolistic market purchasing all the supplied quantity (which is produced, we recall, by both the monopolist and the counterfeiter)

Step 3 – At time $t = t_1 := t_0 + 1$ the monopolist notices that the equilibrium market price determined at t_0 conforms with a higher supplied quantity than the one produced by herself/himself; therefore, the monopolist becomes aware of the presence of another manufacturer: the counterfeiter. Because of such a presence, the monopolist puts in practise some kind of costly reputation investments (tipically, advertising strategies) in order to spread among the potential consumers the information about the existence in the market of counterfeited products. Of course, these marketing strategies change the monopolist starting cost structure and, at time $t = t_1$, she/he maximizes the profit according to her/his new cost structure.

Step 4 – At the same time $t = t_1$ the consumers may, or not, react to the monopolist reputation investments by varying their total demand.

Step 5 – From time $t = t_0 := t_1 + 1$ one iterates Step 2 to Step 5.

Notice that, although our market model contemplates two producers, it can not considered some kind of duopoly because of the assumptions we made on the consumers and the counterfeiter (see, for more details, respectively section **3** and section **5**).

3.   THE DYNAMICAL INVERSE DEMAND FUNCTION

As sinthetically described in the previous section **2**, the inverse demand function is characterized, beyond the classical terms, by both the presence of counterfeited products and the reaction of the consumers to the monopolist reputation investments. In particular, we formalize its dynamics as follows:

$$p(t) = a - b \cdot y(t) - b \cdot y_C^S(t) + k(t) \cdot I(t), \text{ with } a, b > 0, \qquad (3.1)$$

where
$p(t)$ denotes the good or service price at time t,
$y(t)$ indicates the classical demand at time t,
$y_C^S(t)$ shows the fraction of the part of the consumers' demand not satisfied by the monopolist which is satisfied by the counterfeiter at time t,
$k(t)$ denotes the reaction of the consumers to the monopolist reputation investments at time t, and
$I(t)$ indicates the monopolist reputation investments at time t.
    With regard to this dynamics, some remarks are needed:

(3.1) both the classical demand $y(t)$ and the counterfeited supplied quantity $y_C^S(t)$ are inversely linked to the price $p(t)$ by the same constant parameter b because the consumers are not able to distinguish the original products from the counterfeited ones;

(3.2) as the reaction of the consumers to the monopolist reputation investments consists or in reducing their total demand,[1] or in letting it unchanged, or in increasing it,[2] the time-varying parameter $k(t)$ may take, respectively, a negative, a null, or a positive value; in particular, we assume the dynamical behaviour of $k(t)$ as fully exogenous to our market model because its determination may depend on the consumers' psychology, tastes, ... we do not take into account;

(3.3) as for the monopolist reputation investments, we assume that $I(t)$ is proportional to the counterfeited supplied quantity the monopolist expects is produced at time t, that is

$$I(t) = d(t) \cdot E_{M,t}[y_C^S(t)] = d(t) \cdot y_C^S(t-1), \tag{3.2}$$

where

$d(t) \geq 0$ denotes the time-varying proportionality factor, and $E_{M,t}[\cdot]$ indicates the expectation operator conditional on relevant information available to the monopolist at time t or before.

Also, concerning the dynamical behaviour of the proportionality factor $d(t)$, we assume it as wholly exogenous to the considered market model because its determination is mainly due to some kind of "manager sensitiveness" of the monopolist.

Now, arranging equations (3.1) and (3.2) together, we obtain the dynamical inverse demand function in the form we cope with in sections 4 and 5, that is

$$p(t) = a - b \cdot [y(t) + y_C^S(t)] + k(t) \cdot d(t) \cdot y_C^S(t-1). \tag{3.3}$$

4. THE MONOPOLIST DYNAMICAL BEHAVIOUR

As is well known, a monopolist supplies that good or service quantity which maximizes her/his profit, and this quantity is determined by equating his/her marginal revenues to his/her marginal costs. In our discrete time frame, we proceed in a similar way; in fact, in order to determine the monopolist supplied product quantity at time t, $y_M^S(t)$, we deal with the following equation:

$$MR_M(t) = MC_M(t), \tag{4.1}$$

where

$MR_M(t)$ denotes the monopolist marginal revenues at time t, and $MC_M(t)$ denotes the monopolist marginal costs at time t.

In particular, with regard to the monopolist marginal revenues $MR_M(t)$, we typically obtain it, in the assumed discrete time frame, as the partial derivative of the monopolist total revenues at time t, $TR_M(t)$, with respect to the classical demand at the same time t, that is

$$\frac{\partial TR_M(t)}{\partial y(t)} = \frac{\partial}{\partial y(t)}[p(t)y(t)]$$

$$= \frac{\partial}{\partial y(t)}\{\{a - b[y(t) + y_C^S(t)] + k(t)d(t)y_C^S(t-1)\}y(t)\}$$
$$= a - b[2y(t) + y_C^S(t)] + k(t)d(t)y_C^S(t-1); \qquad (4.2)$$

moreover, also with respect to the monopolist marginal cost we consider a classical structure simply modified by the introduction of the cost incurred by the monopolist to build up his/her reputation, that is

$$\begin{aligned} MC_M(t) &= c_0 + c_1 \cdot y(t) + I(t) \\ &= c_0 + c_1 \cdot y(t) + d(t) \cdot y_C^S(t-1), \qquad (4.3) \end{aligned}$$

with
$0 < c_0 < a$ and $c_1 > 0$.

In particular, we assume that also the counterfeiter marginal costs, $MC_C(t)$, have the same structure because the counterfeited good or services, in order to be undistinguishable from the original ones, need a productive activity quite similar to the monopolist one.

Now, equating equation (4.2) to equation (4.3), after some simple algebraic manipulation, we obtain the following dynamics for the monopolist supplied product quantity at time t:

$$y_M^S(t) = \frac{a - c_0}{c_1 + 2 \cdot b} - \frac{b}{c_1 + 2 \cdot b} \cdot y_C^S(t) + \frac{d(t) \cdot [k(t) - 1]}{c_1 + 2 \cdot b} \cdot y_C^S(t-1),$$
$$(4.4)$$

with
$\dfrac{a - c_0}{c_1 + 2 \cdot b}$ and $\dfrac{b}{c_1 + 2 \cdot b}$ constant and positive coefficients, and
$\dfrac{d(t) \cdot [k(t) - 1]}{c_1 + 2 \cdot b}$ time-varying coefficient; in particular, recalling that $d(t)$ may be greater or equal to 0, the sign of this coefficient depends on the fact that $k(t)$ is lower, equal, or greater than 1.

5.   THE COUNTERFEITER DYNAMICAL BEHAVIOUR

In a standard monopolistic market, the product quantity, which is totally supplied by the monopolist, is lower than the so-called socially optimal one (solely in such a situation the monopolist attains a profit greater than 0). In the monopolistic market we consider, the counterfeiter supplies at time t a fraction of the positive difference between these latest quantities, that is

$$y_C^S(t) = f(t) \cdot \{E_{C,t}[y^*(t)] - E_{C,t}[y_M^S(t)]\}$$
$$= f(t) \cdot [y^*(t-1) - y_M^S(t-1)], \text{ with } 0 < f(t) < 1, \quad (5.1)$$

where

$f(t)$ denotes the time-varying percentage of the demand not satisfied by the monopolist which is satisfied by the counterfeiter,

$E_{C,t}[\cdot]$ indicates the expectation operator conditional on relevant inform-ation available by the supply counterfeiter at time t or before, and

$y^*(t)$ shows the socially optimal product quantity.

Before determining the dynamics for the socially optimal product quantity $y^*(t)$, we synthetically specify the dynamics of the time-varying percentage $f(t)$:

Step 1 – At time $t = t_0 := 0$, when the good or service counterfeiting starts, the supply counterfeiter sets $f(t_0)$ to a costant level f, with $0 \le f \le 1$; in particular, we reasonably assume that such a setting is entirely exogenous to the market model we are dealing with because its determination does not derive from any "institutional" economic optimization problem, but, rather, follows some kind of unlawfulness-based logic.

Step 2 – Recalling that at time $t = t_i := t_0 + i$, with $i := 1$, the market equilibrium does not conform with just the monopolist productive activity (see, for more details, Step 3 of section **2**), we assume that such an economic situation makes, besides the monopolist, also some kind of market Authority aware of the presence of the supply counterfeiter. Moreover, we assume that, on account of this presence, the considered market Authority puts in practise some legal action against the counterfeiter; in particular, notice that this legal operation is, by economic construction, completely exogenous to our market model, and, of course, that it may be less or more succesful.

Step 3 – At same time $t = t_i$, in order to formalize such features of the market Authority action, we put the time varying percentage as $f(t_i) = f(t_0) + \varepsilon(t_i)$, where $\varepsilon(t_i)$ are identically and independ-ently distributed random variables with mean equal to 0 and finite variance; of course, these random variables have to be eventually truncated in such a way as to respect the economic constraint fol-lowing which $f(t_i)$ must belong to $[0, 1]$ for each $t_i \in \{t_1, t_2, \ldots\}$.[3]

Step 4 – Once i is updated by an unit increase, one iterates Step 3 to Step 4.

With respect to the socially optimal product quantity $y^*(t)$, we clas-sically determine its dynamics in the assumed discrete time framework by solving, at each time t, the equation between the inverse demand function $p(t)$ (see equation (3.1)) and the productive marginal costs $MC_M(t)$, or, equivalently, $MC_S(t)$, (see equation (4.3)), that is by solving

$$a - b[y(t) + y_C^S(t)] + k(t)d(t)y_C^S(t-1) = c_0 + c_1 y(t) + d(t)y_C^S(t-1);$$
$$(5.2)$$

after some algebraic manipulations, we obtain the following solution:

$$
\begin{aligned}
y^*(t) &= \frac{a - c_0}{c_1 + b} - \frac{b}{c_1 + b} \cdot y_C^S(t) + \frac{d(t) \cdot [k(t) - 1]}{c_1 + b} \cdot y_C^S(t-1) \\
&= \frac{c_1 + 2 \cdot b}{c_1 + b} \cdot \left\{ \frac{a - c_0}{c_1 + 2 \cdot b} - \frac{b}{c_1 + 2 \cdot b} \cdot y_C^S(t) + \right. \\
&\quad + \left. \frac{d(t) \cdot [k(t) - 1]}{c_1 + 2 \cdot b} \cdot y_C^S(t-1) \right\} \\
&= \frac{c_1 + 2 \cdot b}{c_1 + b} \cdot y_M^S(t).
\end{aligned}
$$
$$(5.3)$$

Now, arranging equation (5.1) and (5.3) togheter, we get the following dynamics for the counterfeiter supplied product quantity at time t:

$$
\begin{aligned}
y_C^S(t) &= f(t) \cdot \left[\frac{c_1 + 2 \cdot b}{c_1 + b} \cdot y_M^S(t-1) - y_M^S(t-1) \right] \\
&= \frac{f(t) \cdot b}{c_1 + b} \cdot y_M^S(t-1).
\end{aligned}
$$
$$(5.4)$$

6.   THE MARKET MODEL

As previously illustrated in section **2** to section **5**, the dynamical behaviour of the economic agents acting in the considered market are wholly formalized in the dynamical monopolist supplied product quantity $y_M^S(t)$ (see equation (4.4)) and in the dynamical counterfeiter supplied one $y_C^S(t)$ (see equation (5.4)). Because of it, we can fully describe our market model by jointly considering both such dynamics in the following system:

$$
\begin{cases}
y_M^S(t) = \dfrac{a - c_0}{c_1 + 2 \cdot b} - \dfrac{b}{c_1 + 2 \cdot b} \cdot y_C^S(t) + \dfrac{d(t) \cdot [k(t) - 1]}{c_1 + 2 \cdot b} \cdot y_C^S(t-1) \\
y_C^S(t) = \dfrac{f(t) \cdot b}{c_1 + b} \cdot y_M^S(t-1)
\end{cases}
$$
$$(6.1)$$

or, equivalently, by arranging them togheter, obtaining the following nonlinear and stochastic dynamical market model:

$$y_M^S(t) = \alpha(t) \cdot y_M^S(t-1) + \beta(t) \cdot y_M^S(t-2) + \gamma, \qquad (6.2)$$

with

$\alpha(t) = -\dfrac{f(t) \cdot b^2}{(c_1 + b) \cdot (c_1 + 2 \cdot b)}$ time-varying and negative coefficient,

$\beta(t) = \dfrac{f(t) \cdot b \cdot d(t) \cdot [k(t) - 1]}{(c_1 + b) \cdot (c_1 + 2 \cdot b)}$ time-varying coefficient; in particular, recalling that $f(t)$ belongs to $[0, 1]$ and that $d(t)$ may be greater or equal to 0, its signum depends on the fact that $k(t)$ is or lower, or equal, or greater than 1, and

$\gamma = \dfrac{a - c_0}{(c_1 + b) \cdot (c_1 + 2 \cdot b)}$ constant and positive coefficient.

Generally, in order to characterize a dynamics, the determination of its analytical properties is enough. In such a respect, in the rest of this section we propose our main theoretical results relevant to the solution of the considered dynamical market model and to its asymptotic behaviour. Nevertheless, because of the presence of some nonlinearities and some stochastics, such results cannot fully characterize our dynamics; so, in order to fill this deficiency, a numerical investigation is also needed (see, for more details, sections **7** and **8**).

Proposition 6.1 - Let dynamics (6.2) be given. Its closed form solution is

$$y_M^{S,*}(t) = \begin{cases} \gamma[1 - 2\alpha(0)] & \text{if } t = 0 \\ c_1 \displaystyle\prod_{i=1}^{t} \lambda_1(i) + c_2 \displaystyle\prod_{i=1}^{t} \left[i^{j(i)} \lambda_2(i) \right] + \dfrac{\gamma}{1 - \alpha(t) - \beta(t)} & \text{if } t \geq 1 \end{cases},$$

$$(6.3)$$

with

c_1 and c_2 constant coefficients,

$\lambda_{1,2}(i) = \dfrac{\alpha(i) \pm \sqrt{\alpha^2(i) + 4 \cdot \beta(i)}}{2}$, and

$j(i) = \begin{cases} 0 & \text{if } \lambda_1(i) \neq \lambda_2(i) \\ 1 & \text{if } \lambda_1(i) = \lambda_2(i) \end{cases}$. $\blacksquare$

With regard to the proof of this proposition, in consequence of the really huge amount of the implied calculations, we only give the following outline:

Sketch of proof - The closed form solution contained in the first "branch" of the equation (6.3), the one conforming with time $t = 0$, is simply obtainable by substituting in the dynamics (6.2) the proper quantities evaluated at time $t = 0$; the closed form solution contained in the second "branch" of the same equation, the one conforming with time $t \geq 1$, is obtainable by applying a classical induction-based method. ∎

Notice that, starting from the result enunciated in the previous proposition, in order to evaluate the market state at any time $\bar{t} \geq 1$, one needs the whole time series up to $t = \bar{t}$ of both $\lambda_1(t)$ and $\lambda_2(t)$. In particular, the asymptotic market state, and its final stability, becomes undeterminable. The next proposition gives some conditions by which the existence of a finite asymptotic state market is assured.

Proposition 6.2 - Let $k_{\text{low}}(t) := 1 - \dfrac{(c_1 + b) \cdot (c_1 + 2 \cdot b)}{d(t) \cdot b \cdot f(t)}$ and $k_{\text{up}}(t) :=$ $1 + \dfrac{(c_1 + b) \cdot (c_1 + 2 \cdot b) - b^2 \cdot f(t)}{d(t) \cdot b \cdot f(t)}$ be. If

$$k_{\text{low}}(t) < k(t) < k_{\text{up}}(t)$$
$$\text{for all } t \geq 1 \quad , \tag{6.4}$$

if $\alpha(i)$ is equal to $\pm 2 \cdot \sqrt{-\beta(i)}$ at most a finite number of times for all $i \geq 1$, and if t tends to ∞, then the market state tends to the finite value

$$\frac{\gamma}{1 - \alpha(\infty) - \beta(\infty)}, \tag{6.5}$$

with
$\alpha(\infty) = \lim_{t \to \infty} \alpha(t)$ and
$\beta(\infty) = \lim_{t \to \infty} \beta(t)$. ∎

Proof - As, by hypothesis, $k(t)$ belongs to the interval (6.4) for all $t \geq 1$, then, after some calculations, one proves that $\|\lambda_1(t)\|$ and $\|\lambda_2(t)\|$ are both lower than 1 for all $t \geq 1$, where $\| \cdot \|$ denotes the Eucledean norm. As, by hypothesis again, $\alpha(i)$ is equal to $\pm 2 \cdot \sqrt{-\beta(i)}$ at most a finite number of times for all $i \geq 1$, then also $j(i)$ is equal to 1 at most a finite number of times for all $i \geq 1$, by which

$$
\lim_{t\to\infty} y_M^{S,*}(t) = \lim_{t\to\infty} \left\{ c_1 \cdot \prod_{i=1}^{t} \lambda_1(i) + c_2 \cdot \prod_{i=1}^{t} \left[i^{j(i)} \cdot \lambda_2(i) \right] + \right.
$$
$$
\left. + \frac{\gamma}{1 - \alpha(t) - \beta(t)} \right\} =
$$
$$
= c_1 \cdot \lim_{t\to\infty} \prod_{i=1}^{t} \lambda_1(i) + c_2 \cdot \prod_{i\in I} i^{j(i)} \cdot \lim_{t\to\infty} \prod_{i=1}^{t} \lambda_2(i) +
$$
$$
+ \lim_{t\to\infty} \frac{\gamma}{1 - \alpha(t) - \beta(t)}
$$
$$
\tag{6.6}
$$

where
I indicates the set of indexes conformably to which $j(i)$ is equal to 1.
Now, recalling that, by construction, $\|\lambda_1(t)\|$ and $\|\lambda_2(t)\|$ are both lower
than 1 for all $t \geq 1$, as t tends to ∞, then one gets the following asymptotic market state:

$$
y_M^{S,*}(\infty) = \frac{\gamma}{1 - \alpha(\infty) - \beta(\infty)}. \tag{6.7}
$$

Finally, again as $k(t)$ belongs to the interval (6.4) for all $t \geq 1$, it is
possible to prove that $1 - \alpha(t) - \beta(t)$ is never equal to 0 for any $t \geq 1$
and, consequently, that the value (6.5) is finite.[4]∎

Of course, the result enunciated in the latest proposition does not completely characterized the asymptotic state market because of its strong
assumptions.

7. NUMERICAL APPROACH: THE FRAME

In general, one of the major drawbacks concerning quantitative social
sciences is the impossibility of carrying out physical-like experiments by
which to check the validity of proposed theoretical models. Tipically,
such a want may be filled by numerical investigations, whose effectiveness, of course, depends on the utilized computer science tools. In
particular, in this context a crucial role is played, *ex ceteris paribus*, by
the software development environment, whose "logic" have to be close
as much as possible to the one of the considered social sciences.

A software development environment such as to conform with this
basic requirement is surely Swarm; in fact, Swarm is a software package mainly addressed to individual agents' interacting simulation by an

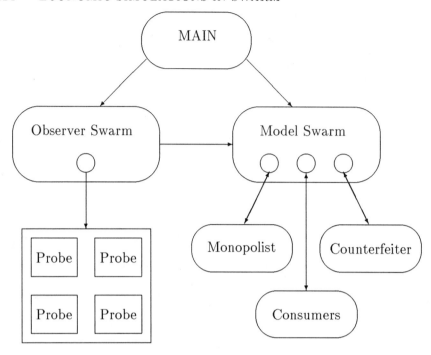

Figure 8.1   Architecture of Simulation Model

object-oriented approach. Tipically, a Swarm based code is structured as a set of precoded individual agents interacting togheter following a common schedule, each of them characterized by its own set of internal state variables;[5] all that is called "Model Swarm". Moreover, it is also characterized by a suitable interface object, which is called "Observer Swarm", which manages both the simulation and the user input/output.

With regard to the Swarm code we developed in order to implement the previously proposed supplied counterfeited monopolistic market, we defined three "simple" agents (that is, not organized as a set of sub-agents) corresponding with, respectively, the monopolist, the supply counterfeiter and the consumer collectivity; moreover, we also implemented some probes in order to monitor in real-time the market's dynamical evolution. A graphic representation of the structure of this code is sketched in figure 7.1.

8. NUMERICAL APPROACH: THE RESULTS

The presence of nonlinearities and stochastics in our market model makes its dynamics not completely characterizable from a theoretical stand-point (see, for more details, section **6**). In order to fill this deficiency, in this section we present some results forecoming from the numerical investigation of our dynamical model.

Of course, at first we need to specify some dynamical behaviour for the time varying parameters we assume exogenous to our market model, i.e. the consumers' reaction to the monopolist reputation investments, $k(t)$, and the proportionality factor to the counterfeited supplied quantity the monopolist expects to be produced, $d(t)$.[6]

As for $k(t)$, we assume that the consumers react, at each time t, to the monopolist reputation investments in a proportional way to the "asymptotic-market-state-convergence" interval (6.4), that is

$$k(t) = \begin{cases} 1 - k[1 - k_{\text{low}}(t)] & \text{if consumers react less than proportionally} \\ 1 + k[k_{\text{up}}(t) - 1] & \text{if consumers react more than proportionally} \end{cases},$$
(8.1)

with
$k \in [0, 1]$.

Notice that, for all $t \geq 1$, $k(t)$ belongs to the interval (6.4) for each $k \in [0, 1]$.

Concerning $d(t)$, we assume that the monopolist determines its dynamics in order to extrude the counterfeiter from the considered market, or, equivalently, in order to make void the counterfeited product quantity at each time $t \geq 1$. So, by putting $y_C^S(t) = 0$ in the equation (5.4), after some re-arrangements we obtain the equation solution

$$d^*(t) = \frac{c_0 - a + b \cdot y_C^S(t-1)}{[k(t) - 1] \cdot y_C^S(t-2)} \quad \text{for all } t \geq 2$$
(8.2)

with
$k(t) \neq 1$ and $y_C^S(t-2) \neq 0$;
moreover, recalling that $d(t)$ has to be greater or equal to 0 (see, for more details, section **3**), and recalling that, at time $t_1 := 1$, $y_C^S(t_1 - 2) = y_C^S(-1) = 0$, we get the searched for dynamics:

$$d(t) = \begin{cases} 0 & \text{if } t = 1 \\ \max\{0, d^*(t)\} & \text{if } t \geq 2 \end{cases}.$$
(8.3)

Of course, such a dynamics is not so effective as the monopolist would like, because, at each time $t \geq 1$, it basicly depends on the counterfeited goods or services the monopolist expects to be produced, instead of their current quantity.

In the rest of this section we present six numerical investigations of the proposed market model, each of them organized in four graphs: "Quantity *vs.* Time", "Price *vs.* Time", "Quantity$(t-1)$ *vs.* Quantity(t)" and "Price$(t-1)$ *vs.* Price(t)". Moreover, each of these graphs are characterized by proper labels, in which "CQ" means "Counterfeiter Quantity", "MP" means "Market Price", "MQ" means "Monopolist Quantity", "SMP" means "Standard Monopoly Price", and "SMQ" means "Standard Monopoly Quantity". In particular, in order to emphasize the role played by the time varying parameters (that is, $k(t)$, $d(t)$, and $f(t)$) in the time evolution of the considered dynamical market model, in all the investigations we give the same numerical values to the constant parameters; more in detail we set $a = 100$, $b = 1$, $c_0 = 50$, and $c_1 = 1$.

In the first numerical investigation we propose (see *Figures 8.1.1* to *8.1.4*), we set $k = -0.25$, $d(t)$ constant and equal to 5, $f = 0.\bar{3}$, and $\varepsilon(t)$ as Uniformly identically and independently distributed random variables taking values in the interval $[-0.1, 0.1]$.

Particularly, notice that, in order to provide at least a highly legible example of our numerical approach, we intentionally propose the four graphs concerning this first investigation in a largest size than the graph concerning the remaining numerical analyses.[7]

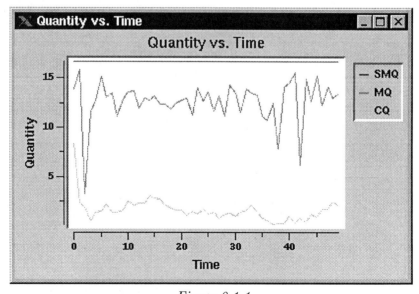

Figure 8.1.1

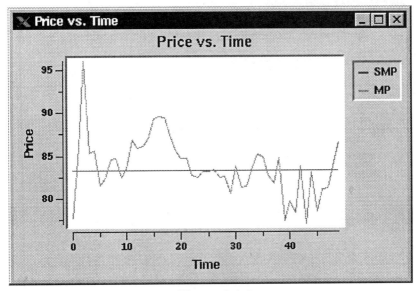

Figure 8.1.2

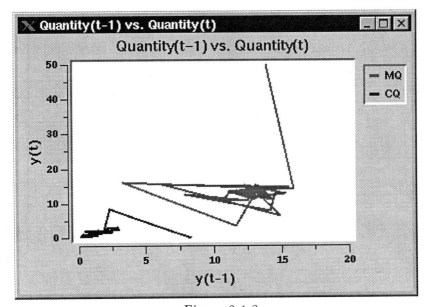

Figure 8.1.3

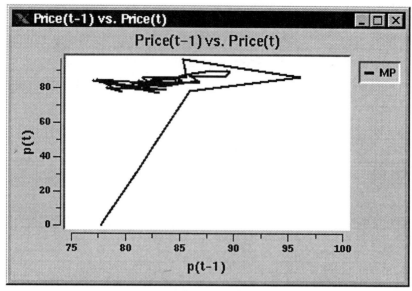

Figure 8.1.4

The second numerical investigation we present (see *Figure 8.2*) differs from the previous one only in the value of k that, here, we set equal to 0.25.

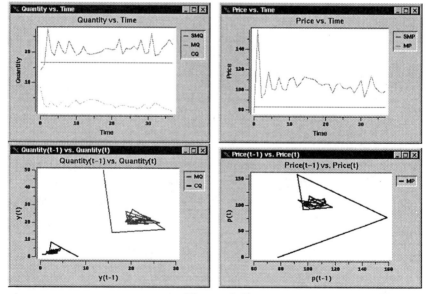

Figure 8.2

The third numerical investigation we propose (see *Figure 8.3*) differs from the first one because, here, we set $\varepsilon(t)$ as Normally identically and independently distributed random variables with mean equal to 0 and variance equal to 0.0005.

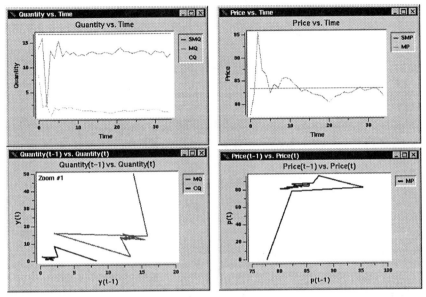

Figure 8.3

The fourth numerical investigation we present (see *Figure 8.4*) differs from the previous one only in the value of k that, here, we set equal to 0.25.

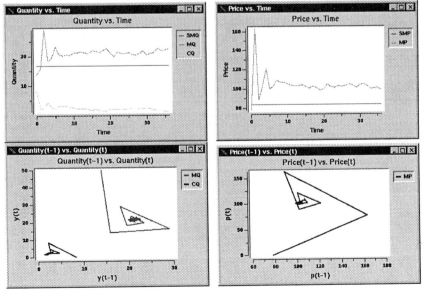

Figure 8.4

The fifth numerical investigation we propose (see *Figure 8.5*) differs from the third one in $d(t)$ that, here, we set dynamical.

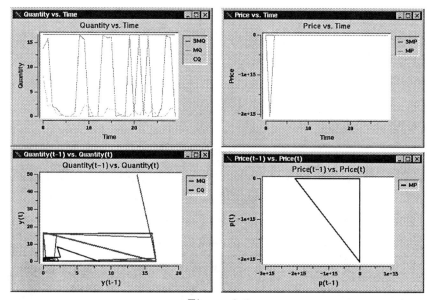

Figure 8.5

Notice that, in the latest investigation, the numerical approach is quite important because, unlike the analytical one, it can emphasize a setting of parameters for which the time evolution of the considered dynamical model, implying negative price $p(t)$ for some t, is meaningless from an economic point of view.

The sixth numerical investigation we propose (see *Figure 8.6*) differs from the fourth one in $d(t)$ that, here, we set dynamical.

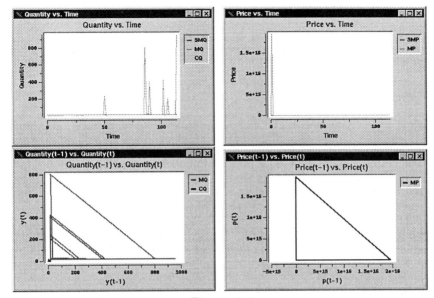

Figure 8.6

Notice that, also in this latest investigation, the numerical approach is quite important because, unlike the proposed theoretical results, it detects a setting of parameters for which the considered market model is characterized by some kind of diverging time evolution.

9. CONCLUDING REMARKS AND OPEN ITEMS

The dynamical counterfeited monopolistic market model we propose may be considered as one of the possible generalization of the static standard monopolistic market. In fact, if we assume the absence of the counterfeiter from our generalized model, or, equivalently, we put $y_C^S(t) = 0$, $k(t) = 0$, $d(t) = 0$, and $f(t) = 0$ for all $t \geq 0$, then the developed market model (6.2) becomes

$$y_M^S(t) = \gamma = \frac{a - c_0}{(c_1 + b) \cdot (c_1 + 2 \cdot b)} \text{ for all } t, \tag{9.1}$$

which is the constant equilibrium state of the standard monopolistic market.

Then, the numerical analysis has to be refined in order to detect as meaningless from an economic point of view and to manage all those parameter settings by which $y_M^S(t)$, and/or $y_C^S(t)$, and or $p(t)$ may be negative for some t.

Finally, the proposed dynamical model offers evidence for further possible generalizations. In fact, it should be properly developed in order to make endogenous some, or, perhaps, all of the time varying parameters characterizing its dynamics.

Notes

1. Like, for instance, in the case of faked works of art, adulterated pharmaceutical products, ...

2. Like, for instance, in the case of counterfeited status symbol goods as "griffed" wear, watches, ...

3. Notice that, consequently, the percentages $f(t_i)$ are identically and independently distributed, eventually truncated, random variables with mean equal to f and finite variance for each $t_i \in \{t_1, t_2, \ldots\}$.

4. Notice that solely for $k(t) = [1 + (c_1 + b) \cdot (c_1 + 2 \cdot b) + f(t) \cdot b^2]/[b \cdot f(t) \cdot d(t)]$, which does not belong to the interval (6.4), the value of $1 - \alpha(t) - \beta(t)$ is equal to 0.

5. In particular, an agent, in its turn, may be a set of predefined sub-agents, and so on.

6. We recall that the dynamical behaviour for the percentage of the demand not satisfied by the monopolist which is satisfied by the counterfeiter, $f(t)$, is already specified in section 5.

7. Going into simple technical details, we ran our Swarm code on an Apple i-Mac computer, by using Linux PPC as operating system, and managing all the graphs by the XV software package.

References

Bamossy, G.J. and Scammon, D.L., "Counterfeiting. A Worlwide Problem: What is the Role of Channel Members", in Pellegrin, L. and Reddy, S.K. (eds.), *Marketing Channels: Relationship and Performance. Advances in Retailing Series*, Lexington Books, 1986.

Comité Colbert (ed.), "La Contrefaçon en Italie", *Working Paper*, Paris (France), February, 1992.

Corazza, M. and Funari, S., "Un Approccio Dinamico alla Contraffazione dell'Offerta nei Mercati Monopolistici", lecture presented at the *XX Convegno A.M.A.S.E.S.*, Urbino (Italy), 1996.

Corazza, M. and Funari, S., "Un Approccio Dinamico alla Contraffazione dell'Offerta nei Mercati Monopolistici", *Quaderno del Dipartimento di Matematica Applicata*, Department of Applied Mathematics - University "Ca' Foscari" of Venice (Italy), 66/98, 1998a.

Corazza, M. and Funari, S., "Quantitative Dynamics for the Pedlar Model", lecture presented at the international seminar *The Economics of Copying and Counterfeiting*, Istituto Veneto di Scienze Lettere ed Arti, Venice (Italy), 1998b.

Grossman, G.M. and Shapiro, C., "Counterfeit-product Trade", *The American Economic Review*, 78(1), 59–75, 1988a.

Grossman, G.M. and Shapiro, C., "Foreign Counterfeiting of Status Goods", *Quarterly Journal of Economics*, 103(1), 79–100, 1988b.

Guerraggio, A. and Salsa, S., *Metodi Matematici per l'Economia e le Scienze Sociali*, G. Giappichelli Editore, 1988.

Higgins, R.S. and Rubin, P.H., "Counterfeit Goods", *Journal of Law and Economics*, 29(2), 211–230, 1986.

Johnson, P., "An Agent Based Model of the Exchange Theory of Interest Groups", available at web site *http://lark.cc.ukans.edu/~pauljohn/ResearchPapers*, 1998.

Medio, A., *Chaotic Dynamics. Theory and Applications to Economics*, Cambridge University Press, 1992.

Mossetto, G., "L'Economia della Contraffazione", *Working Paper*, Department of Economics - University "Ca' Foscari" of Venice (Italy), 92.16, 1992.

Mossetto, G., "Some Economics of Counterfeiting", lecture presented at the international seminar *The Economics of Copying and Counterfeiting*, Istituto Veneto di Scienze Lettere ed Arti, Venice (Italy), 1998.

Perrone, A., "SwarmJournal", available at web site *http://venus.unive.it/~alex/swarm*, 1999.

Perrone, A., "How to Use Gdb and Emacs to Write Simulations in Swarm", available at web site *http://venus.unive.it/~alex/swarm* 1999.

Rowley, C., Tollison, R. and Tullock, G., *The Political Economy of Rent-seeking*, Kluwer Academic Publishers, 1991.

Rushing, F. and Ganz Brown, C., *Intellectual Property Rights in Science, Technology and Economic Performance*, Westview Press, 1990.

U.S. International Trade Commission (ed.), "The Effects of Foreign Product Counterfeiting on U.S. Industry", *USITC Publication*, 1479, 1984.

Chapter 9

USING SWARM FOR SIMULATING THE ORDER FULFILLMENT PROCESS IN DIVERGENT ASSEMBLY SUPPLY CHAINS

Fu-ren Lin,
Department of Information Management
National Sun Yat-sen University
Kaohsiung, Taiwan, R.O.C.
frlin@mis.nsysu.edu.tw

Troy J. Strader,
Department of Logistics, Operations, and MIS
Iowa State University
Ames, Iowa 50011
U.S.A.
tstader@iastate.edu

Michael J. Shaw
Department of Business Administration, and
Beckman Institute for Advanced Science and Technology
University of Illinois at Urbana-Champaign
Champaign, IL 61810 U.S.A.
m-shaw2@uiuc.edu

Abstract   Management of supply chains is a difficult task involving coordination and decision-making across organizational boundaries. Computational modeling using multi-agent simulation is a tool that can provide decision support for supply chain managers. We identify the components of a supply chain model and implement it in the Swarm multi-agent simulation platform. The model is used to study the impact of information sharing on order fulfillment in divergent assembly supply chains (commonly associated with the computer and electronics industries).

We find that efficient information sharing enables inventory costs to be reduced while maintaining acceptable order fulfillment cycle times. This is true because information, which provides the basis for enhanced coordination and reduced uncertainty, can substitute for inventory.

Keywords: supply chain management, multi-agent simulation, Swarm, decision support systems, electronic commerce, computer industrycomputer, electronics industry

Introduction

Supply chain management is a difficult task involving coordination and decision making across organizational boundaries. It is an outgrowth of organizations realizing that efficiency of individual business units alone is insufficient for maintaining competitiveness in today's business climate. The revolution of the 1990's is driven not by changes in production and transportation but by changes in coordination. Whenever people work together they must somehow communicate, make decisions, allocate resources and get products and services to the right place at the right time. Managers, clerks, salespeople, buyers, brokers, accountants - in fact, almost everyone who works - must perform coordination activities (Malone and Rockart, 1991)." Coordination in the past was facilitated through large hierarchical organizational structures. Today, large hierarchies are separating into smaller specialized companies where coordination can not be mandated. This has created a situation where uncoordinated interorganizational business processes result in unacceptable overall organization performance even if individual business units are operating efficiently. Supply chain management expands the scope of the organization being managed beyond the enterprise level to include interorganizational relationships. Examples include improving coordination between suppliers and manufacturers, as well as between manufacturers and distributors. As improvements in information technology have enabled the costs of coordination to decrease (Malone, Yates and Benjamin, 1987), there has been a general movement toward organizing as partnerships between more specialized firms or business units. Supply chain management is an important topic to study because it is an instance of these partnerships. Most MIS research related to supply chain management has concentrated on identifying the information requirements of local supply chain node decision-making (Billington, 1994; Davis, 1993; Lee and Billington, 1992; Lee and Billington, 1993; Lee, Billington and Carter, 1993; Swaminathan, Smith and Sadeh, 1994). Often this involved development of models of material and information flow through the supply chain network (SCN). The purpose of our research is twofold. First we investigate the feasibility of using multi-agent systems to simulate order fulfillment in supply chains to provide a decision support tool for managers. Multi-agent systems are appropriate for modeling supply chains because they involve divisible processes with loosely coupled command and control. Multi-agent techniques are most useful for modeling these processes. Traditional operations research methods were useful for simulating hierarchical production systems where decision making is centralized. A supply chain, with its decentralized command and control, is more appropriately modeled as a social simulation. Our multi-agent system is simplistic, but it does provide a basis for modeling negotiation between supply chain partners, as well as supply chains where there are power differentials between partner firms (for example a supply chain involving large companies like Wal-Mart or General Motors, and a number of smaller firms). Our second purpose is to use the system to identify the impact that information sharing has on the performance of divergent assembly supply chains commonly associated with the computer and electronics industries. A link to the simulation code is provided in Section 4.3 where the verification and validation of the model are discussed. We investigate the impact of several characteristics of supply chain management in an environment of electronic commerce. These include (1) centralized, global business and management strategies (e.g. make-to-order, assembly-to-order and make-to-stock), (2) on-line, real-time distributed information processing to the desktop, providing total supply chain information visibility, and (3) the ability to manage information not only within a company but across industries and enterprises (Kalakota and Whinston, 1996). Within an overall framework for studying electronic commerce, our research is at the application level (e.g. supply chain management) enabled by the information superhighway, multimedia content and network publishing, messaging and information distribution, and common business services infrastructures (Applegate, Holsapple, Kalakota, Radermacher and Whinston, 1996). We discuss our findings in the following sections. In Section 1. we present a brief overview of supply chain management to provide background for understanding the later material. In Section 2. we discuss the information technology currently available that enables information sharing across organizational boundaries. In Section 3. we describe the simulation and evaluation of the order fulfillment process using the Swarm simulation system. Section 4. illustrates how information-sharing impacts overall supply chain network performance through a set of simulations. In Section 5. we present our conclusions.

1.   SUPPLY CHAIN MANAGEMENT

We introduce supply chains by presenting (1) a general overview of supply chain management, and (2) a summary description of supply chain management.

1.1   GENERAL OVERVIEW OF SUPPLY CHAIN MANAGEMENT

A supply chain is a network of facilities that procures raw materials, transforms them into intermediate subassemblies and final products and then delivers the products to customers through a distribution system (Billington, 1994). It is commonly referred to as a network because it involves bi-directional flows of materials, information and payments. Supply chains exist in virtually every industry, especially industries that involve product manufacturing, and management of supply chains is not an easy task because of the large amount of activities that must be coordinated across organizational and global boundaries. The most common problems involve coordinating materials inventory and production capacity availability across several organizations to produce products that can satisfy forecasted demand in an environment with a high level of uncertainty. Several factors are making supply chain management an important issue for today's managers. These factors include (1) more instances of multisite manufacturing, where several independent entities are involved in the production and delivery process, (2) increasingly cut-throat marketing channels, (3) the maturation of the world economy, with heightened demand for "local" products, and (4) competitive pressures to provide exceptional customer service, including quick, reliable delivery (Davis, 1994). In the past, management would concentrate on making each node of the supply chain network efficient. What managers are now realizing is that efficiency at each node does not result in the supply chain as a whole operating optimally. Increasingly, the challenges related to improved product quality, customer service and operating efficiency cannot be effectively met by isolated change to specific organizational units, but instead depend critically on the relationships and interdependencies among different organizations (or organizational units) (Swaminathan, Smith and Sadeh, 1994). Supply chain management is a management process that attempts to optimize the operation of the entire supply chain. Different entities in a supply chain typically operate subject to different sets of constraints and objectives. Even when belonging to the same company, supply chain entities often report to different divisions. Supply chain entities are highly inter-dependent when it comes to improving due date performance, increasing quality or reducing costs. As a result, the welfare of any entity in the system directly depends on the performance of the others and their willingness and ability to coordinate (Swaminathan, Smith and Sadeh, 1994). Specifically, supply chain management involves balancing reliable customer delivery with manufacturing and inventory management costs (Billington, 1994). Two metrics commonly used to measure overall supply chain performance are (1) order fulfillment cycle time, and (2) inventory level and cost. One major problem involved in supply chain management is understanding and managing the uncertainties involved in the supply chain. This is especially true in industries such as fashion skiwear where demand is heavily dependent on a variety of factors that are difficult to predict - weather, fashion trends, the economy - and the peak of the retail selling season is only two months long (Fisher, Hammond, Obermeyer and Raman, 1994). Three fundamental sources of uncertainty exist along a supply chain. They include demand (volume and mix), process (yield, machine downtimes, transportation reliabilities), and supply (part quality, delivery reliabilities) (Billington, 1994; Lee and Billington, 1993; Lee, Billington and Carter, 1993). Inventories are often used to protect the chain from these uncertainties. Another major problem involved in supply chain management is the management of lead-time. A role of information technology (IT) in supply chain management is to assist managers in managing uncertainty and lead time through improved collection and sharing of information between supply chain nodes. It is felt that this will result in better customer service, through better coordination, and improve asset management, by giving decision-makers the information necessary to optimize inventory and capital asset costs. Many of these improvements occur because IT enables changes to be made in inventory management and production planning dynamically. The difficulty arises when trying to design an information system that can handle the information needs of each of the supply chain nodes to allow efficient, flexible, and decentralized supply chain management. The information technology that enables information sharing across a supply chain is discussed in Section 3.

1.2   SUMMARY DESCRIPTION OF SUPPLY CHAIN MANAGEMENT

The information infrastructure that is required by supply chain management is by nature supported by a distributed information system. Because of this, we feel that a distributed system model is most appropriate to describe a supply chain network. Distributed problem solving is the cooperative solution of problems by a decentralized and loosely

Table 9.1 Supply Chain Management Summary Description

1. Actors	Suppliers, manufacturers, assemblers, distributors, and customers
2. Activities	Material and information processing
3. Interdependencies	Material shipments and orders, Funds transfer, Information sharing, and Command and control
4. Goals	Minimize order fulfillment cycle time, Minimize inventory levels and costs, Minimize uncertainty, and Preserve robustness.
5. Overall Objective	Balance individual goals based on priorities to produce the best "average" performance, or the best "worst case" performance

coupled collection of knowledge sources (KS's) located in a number of distinct processor nodes (Smith and Davis, 1988). Distributed problem solving is often necessary because no one node has sufficient information to solve the entire problem. The components of a distributed, coordination intensive, problem include goals, activities, actors, and interdependencies (Malone and Crowston, 1990). We feel that a supply chain can be described by identifying its actors, activities, interdependencies, goals and objective. Our supply chain description is summarized in Table 9.1. The overall supply chain objective is to balance each of the goals based on their importance to supply chain managers. In some situations costs may be the priority, while in other situations customer service may be the priority. In all situations it is important to operate in a manner that allows the supply chain to adapt to changes in the business environment.

2. CURRENT TECHNOLOGY THAT ENABLES SUPPLY CHAIN INFORMATION SHARING

In this section we discuss current technologies that enable information sharing across supply chains. Details of how to implement these systems into a complete supply chain information infrastructure are outside the scope of this paper. The technologies that we discuss include electronic data interchange (EDI), the Internet-based World Wide Web (WWW), intranets, and extranets. EDI is an existing information technology that provides a method of electronic transaction transfer. It is the process of computer-to-computer business-to- business transaction transfer. EDI involves the direct routing of information from one computer to another without interpretation or transcription by people, and to achieve this the information must be structured according to predefined formats and rules which a computer can use directly (Holland, Lockett and Blackman, 1992). One example of where EDI has been shown to improve part of supply chain management is in inventory management, specifically a just-in-time (JIT) system. EDI technology was shown to facilitate accurate, frequent, and timely exchange of information to coordinate material movements between trading partners. Suppliers receiving JIT schedule information achieved better shipping performance. Similarly, suppliers with the ability to directly map incoming information to internal production control systems were found to enjoy even greater benefits. Moreover, as the supplier handles a higher fraction of customers electronically, it was found that shipment errors continued to diminish (Srinivasan, Kekre and Mukhopadhyay, 1993). Each year the use of EDI increases as organizations look for methods to improve enterprise integration and interorganizational coordination. Numerous studies have been done on various aspects of EDI and they all draw the same conclusion. EDI increases the speed and the accuracy of processes compared with non-electronic transfer of information (Snapp, 1990), and it is a potential source of competitive advantage (Johnston and Vitale, 1988). When a supplier and a procurer use information technology to create joint, interpenetrating processes at the interface between value-adding stages, they are taking advantage of the electronic integration effect. This effect occurs when information technology is used not just to speed communication, but to change - and lead to tighter coupling of - the processes that create and use information. One simple benefit of this effect is the time saved and the errors avoided by the fact that data need only be entered once (Malone, Yates and Rockart, 1991). This is just one of several benefits derived from supply chain partners using more highly integrated information systems. A practical problem that must be addressed when designing an EDI process is the lack of a globally recognized standard format for data storage and transfer (Snapp, 1990). Because of this lack of standards, organizations must agree upon the translation software and data format on a project by project basis. Without an agreement upon a standard the EDI process will not work. This is one of the reasons why there will be a general movement away from these transaction specific connections to more flexible methods of electronic information transfer. One solution that has been considered by a number of businesses is using the Internet-based WWW and Net browsers (such as Netscape Navigator). The Internet is an example of a global information network composed of an existing set of information technologies that provide a method for electronic information sharing. One component of the Internet is the WWW. Although the WWW was not developed specifically for sharing of information among supply chain partners, it provides a model for these types of systems. The Web was developed to be a pool of human knowledge, which would allow collaborators in remote sites to share their ideas and all aspects of a common project (Berners-Lee, Cailliau, Luotonen, Nielsen and Secret, 1994). Because supply chain management is similar to the projects the WWW was designed for (remote sites, shared knowledge, common project) it can serve as a method for sharing of information in a supply chain. Netscape Navigator is an example of a WWW browser (which can also be viewed as a global network interface) that provides seamless access to a wide range of data through the WWW. The major problem with using the Internet for supply chain management is security. This includes security of information stored in databases as well as transfers of information between servers. Experts say reports of Internet-related security breaches are rising. Nearly one in four respondents to an Information Week survey conducted in February 1996 say fear of Net break-ins is keeping them from using the Net (Violino, 1996). The solution seems to be a more secure version of the Internet, an Intranet. An intranet is essentially any site based on Internet technology but placed on private servers and designed not to allow outsiders in (Miller, 1996). The outsiders in this case would be individuals and companies not directly involved in the management of the supply chain. Intranets use Web-based and Internet technology to inexpensively and easily share [organizational] data across a private network (Carr, 1996). We feel that the "organization" can encompass several separate firms such as in a supply chain. Intranet usage is predicted to overwhelm external Internet usage before the turn of the century. The key enablers of WWW growth are: (1) the proliferation of PCs, LANs, and modems, (2) open standards such as TCP/IP, HTTP, and

HTML, (3) cross-platform support, (4) multimedia support and ease of use, and (5) support for secure transactions. [Organizational] intranets can provide information in a way that is immediate, cost-effective, easy to use, rich in format, and versatile (Netscape, 1996). What we have described is an extended Intranet (or Extranet). This is in line with the third wave of Internet usage identified by Netscape's Marc Andreessen. "We are ready for a new era: the emergence of the extranet, or extended Intranet, connecting companies with their suppliers and customers via Web links" (Karpinski, 1997). Extranets, utilizing the WWW, its middleware, and browser software, provide a set of existing technologies that make supply chain information sharing feasible.

3. SIMULATING AND EVALUATING THE OFP USING THE SWARM SIMULATION SYSTEM

In this section we describe our supply chain management computational model and how it is used to identify the performance gains arising from information sharing. We focus on one of the core business processes, the order fulfillment process (OFP), and use the Swarm simulation platform (Santa Fe Institute, 1996) to simulate the OFP in supply chain networks (Lin, 1996; Lin, Tan and Shaw, 1996). Swarm is a multi-agent simulation platform developed for the study of complex adaptive systems. It was developed at the Santa Fe Institute and aims at providing a general-purpose tool for building simulation models. An order fulfillment process begins with receiving orders from customers and ends with having the finished goods delivered (Lin, 1996). It consists of several activities (sub-processes), such as order management, manufacturing, and distribution. The main objectives of the OFP can be generalized into two dimensions (Christopher, 1993; Goldman, Nagel and Preiss, 1995; Lin, 1996):

1. delivering qualified products to fulfill customer orders at the right time and right place, and

2. achieving agility to handle uncertainties from internal and external environments.

3.1 ISSUES IN MANAGING SCNS FOR SUPPORTING THE OFP

Because of the complexity of a SCN, it is a challenge to coordinate the actions of entities within the network to perform in a coherent manner. When orders come into an entity in a SCN, the lead time for delivering products (called the order fulfillment cycle time) is composed of (1) order processing times, including the order transfer time from customers to manufacturers or distributors, and the due date assignment process, (2) material lead times, including material planning and purchase lead time, supplier lead time, transport lead time, receipt and inspection lead time, assembly release time, and material order picking time, (3) assembly lead times, including waiting time, processing times, and transport time to the next stage, (4) distribution lead times, including dispatch preparation time (documents, packages), and transportation time to the customer, and (4) installation lead times. These components of the order fulfillment cycle time distribute across the network, and the variation of lead times at any stage will affect the execution of the other stages and result in uncertainties for the overall order cycle time. This is called the *ripple effect*. Take, for example, a product that is assembled by component parts from several different suppliers. The cycle time for assembling the product can be affected by the lead-time of material supply from different suppliers. If parts from some of the suppliers come later than the other parts for assembly, the assembly will be delayed due to the unavailability of required parts. This also increases the inventory costs for those available parts. If the product is a component for the downstream manufacturing process, the delay for shipping this product will affect the consequent stages, and in turn, influence the whole network. Therefore, the first issue in managing a SCN is how to control the ripple effect of lead-time so that the variability of a SCN can be mitigated. How to coordinate the policies of up and down stream entities in facilitating such variability reduction is the main concern. Demand forecasting is used to estimate demand for each stage, and the inventory between stages of the network is used for protecting against fluctuations in supply and demand across the network such as machine breakdown, extra large demand, etc. Due to the shortening of product life cycles, such protection seems unwise and actually reduces flexibility. Because of the decentralized control properties of the SCN, control of the ripple effect requires coordination between entities in performing their tasks. The management of interdependencies is the key to smooth material flow within the SCN. The interdependencies between entities of the SCN can be described in the following situations:

1. Producer/consumer dependence can be used to describe the supplier/manufacturer relationship in the SCN. This requires cooperation between suppliers and manufacturers in an efficient and effective way. Efficiency means to reduce material lead times, and effectiveness means to supply only the needed materials. This depend-

Table 9.2 The Properties of Type I, II, and III SCNs

ATTRIBUTES	TYPE I	TYPE II	TYPE III
Manufacturing process	Convergent assembly	Divergent assembly	Divergent differentiation
Primary business objectives	Lean production	Customization	Responsiveness
Product differentiation	Early	Late	Late
Number of product model	Concentrating at the manufacturing stage	Distributed to the distribution stage	Concentrating at the manufacturing stage
Assembly process	Concentrating at the manufacturing stage	Distributed to the distribution stage	Concentrating at the manufacturing stage
Product life cycle	Years	Months to Years	Weeks to Months
Main inventory type	End products	Semi-products	Raw materials

ence also implies a constraint satisfaction problem, and through the network it is a constraint propagation issue too.

2. Material flows within the SCN implies a synchronization problem, where related materials for a product are delivered to the manufacturer at a coherent speed which incurs minimal inventory and delay.

Inventory is an unwise approach to dealing with highly changing market demand and short life cycle products. What would be the substitution for inventory? Information can do. The material lead-time information from different suppliers can be used for planning the material arrival, instead of building up inventory. The demand information can be transmitted to the manufacturers on a timely basis, so that orders can be fulfilled with less inventory costs. The second main issue is how to manage the information flow within a SCN so that decisions made by business entities can take more global factors into consideration. In this way, we can increase SCN visibility. These issues are brought up because of the essential concern: how to make the network respond effectively and efficiently to satisfy customer demand, which leads to the motivation for managing SCNs to support the OFP. In (Lin, 1996), Lin identified three main types of SCNs, Type I, II and III, based on such attributes as manufacturing process, primary business objective, product differentiation, range of product variation, assembly stages, product life cycle, and main inventory type as shown in Table 9.2.

The automobile and aerospace industries are associated with Type I SCNs, where how to efficiently meet customer demand without carrying excessive inventory, and how to coordinate suppliers and assemblers to smooth material flow, are two main issues and challenges. Structurally, there are many suppliers. The wide range of materials and subcomponents that come from these suppliers converges through a series of manufacturing stages until the final product is assembled at one location. The final product is then shipped to several distributors and ultimately to a large number of retailers. The appliance, electronics, and computer industries can be classified as Type II SCNs, where reducing the lead-time of the assembly-to-order process, and managing the inventory and purchasing for the assembly, are two main issues and challenges. In these SCNs, a relatively small number of suppliers provide materials and subcomponents that are used to produce a number of generic product models. Complex assembly processes for generic models (semi-products) are executed at factory sites, and simple assembly processes for customized models are executed at distribution sites. A number of distribution points may be needed to quickly respond to customized orders. The apparel/fashion industry is a Type III SCN, where acquiring market information to respond to demand, and deferring product differentiation to maintain flexibility to handle constantly changing markets, are two main issues and challenges. In these SCNs, the number of end items is larger than the number of raw materials. There are a small number of suppliers and manufacturers, but a larger number of distributors and retailers. These three types of SCNs serve as the foundation to understand the issues and challenges for improving the OFP in SCNs.

3.2   USING SWARM FOR SIMULATING ORDER FULFILLMENT IN SCNS

The Swarm simulation platform is suitable for modeling supply chain networks based on the following analysis on their properties (summarized in Table 9.3). A supply chain network is composed of several autonomous or semi-autonomous business entities which can be viewed as a swarm of agents. Each business entity has its capability and capacity and can be assigned to, or take certain types of tasks, according to its organizational roles in the SCN. These capability, capacity, and organizational roles can be modeled by individual-based models. The SCN can be decomposed according to the multiple layer abstraction, which can be modeled by Swarm's nested inherent hierarchy property. The material flow is controlled by business entities within the SCN. These business entities can be represented as physical agents, while logical agents are

Table 9.3   The Mapping of Properties between SCNs and Swarm

Supply Chain Networks	Swarm Simulation System
Composition of autonomous and semi-autonomous business entities	A swarm of agents with individual based modeling
Business entities act different organizational roles	Agents are constructed with internal state variables and action functions
Multiple layer abstraction	Message passing between agents
Information flow between business entities	Message passing between agents
Material flow during procurement, manufacturing, and distribution activities	Discrete event simulation and time-stepped scheduling to trigger agent actions
In a SCN, the processes of individual entities contribute to the global SCN performance	In Swarm, the combination of individual behaviors determines the collective group behavior
The visibility of a SCN is determined by the information boundary	The boundaries of message passing determine the visibility

used for controlling actions for material movement. These operational and control actions can be simulated by Swarm's hybrid scheduling capability (i.e., discrete event and time-stepped scheduling). SCN visibility depends on the boundary of information sharing which is an analogy to the boundaries of message passing in Swarm. In a SCN, the processes of each individual entity contribute to the global performance of the SCN, while in Swarm, the combination of individual behaviors determines the collective performance of the whole group.

Figure 9.1 illustrates the mapping between a SCN and the Swarm platform. The supply chain network can be well represented by Swarm which consists of several layers of swarms. At the topmost layer, the whole supply chain network is viewed as a swarm denoted as Swarm M. Swarm A is composed of agents within the organization bounded by Circle A. Supplier S5 is represented as a collection of agents in Swarm B, and machines in Assembler F6 are formed as agents in Swarm C.

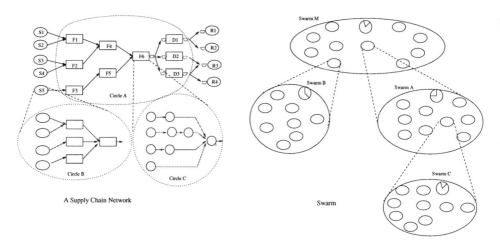

Figure 9.1 The Mapping between a SCN and Swarm

3.3   SCN IMPLEMENTATION ON THE SWARM

We consider two tasks in using the Swarm simulation platform to simulate the OFP in SCNs: (1) Simulating the OFP under the SCN environment, which includes forming agents in SCNs, defining functions and relations of agents, and designing the business environments. (2) Evaluating the OFP in SCNs, which includes specifying evaluation criteria, conducting experiments, and evaluating potential strategies for improving the OFP. Following the framework denoted in Figure 1 we implemented SCNs on the Swarm platform. Figure 9.2 describes the SCN implementation on the Swarm platform. The topmost swarm, the OFP Batch Swarm, is designed to control the whole simulation. It creates two swarms, the OFP Model Swarm and the Statistics Swarm, creates actions, and then activates the simulation process. The OFP Model Swarm is composed of an array of SCN Entities created while building objects. The SCN configuration with each entity's properties and product information are fed in during the entity's creation. The OFP model actions are composed of each SCN entity's actions, and are activated when the OFP Model Swarm is activated. A SCN entity is composed of several agents, such as an order management agent, an inventory management agent, and a SCN management agent. An entity with manufacturing capability includes a production planning agent, a capacity planning agent, a materials planning agent, a shop floor control agent, and manufacturing systems agent. A SCN Entity Swarm holds entity level information such as suppliers, customers, order transfer delay

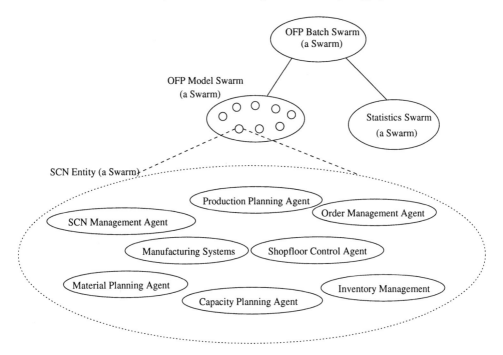

Figure 9.2 The Implementation of Swarm in Modeling SCN

time, and product delivery time, which are accessible by internal agents and other entities. The encapsulated agents perform certain functions in enabling the movement of information and material within the entity and between entities. The Statistics Swarm is used to compute the statistics data gathered through the simulation for analysis purposes.

The functions of agents are described as follows:

1. Order management agent – It processes orders coming from outside entities or other agents inside the entity. Tasks include estimating due dates, checking inventory availability, and forwarding orders to upstream suppliers if needed. It obtains orders from the SCN Swarm, and queries inventory availability through the inventory management agent. If the entity has manufacturing capability, the estimation of due dates also requests product availability from the production planning agent and the shop floor control agent.

2. Inventory management agent – It handles the inventory related tasks, such as keeping track of inventory records, determining the reordering point, and responding to the inventory availability queries from other agents, such as order management, material planning, and shop floor control agents.

3. Production planning agent – It takes the orders from the order management agent, and then, according to the product due dates, capacity and material availability, generates *build plans* under different planning horizons. The build plan will be used by the material planning and the shop floor control agents to execute the production process.

4. Capacity planning agent – It keeps track of the capacity consumption of manufacturing systems, and provides capacity availability information for the production planning agent in production planning.

5. Material planning agent – It has two main roles: one to plan the required materials for the manufacturing process, including the allocation of parts from inventory, or the purchase of materials from suppliers; the other is to provide material availability information for the production planning agent to generate build plans.

6. Shopfloor control agent – It dispatches parts from inventory to the manufacturing systems according to the work order derived from build plans. It also provides capacity utilization information for other agents.

7. Manufacturing agent – It executes the manufacturing processes by providing the components and utilizing capacity information.

8. SCN management agent –It chooses suppliers for the entities in acquiring components for manufacturing or end products for distribution.

The following scenario describes the interactions among these agents, and Figure 9.3 summarizes them. For example, an entity ScnESwarm A receives an order from its customer ScnESwarm C. The order flows to the order management agent (OrdM). According to the customer lead times, the inventory availability information (from InvM), the production plan (from PrdP), and the manufacturing capacity (CapP), the order management agent assigns a due date to the order. If the products are in stock, the order is filled by shipping the products from inventory. If the products are in receiving, the due date is set according to the delivery date of the products. For an entity with manufacturing capability, the order is forwarded to the production-planning agent (PrdP) where the schedule for making the products is planned. The capacity-planning agent (CapP) and the material-planning agent (MatP) are partner agents in generating achievable build plans. The material planning

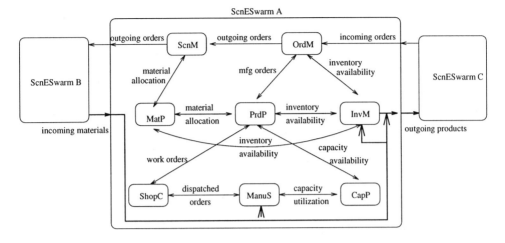

Figure 9.3   SCN Agent Interaction in the Swarm Implementation

obtains build plans from the production-planning agent to allocate materials for manufacturing. It also contributes information about material availability to production planning for scheduling. The capacity planning agent (CapP) plans capacity by taking the build plan from PrdP and sends capacity usage information to PrdP for scheduling the build plan. The SCN management agent (ScnM) takes the order information to choose suppliers in allocating material sources. The outgoing orders are transferred through its SCN Entity (ScnESwarm A) to be transferred to other entities (i.e. ScnESwarm B). This describes the information within an entity. If the entity is a distribution center or a retailer without manufacturing capability, the ordered products are delivered from suppliers as end products to ship to its customers. For an entity with manufacturing capability, the ordered end products are supplied from the shop floor (ManuS) to its customers. The input materials are components for the end products. This represents the material flow with an entity. The interaction of these agents enables the flow of materials and information within an entity, and, through the SCN Entity Swarm (ScnESwarm), the information and materials flow across the supply chain network.

4.   PERFORMANCE IMPROVEMENTS ENABLED BY INFORMATION SHARING

We implemented a supply chain designed to simulate order fulfillment in a Type II SCN to investigate the impact of Information Sharing on Divergent Assembly (Type II) Supply Chains. The model and Swarm system both include the major components (as shown in Table 1) of a divergent assembly SCN. Suppliers, manufacturers/assemblers, and distributors are included as entities (actors) in the system. Entities are composed of agents (activities) that represent the agents shown in Figure 2. These agents incorporate the decision making, and information and material processing. (Goals) are incorporated into the decision-making rules of the agents. Message passing between agents (as shown in Figure 9.3) represents information and material transfer (interdependencies). Modeling of a divergent assembly supply chain is done by structuring the entity interactions to match a generic supply chain structure (as shown in Figure 4), and product structure, seen in the computer or electronics industry (i.e. Hewlett-Packard, Motorola). We verified that the entities, agents, activities, and interdependencies included in the system are those that are typically described in the supply chain management literature. Performance (overall objective) is based on cycle time and inventory levels resulting from the implementation of the other model components. The system performed as expected with positive impacts resulting from increased information sharing. Our Swarm-based divergent assembly supply chain model is valid because it encompasses all of the major components of a real-world supply chain, and it involves a detailed view of the inner-workings that is not seen in high level analytical models. Validity beyond this level is difficult and would require implementation of one specific real-world divergent assembly supply chain. This is a potential topic for future research. "Scn-II" in Figure 9.4 represents a Type II SCN consisting of 15 business entities aligned into five tiers. Entities in tiers 1, 2 and 3 perform complicated manufacturing and assembly processes, entities in tier 4 execute simple assembly processes, and those at tier 5 do not have manufacturing capability. Scn-II shares some features with a Type II SCN such as divergent assembly, late product differentiation, and distributing assembly to the distribution stage.

We conducted experiments to evaluate OFP performance using various information-sharing strategies. Information sharing between business entities considers three issues: (1) the information contents, (2) the depth of information penetration (the number of tiers for which information is accessible), and (3) the information acquisition direction (upward or downward sharing). Agent decision- making processes are held constant to isolate the impact of information sharing. The experiments were designed to test two hypotheses related to the importance of different information types, and the importance of different demand management policies. The hypotheses are identified later in this section. In the design of the simulation platform, the information acquired by downstream en-

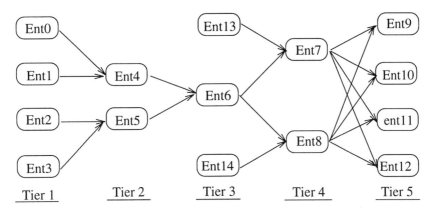

Figure 9.4   Simulated SCN Structure - "Scn-II"

tities is mainly material and capacity availability information from their suppliers. The information acquired by an upstream entity is information about customer demand and orders. The depth of information penetration can be specified in various degrees, e.g., isolated, upward one tier, upward two tiers, downward one tier, downward two tiers, and so forth. The obtained capacity and material information from suppliers is used to estimate the due dates of incoming orders, which are the basis for generating build plans or re-ordering schedules. The obtained customer demand information is used to estimate the demand for the next period, so that the production or re-ordering schedules can adapt to external demand. Demand management policies, such as make-to-order (MTO), make-to-stock (MTS), and assembly-to-order (ATO) have their characteristics and application situations described in Table 9.4 (Lin, 1996; McCutcheon, Amitabh and Meredith, 1994).

If the amount of customization is low, the firm can usually employ a make-to-stock approach and then use inventories of finished goods to provide short lead times. For products with high customization, the make-to-stock strategy cannot efficiently and effectively match customer preferences. If customers are willing to wait for customized products after submitting orders, the make-to-order strategy can be applied to high-customization firms. When the product design allows the product differentiation stage to occur late enough in the production process, the firm can employ an assembly-to-order approach. The experiments were designed to test two hypotheses. The first hypothesis (H1) relates to identifying the best demand management policy for divergent assembly supply chains. An ATO demand management policy should result in the best supply chain performance because divergent assembly supply chains are associated with late product differentiation in an environment

Table 9.4   Some Demand Management Policies for the Order Fulfillment Process

POLICIES	CHARACTERISTICS	APPLICATION SITUATIONS
Make-To-Order (MTO)	Production is triggered by customer orders	High customization pressure but low responsiveness
Assembly-To-Order (ATO)	Final assembly is order-driven, but the component parts are forecast-driven and built to stock	High customization pressure, high responsiveness, and products with late differentiation
Make-to-Stock (MTS)	Production is triggered by inventory replenishment points	Low customization pressure

where product variations are not small and efficient matching of assembly to demand is essential given the short length of product life cycles. *H1.* An ATO demand management policy results in the best divergent assembly supply chain performance when compared to MTO and MTS. The second hypothesis (H2) relates to the importance of demand information sharing. Demand information should be critical because divergent assembly supply chains have a primary business objective of product customization to fulfill customer orders in an environment where product variations are not small. *H2.* Demand information sharing is critical to divergent assembly supply chain performance. The results from evaluating various information-sharing strategies under these three types of demand management policies in the Type II SCN are shown in Figures 5 and 6. The three information sharing strategies are (1) no information sharing, (2) supply information sharing, and (3) supply and demand information sharing. The three demand management policies are listed were listed above. From Figure 5 we see that cycle time is stable for MTO and ATO policies as more information is shared. From Figure 6we see that the same is true for inventory costs for MTO policies. ATO policies result in lower inventory levels when supply and demand information is shared. The addition of demand information is critical. This supports H2. Cycle time and inventory costs are stable for MTS policies when supply information is shared, but when demand information is ad-

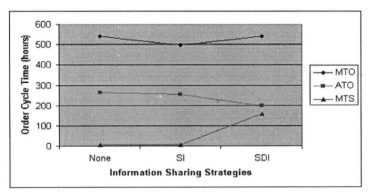

NONE: No information sharing

SI: Supply information is shared

SDI: Supply and demand information is shared

MTO: Make-to-order

ATO: Assembly-to-order

MTS: Make-to-stock

Figure 9.5 OFP Improvement in Order Cycle Time Reduction Using Various Information Sharing Strategies in a Type II SCN

ded, cycle time increases, but inventory costs decline. From the figures we clearly see the tradeoff between cycle time and inventory costs in Type II SCNs. In a Type II SCN, the number of shared components and the range of product variations are higher than in Type I SCNs. Based on our findings, we feel that the best demand management policy is ATO. This supports H1. It results in reasonable cycle times and lower inventory levels. Information can substitute for inventory when a SCN faces a market with high product variations. Indeed, we have seen this ATO strategy implemented in some typical Type II SCNs, such as those in the PC industry.

5. CONCLUSIONS

This study provides two sets of conclusions related to both the feasibility of multi-agent systems as a decision support tool for supply chain managers as well as supply chain performance enhancements arising from information sharing. It is apparent that computational modeling

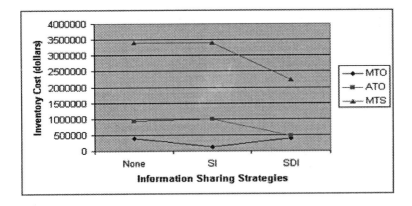

NONE: No information sharing

SI: Supply information is shared

SDI: Supply and demand information is shared

MTO: Make-to-order

ATO: Assembly-to-order

MTS: Make-to-stock

Figure 9.6 OFP Improvement in Inventory Cost Reduction Using Various Information Sharing Strategies in a Type II SCN

can be feasibly used to simulate order fulfillment in supply chains. It incorporates the major components of the supply chain including its actors, activities, interdependencies and goals. It also enables supply chain managers to identify the impact of various decision-making scenarios on performance measures such as cycle time and inventory levels to accomplish their overall objective. This is a first try at decision support for supply chain managers, but it is apparent that it has many potential applications. This model provides a basis for modeling more complex supply chain issues such as negotiation between supply chain partners (the market mechanism), and power differentials between supply chain partners. We can also draw conclusions from our simulation results. In Type II (divergent assembly) supply chains, supply chain management is most effective when using an assembly-to-order (ATO) demand management policy coupled with sharing of both supply and demand (forecast and order) information. This supports both H1 and H2. Inventory costs are reduced while cycle times remain relatively stable. These specific findings produce some interesting overall conclusions. The findings from these experiments enhance the assertion that information technology is important for supporting the order fulfillment process in supply chain networks. We can draw a common conclusion that information can substitute for inventory. Finally, supply chain management involves a fundamental tradeoff between cycle time, inventory and information. In many cases information can replace inventory while maintaining acceptable cycle times. In the past, when information costs were high, inventory was held to manage uncertainty. Today, when information technology continues to reduce information costs, uncertainty can be reduced resulting in lower inventory requirements. Our results illustrate some of the potential impacts of the electronic integration effect (Malone, Yates and Benjamin, 1987). The benefits that we illustrate related to this effect are that supply chain managers may reduce cycle time or inventory costs (or possibly both) because of reduced uncertainty in decision making. This is possible because IT (incorporated into electronic hierarchies) reduces coordination costs. The development of an analytical model to describe this tradeoff is an issue that should be addressed by future research.

References

Applegate, L.M, C.W. Holsapple, R. Kalakota, F.J. Radermacher, and A.B. Whinston (1996), 'Electronic Commerce: Building Blocks of New Business Opportunity', *Journal of Organizational Computing and Electronic Commerce* **vol. 6, no. 1**, pp. 1–10.

Berners-Lee, T, R. Cailliau, A. Luotonen, H.F. Nielsen, and A. Secret (1994), 'The World-Wide Web', *Communications of the ACM*, **vol. 37, no. 8**, pp. 76–82.

Billington, C. (1994), 'Strategic Supply Chain Management', *OR/MS Today*, April 1994. pp. 20–27.

Carr, J. (1996), 'Intranets Deliver', *InfoWorld*, **vol. 18, no. 8**, pp. 61–63.

Christopher, M. (1993), *Logistics and Supply Chain Management*, Pitman Publishing: London.

Davis, T. (1993), 'Effective Supply Chain Management', *Sloan Management Review*, Summer 1993. pp. 35–73.

Fisher, M. L., J.H. Hammond, W.R. Obermeyer, and A. Raman (1994), 'Making Supply Meet Demand in an Uncertain World', *Harvard Business Review*, May–June 1994, pp. 83–93.

Goldman, S.L., R.N. Nagel, and K. Preiss (1995), *Agile Competitors and Virtual Organizations: Strategies for Enriching the Customer*, Van Nostrad Reinhold: New York.

Holland, C., G. Lockett, and I. Blackman (1992), 'Planning for Electronic Data Interchange', *Strategic Management Journal*, **vol. 13**, pp. 539–550.

Johnston, H.R., and M.R. Vitale (1988), 'Creating Advantage with Interorganizational Information Systems', *MIS Quarterly*, **vol. 12, no. 2**, pp. 153–166.

Kalakota, R., and A.B. Whinston (1996), *Frontiers of Electronic Commerce* Addison-Wesley Publishing Company, Inc.: Reading, MA.

Karpinski, R. (1997), 'Extranets emerge as next challenge for marketers', *Netmarketing*, April 1997, pp. M–4.

Lee, H.L., and C. Billington (1992), 'Managing Supply Chain Inventory: Pitfalls and Opportunities', **Sloan Management Review**, spring 1992. pp. 65–73.

Lee, H.L., and C. Billington (1993), 'Material Management in Decentralized Supply Chains', *Operations Research*, **vol. 41, no. 5**, pp. 835–847.

Lee, H.L., C. Billington, and B. Carter (1993), 'Hewlett-Packard Gains Control of Inventory and Service through Design for Localization', *Interfaces*, **vol. 23, no. 4**, pp. 1–11.

Lin, F.-R. (1996), *Reengineering the Order Fulfillment Process in Supply Chain Networks: A Mutliagent Information Systems Approach*, Ph.D. Thesis, University of Illinois at Urbana-Champaign.

Lin, F.-R., G.W. Tan, and M.J. Shaw (1996), 'Multi-Agent Enterprise Modeling', University of Illinois at Urbana-Champaign, College of

Commerce and Business Administration, Office of Research, Working Paper 96–0134.

Malone, T.W., and K. Crowston (1990), 'What is Coordination Theory and How Can It Help Design Cooperative Work Systems?' In *Proc. CSCW '90*, pp. 375–388.

Malone, T.W., and J.F. Rockart (1991), 'Computers, Networks, and the Corporation', *Scientific American*, **vol. 265, no. 3**, pp. 128–136. Malone, T.W., J.Yates, and R.I. Benjamin (1987), 'Electronic Markets and Electronic Hierarchies', *Communications of the ACM*, **vol. 30, no. 6**, pp. 484- -497.

McCutcheon, D.M., S. Amitabh, and J.R. Meredith (1994), 'The Customization Responsiveness Squeeze', *Sloan Management Review*, Winter 1994. pp. 89–99.

Miller, M.J. (1996), 'Your Own Private Internet', *PC Magazine*, **vol. 15, no. 5**, pp. 29.

Netscape Communications Corporation (1996), Intranets Redefine Corporate Information Systems, http://home.netscape.com/comprod/ /at_work/white_paper/indepth.html.

The Sante Fe Institute (1996), The Swarm Simulation System, http://www.santafe.edu/projects/swarm/.

Smith, R.G., and R. Davis (1988), 'Frameworks for Cooperation in Distributed Problem Solving', In *Readings in Distributed Artificial Intelligence*, (Ed.) Alan H. Bond and Les Gasser, Morgan Kaufmann Publishers, Inc.: San Mateo, CA.

Snapp, C.D. (1990), 'EDI Aims High for Global Growth', *Datamation*, March 1, 1990. pp. 77–80.

Srinivasan, K., S. Kekre, and T. Mukhopadhyay (1993), *Impact of Electronic Data Interchange Technology on JIT Shipments*, Graduate School of Industrial Administration, Carnegie Mellon University.

Swminathan, J.M., S.F. Smith, and N.M. Sadeh (1994), *Modeling the Dynamics of Supply Chains*, The Robotics Institute, Carnegie Mellon University.

Violino, B. (1996), 'Your Worst Nightmare', *Information Week*, February 19, 1996, pp. 34–36.

Chapter 10

ONLINE SUPPLY CHAIN MODELING AND SIMULATION

Christoph Schlueter-Langdon
University of Southern California,
Marshall School of Business
csl@schlueterresearch.com

Peter Bruhn,
Darmstadt University of Technology,
Department of Business Administration, Economics and Law
bruhn@winf.de

Michael J. Shaw
University of Illinois at Urbana-Champaign,
Department of Business Administration
m-shaw2@uiuc.edu

Abstract   Digital interactive services such as web and online services are among
the most dynamic markets. Currently the entire area is in its infancy
stage with industry structure and behavior of firms evolving rapidly. To
identify successful strategies such as for market entry, advanced tools
are required to cope with these dynamics and complexity of emergent
behavior. Swarm has been used to implement a simulator that has been
applied to this research problem.

Keywords: Complex adaptive/multi-agent system, information system strategy, simulation, supply chain design

1.   RESEARCH PROBLEM

1.1   INFORMATION TECHNOLOGY AND DIGITAL INTERACTIVE SERVICES INDUSTRY STRUCTURE

The literature suggests that over time industry structure evolves from industry-level integration ("closed") to industry-level specialization ("open", i.e., Chandler 1990, Arora et al. 1997/98, Farrell et al. 1998). Initially, firms tend to be integrated and firm-level specialization appears to be a dangerous proposition, while later specialization becomes more advantageous than integration. During an industry's infancy, the option of "make or buy" for items unique to that industry is most likely reduced to "make" as a "buy" alternative may simply be not available. This observation has also been made for digital interactive services (DIS) such as consumer online services (Schlueter-Langdon 1999). Only integrated online service providers survived the early 1990s (e.g., America Online, CompuServe). Specialized providers failed (e.g., Delphi, Europe Online).

In general, the erosion of integration advantages and trend toward industry-level specialization is facilitated by technological progress and specifically by the emergence of standards. Many industry studies suggest that the emergence of standards or modular component design coincidences with an increase in the number of specialized producers.[1] As one piece of equipment is broken into compatible components vendors as well as users can specialize. Also, information technology (IT) specifically has been identified to reduce transaction cost (Malone 1987, Table 1, 485). As the division of labor implies trade between specialized agents and as therefore benefits of specialization for any agent also depend on the efficiency of transactions, progress with information technology facilitates specialization.

On a very high level and over time, observations of industry structure and progress of IT can be summarized as follows: As IT advances, industry structure evolves from industry-level integration to industry-level specialization. While specialized firms are at risk initially, they tend to become more successful at a more mature stage of the industry life cycle. The lack of choice of suppliers and upstream competition causes coordination problems and could raise cost of inputs through the increase of market power of vendors and might even lead to upstream foreclosure (e.g., Whinston 1990, Ordover 1990).

In order to keep the research problem simple only two states of technology are distinguished: "old" versus "new" information technology. Overall, DIS information systems have evolved from proprietary, monolithic platforms, such as the original AOL system, to open, compatible component technology, such as the Web browser and server. Therefore, in the context of DIS markets "old" information technology is understood as monolithic, proprietary platforms or dedicated, standalone systems and "new" information systems are considered modular and compatible.

The problem with its two clear cut situations ("old" IT and industry-level integration, "new" IT and industry-level specialization) is not very exciting unless one changes perspectives and switches from the historic view of an industry observer to the situation of a potential entrant looking at the industry at a particular point in time. Suddenly, decisions on scope of activities and choice of IT become difficult as there is neither a linear path toward specialization, nor a recipe of how to build a best practices online platform. Instead, firms integrate and divest frequently and technology presents itself as a steady stream of innovation with promising technology on the horizon every day.

This situation sets the stage for the following research question: What strategy should an entrant adopt with regards to choice of integration and process technology?

Once a DIS market and a position within have been identified as an attractive target, a potential entrant has to make two strategic decisions: (1) What is the scope of business activities to compete with incumbents? and (2) What are the choices of technologies to support these activities? Decisions on these two interdependent questions provide the foundation and skeleton of any financial business plan in DIS. They need to be provided before moving on to specify implementation issues, such as a marketing plan or an organizational chart. The complication with the research question arises from the fact that decisions of firms are not independent. "New" IT may have the potential to reduce transaction cost between business processes (as suggested by Malone 1987) and, therefore, facilitate segregation of labor and market relationships. In order to release this potential, firms would have to adopt the "new" IT and specialize. From the perspective of each firm, its adoption decision clearly depends on the behavior of other firms. In other words, individual decisions depend on industry-level conditions, which, in turn, are the result of the collective behavior of firms.

Answers to the research question fall between the two extremes (considering an industry that is less than 100% integrated or specialized): (1) Enter integrated and use "old" IT or (2) enter specialized and use "new" IT. If the industry is more integrated than specialized then the former appears to be a safer bet. The latter option may only be successful if the advantages from IT such as lower unit cost and increased flexibility are strong enough to support specialized entry. Unfortunately, integrated entry is usually very expensive and if not achieved through a single merger or acquisition but many small steps it can be also very time-consuming. Furthermore, an integrated entrant would be exposed to competition along many processes, while a specialized entrant could focus on a smaller set of activities.

2. THE MODEL

2.1 SUPPLY CHAIN MODELING AND SIMULATION

As of end of 1998, only two models could be found that relate remotely to a supply chain configuration and address the dynamics of industry evolution (Arora et al. 1997/98, Farrell et al. 1998).[2] Both models investigate the process of vertical integration and disintegration and provide similar models of industry structure. They differ in that Arora et al. "explicitly investigates the dynamics of industry structure evolution in a competitive market setting, albeit with boundedly rational firms" (Arora et al. 1997/98, 3), while Farrell et al. consider strategic interaction (Bertrand and Cournot competition).

In order to investigate the dynamics of an entire industry with multiple business segments, the use of simulation experiments is viewed as a promising approach.[3]

2.2 CONCEPTUAL MODEL

In order to model the research problem of an optimal entry strategy, the following key components need to be incorporated: (1) an industry, (2) firms, and (3) a supply chain. Also, the following issues have to be addressed: How to recognize or differentiate (1) the structure of a firm, (2) states of IT, and (3) industry-level feedback.

In the model, an industry is conceptualized as being composed of firms, with similar firms representing a business segment, such as manufacturers and retailers. Firms are composed of at least one business process, which, in turn, is comprised of production and cost functions. A supply chain defines the order of the main business processes or, in other words, the successive stages of value-added.

Combining different processes creates firms with different structures. A firm with one process is considered specialized, while a firm composed of a combination of processes is referred to as an integrated one. Different states of IT are reflected in the shape of cost functions (C_{FIX}, c_{VAR}), which are embedded in a business process.

The industry-level feedback mechanism is achieved by coordinating the interaction of firms along the value chain through markets. Therefore, each firm is at the same time a buyer of inputs and a seller of outputs.

In order to identify viable entry strategies, the success of different types of firms at the same stage in the supply chain has to be studied. The performance of an individual firm within a supply chain configuration is measured by its profits, which are derived by subtracting cost of inputs and production from revenues made by selling output to the firm's most downstream market.[4] Due to market coordination of production activities, the performance of each firm, as well as system performance, is the result of the collective behavior of many agents, as opposed to more traditional approaches—in particular, neoclassic economic models that follow a top-down design with aggregate demand and supply functions representing an economic system.

2.3   COMPLEX ADAPTIVE SYSTEM ARCHITECTURE

2.3.1   Multi-Agent System and Enterprise Integration Modeling.
The conceptual model has been implemented as a multi-agent system (MAS). Its design process has benefited from the application of a formal multi-agent framework of coordination in enterprise integration developed by Sikora and Shaw (1996) and from Holland's complex adaptive system (CAS) modeling methods (1995, 10-40).

The architecture of the MAS model shares characteristics of enterprise integration models, such as multiple level abstraction in representing organizational structures, communication between participants via message-passing, and agent adaptability[5], as well as properties of CAS models, such as flows and aggregation.

Furthermore, the MAS modeling process and, in particular, the implementation of the model have benefited from two CAS simulations: Lin's supply chain network application (1996) and the Anasazi village formation simulator (Kohler and Carr 1996). Lin's model supports the evaluation of approaches for improving order fulfillment performance in supply chain networks in manufacturing. Kohler and Carr's model is utilized in the analysis of the Anasazi village formation, a prehistoric settlement system in Southwest North America.[6] Both models have been among the first applications using the Swarm toolkit.

Both models have been helpful to better understand how to set up the overall program infrastructure for a Swarm implementation. Lin's supply chain network application, in particular, provided insights into the implementation of multiple layer abstractions utilizing Swarm's nested inherent hierarchy property.

2.3.2   Building Blocks, Flows, and Aggregation.   Figure 10.1 provides a high-level overview of the architecture of the MAS model. It

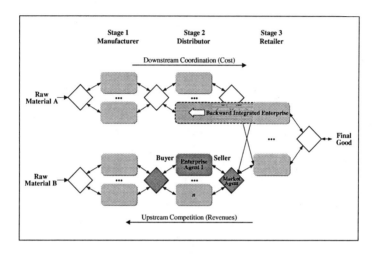

Figure 10.1   Architecture of the Simulation Model

represents a production system or supply chain which can be broken down into three stages of processes which contribute to the transformation of two types of raw materials into one final good. The final stage of processing requires two intermediate goods, each produced in separate process strings. These joint process strings are in turn composed of a two-stage sequence of processes each. This convergent supply chain design is compatible with the high-level abstraction of a generic online supply chain as described in Schlueter and Shaw (1997).

The supply chain stages are implemented as process agents, each of which is assigned to one firm or enterprise agent. Enterprise agents of the same stage represent a business segment. Integration of an enterprise agent into the next stage upstream is achieved by also assigning a process agent of that stage to the same enterprise agent. If input requirements of the enterprise agent's core process can be provided entirely by its upstream process agent, then this configuration is considered 100% vertically integrated. Please note that firms can currently only be integrated backward; although a 100% backward integrated retailer-type firm (stage three) would be no different from a 100% forward integrated stage-two-type firm. Any degree of integration below 100% would make a difference, however.

Enterprise agents interact with each other through market agents. Because each enterprise agent is a seller of its output and, at the same time, a buyer of inputs required to produce the output in the first place, market agents facilitate two flows throughout the system: the flow of goods downstream and revenues upstream.[7] Some of the revenues made from the sale of the final good downstream are passed on to enterprise agents upstream as a reward or return for their contribution to the final value added. The share of revenues distributed upstream depends on conditions with local markets such as the number of buyers and sellers. This decentralized credit-passing scheme provides performance incentives throughout the entire system (i.e., Holland 1995, 42 and 53–60). Backward integration reduces an enterprise agent's dependence on upstream market conditions. As illustrated in Figure 10.1, 100% backward integration would allow bypassing of an upstream market altogether.

Figure 10.1 also reveals an important design method called building blocks (Holland 1995, 34–37; actual building blocks can be perceived as agents in the context of multi-agent systems). The method refers to the decomposition of a complex scene into few, distinct categories of components and relationships. Building blocks can be reused and combined to create relevant, perpetually novel scenes. With decomposition and repeated use of building blocks, novelty arises through combination. Even with only a few sets of categories of components or building blocks and rules for combining them, an exponentially large number of different configurations can be assembled.

The challenge with building blocks is the decomposition of a complex scene into as few and most relevant categories of components and rules for combining them—also referred to as dependencies—as possible. If this can be achieved, building blocks provide great scalability and efficiency with reconfiguration.

Building blocks become even more powerful when applied to aggregation or tiered designs. Aggregation "concerns the emergence of complex large-scale behaviors from the aggregate interactions of less complex agents" (Holland 1995, 11).[8] It is considered a basic characteristic of all complex adaptive systems. Figure 10.2 illustrates how aggregation has been achieved through the nested hierarchies (i.e., enterprise = swarm of processes) and multiple-layer design (i.e., industry, business segments and enterprises) of the multi-agent system: Different low-level process agents are combined to form enterprise agents. Similar enterprise agents aggregate to create different business segments, which in turn represent an industry. This design allows for patterns of high-level events to derive

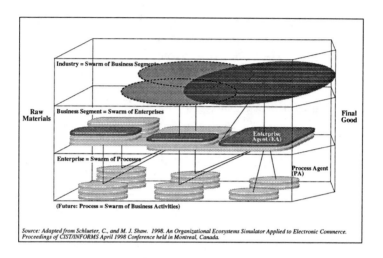

Figure 10.2 Building Blocks and Aggregation

from the settings of low-level building blocks. A change in conditions of process agents, such as an increase in scale economies, trickles up through higher layers to create some aggregate outcome that can be observed at the top layer, such as an increase in industry concentration. In other words, higher-level events, such as changes in industry structures, emerge from lower-level conditions and dynamics of interaction.

Having introduced the three types of agents—enterprise, process and market agents—and high-level relationships, the following paragraph takes a look inside each agent and its dependencies.

2.3.3   Agent Functions and Dependencies.   Figure 10.3—a detail of Figure 10.1 (agents marked in gray)—reveals how tasks have been distributed throughout the system. Each agent carries a distinct functional component: $F_{EA} = \{\text{Adaptation}\}$, $F_{PA} = \{\text{Production}\}$, and $F_{MA} = \{\text{Clearing}\}$. Agents or their embedded functional components are linked with each other through dependencies. In this multi-agent system, four different links are sufficient to create a multi-stage supply chain. If one wishes to turn the selected enterprise agent into a backward integrated firm with production capabilities also in stage 1, then this could be achieved with the current set of components: One process

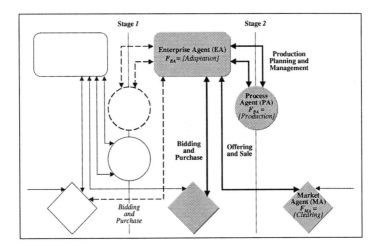

Figure 10.3 Building Blocks and Interdependencies

agent and three interdependencies would have to be added as indicated with dotted lines in Figure 10.3.

The following three paragraphs will explain each of the embedded functions or methods.

Enterprise Agent Activities and Functions.. Enterprises are composed of at least one process agent. They plan and manage production, which is executed by their process agents. Enterprise agents buy non-labor process inputs and fund production of their process agent(s). Purchasing overhead and SG&A (Selling, General & Administration) charges are currently not considered. There is no inventory build-up of either inputs or output; excess supplies and unsold goods are completely written off within one value creation cycle. (This is a very reasonable assumption as direct supplies and the final products in DIS markets are usually services, such as an online newspaper.)

In the case of integrated firms, the enterprise agent is comprised of at least two process agents, internal sourcing is maximized to fully utilize the pre-assigned in-house share (called *InHouseShare* in the software code).

Figure 10.4 illustrates how the *InHouseShare* variable can be utilized to "dial-in" a particular coordination mechanism. As the *InHouseShare* can vary between $\geq 0\%$ and $\leq 100\%$, the entire spectrum of coordination

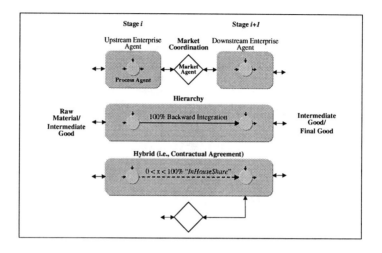

Figure 10.4   Enterprise Agent: Flexibility of Coordination Mechanism

alternatives between the two extremes of hierarchy and market can be implemented (Coase 1937, Williamson 1975). A hybrid configuration, for example, could be chosen to capture the impact of a contractual agreement.

The total enterprise agent costs are given by:

$$C_E = \sum_{k=1}^{n_P} C_{P_k} + C_{EP_k} \qquad (2.1)$$

k Number of enterprise processes
n_P Most upstream process of the enterprise
C_{P_i} Process cost function
C_{EP_i} Cost of process inputs

The costs of inputs for each process are given by:

$$C_{EP}(t_i) = dp_{\alpha P}(t_i)p_{\alpha P}(t_{i-1})\alpha_P(t_i)x_1 + dp_{\beta P}(t_i)p_{\beta P}(t_{i-1})\beta_P(t_i)x_2+$$
$$+p_{\gamma P}x_3$$

$$(2.2)$$

t_i Time step i

$p_{\alpha P}(t_{i-1})$ Unit price of process input α

$dp_{\alpha P}(t_i)$ Unit price change of process input α

$p_{\beta P}(t_{t-1})$ Unit price of process input β

$dp_{\beta P}(t_i)$ Unit price change of process input β

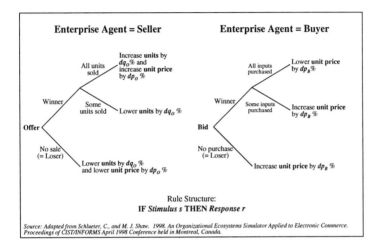

Figure 10.5   Enterprise Agent: Decision Trees for Market Adaptation

Decisions on market interaction (offer price and quantity, bid price) are made on an enterprise level and based on distributed (every firm), primitive "learning" ("IF stimulus s THEN response r" rules) and production requirements (bid quantity). Figure 10.5 depicts the decision trees which underlie the adaptation rules (rules reflect bounded rationalityrationality).

Decision-making is based on rules, which determine the adaptive behavior of an enterprise agent. As sellers, enterprise agents make offers and have to decide on price and quantity; as buyers of inputs, they submit bids and make a decision on bid price. Decisions are made simultaneously; no firm commits to its offer and bid prior to its competitors.

Process Agent Activities and Functions..   For each core process, it is assumed that two inputs are needed to produce one unit of output $[Q_P = f(x_1, x_2)]$. The relationship between inputs is such that output is limited by the most scarce input $[f(x_1, x_2) = \min\{\alpha_P x_1, \beta_P x_2\}$—a

Leontief case, as opposed to a Cobb-Douglas function with substitutive factors]. The effect of input expansion on the amount of output is assumed to be one with constant returns to scale; thus, cost functions are linear, "which is often a reasonable assumption to make about technological structures" (Varian 1984, 18):

$$Q_P(x_1, x_2, x_3) = \alpha_P x_1 + \beta_P x_2 + \gamma_P x_3 \qquad (2.3)$$

x_1 In-system or direct input type 1
x_2 Direct input type 2
x_3 Out-of-system input or indirect input
α_P *InSystemNeed0* (name of variable used in the software code)
β_P *InSystemNeed1*
γ_P *OutSystemNeed*

Each core process exhibits fixed and variable cost:

$$C_P(Q_P) = C_{FIX} + c_{VAR} Q_P \qquad (2.4)$$

C_{FIX} Process fixed cost (*FixCost*; i.e., depreciation and amortization)
c_{VAR} Variable cost of process value added *(CashNeed;* i.e., production set up, talent management)

Market Agent Activities and Functions..   Each of the stages of the supply chain is linked with a market agent. As market agents communicate with enterprises only and as enterprises might be 100% backwards integrated across several stages some market agents might be idle during simulation runs.

The most upstream market of the entire supply chain system is called the raw materials market, the most downstream market is called the final good market and markets in between are also referred to as intermediate good markets.

A market agent matches buyers' bids and sellers' offers, applying a pre-specified mechanism. Figure 10.6 depicts market and enterprise interaction. Currently, a two-sided competitive sealed-bid auction mechanism has been implemented. Kambil and van Heck provide an overview of different auction models and implications (1996). Competitive markets in general have proven to create highly efficient results in allocating scarce resources. The mechanism chosen resembles a stock market. The marketplace agent collects offers and bids (units, unit price) from enterprise agents and sorts them into two separate tables (offer-table and bid-table), with offers in ascending order and bids in descending order. Then a second column is created for each table, accumulating unit

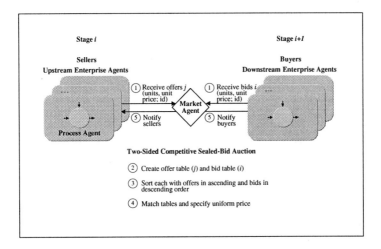

Figure 10.6 Market and Enterprise Interaction

volume for each price position such that any offer table field shows the maximum of what gets offered at same row price, while any bid table field shows the maximum of what will be bought at same row price. Finally, a uniform price is set to be the lowest accepted bid, maximizing exchange revenue (not transactions).

The clearing mechanism can be formally described as:

$$Uniform\_Price = \max_{\forall i}\{p_{B_i}|p_{B_i} \cdot \min[u_{B_i}, \max_{\forall j}(u_{O_j}|p_{O_j} \leq p_{B_i})]\} \quad (2.5)$$

p_{B_i}	Bit unit price
u_{B_i}	Bid units
p_{O_j}	Offer unit price
u_{O_j}	Offer units

Since all successful buyers pay the same market-clearing price, this institution is considered to create an impression of fairness (Kambil and van Heck 1996).

3.   IMPLEMENTATION

Swarm[9] proved to be a very appropriate tool to build simulation applications for the analysis of supply chains.[10]

In order to investigate emergent industry structures, a new simulation application had to be developed and built. Non of the available Swarm-based simulators provided the functionality required for organizational analysis, such as vertical integration and market coordination. The resulting simulator is not just another application, but rather a new tool kit designed to facilitate organizational analysis. It is a library of reusable supply chain modeling components that enable rapid development of customized decision support tools. It features a few relevant, yet simple building blocks (components/agents and rules/dependencies) that can be arranged to quickly create complex scenarios without losing flexibility and ease of modifications. The system is called ORECOS (ORganizational ECOsystems Simulator) (Schlueter and Shaw 1998). It takes advantages of key concepts in object-oriented development, such as inheritance and polymorphism, to increase scalability and flexibility for adaptation and change.

Instances of enterprise types are actual agents employed in simulation runs. In order to run a particular application, six input files are currently required, which shape a specific experimental setting based on ORECOS system functionality: SuperSettings.data (defines number of vertically related steps in the supply chain structure and relations), MarketFile.data (specifies location of markets in step structure), EPTypes.data (defines different types of enterprise agents), EPInstances.data (specifies enterprise agent instances within enterprise agent type parameters), CPTypes.data (defines different types of core process agents), and CPTypesVar.data (specifies randomization of enterprise adaptation). The system architecture has been implemented and the system code written by Peter Bruhn, Christoph Schlueter and Gek Woo Tan.[11]

The functionality of the ORECOS system has been validated through a staged testing of its components (Schlueter-Langdon 1999).

4.   EXPERIMENTAL DESIGN

The goal of the simulation experiments is to facilitate the identification of successful entry strategies for emergent DIS industries. Two scenarios with different industry-level concentration and process cost conditions have been created to reflect conditions in emerging online information markets. Because of the choice of abstraction in the conceptual model and implementation limitations, simulation experiments will only share modest similarities with online information markets.

Because the model is designed to investigate conditions only in intermediate good markets or the inner-workings of the production system, complications for input and output of the system have not been considered. Therefore, in both scenarios, demand for the final good is increasing and linear and supply of raw materials is unlimited.

A simulation experiment advances in time steps. For both scenarios, one time step has been chosen to represent a one-month time period. Each simulation experiment or run is conducted over 24 time steps or two years.[12] At each time step, firms adapt to market conditions as explained in paragraph 2.3.3 (Agent Functions and Dependencies) and illustrated in Figure 10.5 (Enterprise Agent: Decision Trees for Market Adaptation). This decision process is randomized in that values of unit and price change are drawn from a normal distribution with a constant variance (e.g., a 5% change is implemented as $\mu = 5$ with $\sigma = 1$).

The two scenarios differ in industry or supply chain structures; runs differ in cost functions or, more specifically, values for fixed and variable cost (C_{FIX}, c_{VAR}).

Figure 10.7 illustrates how the two scenarios differ in terms of structural conditions in intermediate good markets. The scenario of industry-

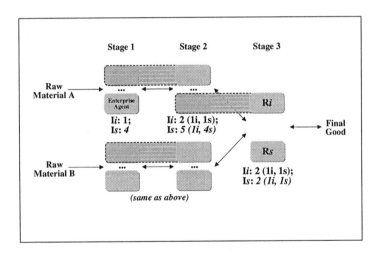

Figure 10.7   Industry-level Integration (Ii) versus Industry-level Specialization (Is)

level integration (Ii) is two firms at stage 1, four firms at stage 2—one backward integrated and one specialized enterprise for each input string, and two firms at stage 3 (one backward integrated firm and a specialized one). Twelve firms have been added to create the settings for the second scenario of industry-level specialization (Is). While conditions at stage 3 remain the same, specialized firms have been added to stages 1 and 2.

Because all integrated firms have been chosen to be 100% backward integrated, the condition in intermediate good markets for scenario Ii, for example, is characterized by a constellation of one seller facing two buyers between stages 1 and 2 and two sellers facing one buyer between stages 2 and 3. 14 and 26 process agents are required in order to implement the scenarios Ii and Is respectively.

Assumptions about cost functions are based specifically on observations of the market for online information services and electronic publishing. Internet/Web technology has significantly altered cost structures. In particular, modularity and compatibility have changed scale and scope economies in IT implementations. In the simulator, economies of scale and scope can be created on a process level through different combinations of fixed and variable cost (C_{FIX}, c_{VAR}).

Scope advantages exist when one firm can produce multiple products more cheaply than single firms can produce each product separately. The actual values for selected parameters of production functions and cost functions do reflect relative differences, however, in order to keep the simulation simple, at the expense of true resemblance of electronic publishing markets.

With "old" IT cost function values reflect the assumption that integrated firms enjoy a clear cost advantage. Fixed cost and variable cost parameters of specialized firms are 25% higher than those of integrated firms.

Furthermore, it is assumed that a scope advantage of 10% remains between integrated firms using "old" IT and specialized firms using "new" IT.

Further details and values for all variables are provided and explained in Schlueter-Langdon (1999, 152–157).

For each of the two scenarios (Ii and Is) many runs have been executed. For each run, the cost functions have been altered to reflect choices of IT ("old" vs. "new"). In order to test the success of a specialized entry for both scenarios, profits of the most downstream (stage 3) firms (Ri vs. Rs) have been measured and compared.[13] In a scenario of industry-level specialization (20 firms in the industry) and availability of "new" IT, for example, the firm Rs can be interpreted as an entrant that is using "new" IT to compete with the incumbent Ri. In this scenario, rival Ri may still use "old" IT (such as a proprietary platform with high fixed cost and low variable cost) or already "new" IT.

5.   SIMULATION RESULTS AND DISCUSSION

A multi-step approach has been devised to start and maintain simulation runs (or steady state). In order to create a "living" system in compliance with the specifications outlined in Section 4., the following features have been added sequentially: First, a linear system (no enterprise adaptation to market results) has been configured with every enterprise agent producing output profitably. Second, adaptation and growth have been introduced.

With industry-level integration, both firms employing "old" IT, and enterprise decisions on units of output only (no price adjustments)—either a unit increase of 5% or a decrease of 5% ($\mu = 5$ and $\sigma = 1$, normal distribution)—the most downstream and specialized firm (Rs-type) did not survive a run of 24 time steps. A 5% increase in unit output per time step would translate into an annual unit growth rate of about 80%. Given fallen DIS prices, the growth rate in the simulation corresponds well with growth in DIS markets. Because volatility appeared to be too high and the rule-based adaptation mechanism not smooth enough, further experiments have been conducted with a reduced rate of change of units of output and prices. A rate of $\pm$ 2.5% has been chosen.

In the scenario of industry-level specialization, when enterprise decisions are based on change of units of output and unit price—price of input(s) (bids) and output (offers)—and specialized firms use "new" IT and integrated firms employ "old" IT, the specialized (Rs-type) firm tends to be more profitable than its integrated rival. In other words, despite lower process cost resulting from scope advantages through integration, specialization appears to be at least as successful, if not more, than integration in the scenario of industry-level specialization.

Figure 10.8 depicts the aggregated results of a series of ten randomly selected runs for the third stage firms (D9s4-0 to D9s4-9; each for 24 time steps and for the first 12 time steps; 3i=integrated third stage firm, 3s=specialized third stage firm).[14] After 24 time steps, the specialized firm is profitable in four out of ten runs versus three out of ten for its integrated rival (upper left diagram in Figure 10.8). Because 24 time steps, or the equivalent of two years, may be too long a time period for the infancy stage of a product life cycle, results after 12 time steps of the same runs have also been considered. After the first 12 time steps, the specialized firm is profitable in seven out of ten runs and the integrated one in five out of ten (lower left diagram in Figure 10.8). While both firms have been profitable in the same run four out of ten times and unprofitable in two out of ten cases at time step 12, the values de-

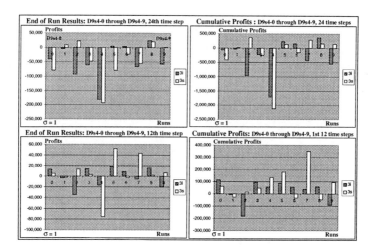

Figure 10.8   Summary of Results

teriorate to one and four out of ten respectively at time step 24. These results suggest that, in this scenario, the industry itself may become less attractive over time. These suppositions are confirmed by the development of cumulative profits. Over 24 time steps, the specialized enterprise agent is profitable in six out of ten runs versus three out of ten for its integrated rival (upper right diagram in Figure 10.8). After 12 time steps, both firms show cumulative profits in seven out of ten runs, however, the total net cumulative results (profits) for the specialized firm exceed the one of its integrated competitor by approximately 245%; lower right diagram in Figure 10.8. Also, cumulative results appear to support the conclusion drawn from point-in-time results that the industry, in this scenario, is becoming less attractive over time. While both firms show cumulative profits in the same run in five out of ten cases and losses in only one run after 12 time steps, these values change to two out of ten and three out of ten after 24 time steps. Even total net cumulative results, which have been profits after 12 time steps, turn into big losses after 24 time steps. Nonetheless, losses of the specialized enterprise agent are still more than 40% lower than those of its integrated rival.

These simulation results conform well with the observation and analysis of DIS markets (Schlueter-Langdon 1999). In DIS markets, the largest and most successful firms have been initially highly vertically integrated. America Online, for example, has built strong vertically integrated competencies, which have been advantageous in becoming and remaining the product innovation leader. Major acquisitions and alliances have facilitated internalization of these competencies such as the purchase of ANS for $35 million in November 1994. Less integrated rivals, such as Delphi or Genie, fell behind the integrated leaders, while others, such as Europe Online, failed outright. More recently the market leader America Online has reduced its degree of backward integration into infrastructural assets and activities and, specifically, high-speed communication networks (sale of its ANS Communications division). This move coincided with the growth of some early Internet service providers like Worldcom's Uunet and GTE's BBN into large, national, first tier providers, which indicates the arrival of a capable, competitive market for Internet services. Specialized entrants like Yahoo! or Excite would not even have been viable without third-party Internet access providers. The same could be said about electronic commerce services. Without technology standards for transaction support and database interoperability as well as third-party platform support few online shops could enter specialized. All these observations suggest that there is empirical evidence mirroring the preliminary simulation results that downstream specialization appears to be at least as successful as integration in the case of industry-level specialization.

Notes

1. An overview of recent case studies is provided by Arora et al. (1997/98). The example of the computer industry is discussed in Farrell et al. (1998, 144–145).

2. "The vertical organization of industry is an important topic that has not received its due attention. There has been a great deal of work on vertical ownership but not on [the competitive characteristics of "open"/horizontal and "closed"/vertical forms of industry organization and their welfare implications]" (Farrell et al. 1998, 170–171). The authors define "open" as a "regime when firms add one stage of value and put the results back in the market, rather than controlling a longer segment of the value chain" (150). This definition is compatible with the one for industry-level specialization as used here.

3. Chaturvedi and Mehta, for example, suggest to use agent-based simulation models as "that for an even moderately complex economic model, there is very little hope of actually solving the problem" (1999, 60). See also Rust (1996).

4. The objective is not to optimize the performance of the entire production system—global performance—which may not maximize each firm's performance—local performance. In Farrell et al.'s model, for example, specialization throughout the supply chain or "open" interaction leads to the socially optimal outcome because it minimizes costs (1998). As a firm's profit is not only determined by cost the socially efficient choice does not need to be the most profitable. In their model and specifically in the case of Bertrand competition, cost heterogeneity drives industry profits, which in turn provides firms with a joint incentive to create a structure that maximizes cost heterogeneity and not necessarily minimizes cost.

5. Lin, Tan, and Shaw provide a brief overview of selected, more recent enterprise integration models (1996, 3–4)

6. While Lin's simulator resembles complicated process chains, albeit with linear interaction, the Anasazi village application features simple processes but adaptive behavior instead of linear interaction. This complication can produce non-linear outcomes, which in turn could allow for the study of emergent behavior such as settlement formation. In the Anasazi village simulator, the smallest unit of analysis or core agent is not a business unit/process but a household. It requires inputs (e.g., food, space for living and farming), generates output (corn), can grow (birth of children) and shrink (death of household member), and engages in trade with other households. The Anasazi village implementation has been a valuable case example, because it features a primitive exchange mechanism.

7. Flows are one of Holland's essential characteristics of a complex adaptive system (1995, 23–27, 38).

8. Aggregation corresponds to the concept of sub-agents in Sikora and Shaw's multi-agent system framework (1996, 1998).

9. Swarm is a general purpose, multi-agent simulation software platform developed at the Santa Fe Institute. It is particularly well-suited for the study of complex adaptive systems, since it allows discrete event simulation of [economic] interactions between heterogeneous agents (firms, markets) and a collective environment (an industry), as well as between agents themselves (Minar et al. 1996a, 1996b; Hiebeler 1994).

10. Lin et al. provide a brief overview of how to use Swarm as a simulation platform (1999, 18–19) and how to apply it to implement a (hierarchical) supply chain network model (20–23). Lin also provides a mapping of supply chain and Swarm properties (21).

11. A first version of the software code is available in Bruhn (1997, Appendix). First simulation experiments and results have been published in Schlueter and Shaw (1998).

12. Two years may already be too long a time period considering that the DIS industry is still in its early phase of the product life cycle, which is usually characterized by rapid product innovation and change of share distribution (i.e., Klepper 1996).

13. If losses are incurred and if cumulative losses exceed cash account balance, then a firm would drop out of the simulation run, or, in other words, exit.

14. All variables and initial conditions were the same across all runs, except for the seed used to generate the random numbers within a run. All initial conditions and the value of the seeds used to generate the random numbers have been recorded, so that any particular simulation run can be recreated.

References

Arora, A., F. Bokhari, and B. Morel. 1997/98. Returns to specialization, transaction costs, and the dynamics of industry evolution. Working Paper, Carnegie Mellon University [electronic document] (accessed 08/08/1999); available from http://econwpa.wustl.edu/eprints/io/ /papers/9606/9606002.abs; Internet.

Bruhn, P. 1997. Enterprise simulation using multi-agent system modeling and the Swarm toolkit. Master Thesis, University of Illinois at Urbana-Champaign, Department of Computer Science, Urbana, IL.

Chandler, A. D. 1990. *Scale and Scope: The Dynamics of Industrial Capitalism.* Harvard University Press: Cambridge, MA.

Chaturvedi, A. R., and S. R. Mehta. 1999. Simulation in Economics and Management. *Communications of the ACM* 42(3) (March): 60–61.

Coase, R. H. 1937. The Nature of the Firm. *Economica* 4: 386–405.

Farrell, J., H. K. Monroe, and G. Saloner. 1998. The Vertical Organization of Industry: Systems Competition versus Component Competition. *Journal of Economics and Management Strategy* 7(2) (Summer): 143–182.

Hiebeler, D. 1994. The Swarm simulation system and individual-based modeling. In: *Proceedings of Decision Support 2001—Advanced Technology for Natural Resource Management—September Conference held in Toronto, Canada.*

Holland, J. H. 1995. *Hidden Order: How Adaptation Builds Complexity.* Helix, Addison-Wesley: Reading, MA.

Kambil, A., and E. van Heck. 1996. Re-engineering the Dutch Flower Auctions: A framework for analyzing exchange organizations. CRIS Working Paper IS-96-23, NYU Stern School, New York, NY.

Klepper, S. 1996. Entry, Exit, Growth, and Innovation over the Product Life Cycle. American Economic Review 86: 562–583.

Kohler, T. A., and E. Carr. 1996. Swarm-based modeling of prehistoric settlement systems in southwestern North America. In: *Proceedings of UISPP XIIIth September 1996 Congress—Colloquium II: Archaeological Application of GIS—held in Forli, Italy.*

Lin, F.-R. 1996. Reengineering the order fulfillment process in supply chain networks: A multi-agent information systems approach. Ph.D. Thesis, University of Illinois at Urbana-Champaign, Department of Business Administration, Urbana, IL.

Lin, F.-R., G. W. Tan, and M. J. Shaw. 1996. Multi-agent enterprise modeling. Working Paper 96-0314, University of Illinois at Urbana-Champaign, College of Commerce and Business Administration, Office of Research, Urbana, IL.

Lin, F.-R., G. W. Tan, and M. J. Shaw. 1999. Multiagent Enterprise Modeling. *Journal of Organizational Computing and Electronic Commerce* 9 (1): 7–32.

Malone, T. W., J. Yates, and R. I. Benjamin. 1987. Electronic markets and electronic hierarchies. *Communications of the ACM* 30(6) (June): 484-497.

Minar, N., R. Burkhart, C. Langton, and M. Askenazi. 1996a. Swarm documentation [electronic document] (accessed 10/20/96); available from http://www.santafe.edu/projects/swarm; Internet.

Minar, N., R. Burkhart, C. Langton, and M. Askenazi. 1996b. The Swarm simulation system: A toolkit for building multi-agent simulations. Technical Report 96-04-2, Santa Fe Institute, Santa Fe, NM.

Ordover, J., G. Saloner, and S. Salop. 1990. Equilibrium Vertical Foreclosure. *American Economic Review* 80: 127–142.

Rust, J. 1996. Dealing with the complexity of economic calculations. *July 31–August 3 Workshop on Fundamental Limits to Knowledge in Economics held at the Santa Fe Institute, Santa Fe, NM.*

Schlueter, C., and M. J. Shaw. 1997. A strategic framework for developing electronic commerce. *IEEE Internet Computing* 1(6): 20–28.

Schlueter, C., and M. J. Shaw. 1998. An organizational ecosystems simulator applied to electronic commerce. In: *Proceedings of CIST/INFORMS April 1998 Conference held in Montreal, Canada.*

Schlueter-Langdon, C. 1999. Dynamics of Emergent Structures in Digital Interactive Services: Organizational Analysis, and Complex Adaptive System Modeling and Simulation. Ph.D. Thesis, Darmstadt University of Technology, Department of Economics, Germany.

Sikora, R., and M. J. Shaw. 1996. A multi-agent framework for the coordination and integration of information systems. Working Paper 96-0140, University of Illinois at Urbana-Champaign, College of Commerce and Business Administration, Urbana, IL.

Sikora, R., and M. J. Shaw. 1998. A Multi-Agent Framework for the Coordination and Integration of Information Systems. *Management Science* 44(11) (November): 65–78.

Whinston, M. 1990. Tying, Foreclosure, and Exclusion. *American Economic Review* 80: 837–859.

Williamson, O. E. 1975. *Markets and Hierarchies: Analysis and Antitrust Implications.* The Free Press: New York, NY.

Chapter 11

THE COEVOLUTION OF HUMAN CAPITAL AND FIRM STRUCTURE

Francesco Luna
Department of Economics
University of Venice Ca' Foscari
30120 Venezia Italy
fluna@unive.it

Alessandro Perrone
Department of Economics
University of Venice Ca' Foscari
30120 Venezia Italy
alex@unive.it

1.   INTRODUCTION

This last paper of the collection is mainly thought of as a pretext to trigger hands-on experience in the interested reader. It will present a "simple" model, some preliminary results and a series of issues that the model could address with "some" modification.

Several of the most recent economic analyses of growth point at the essential role played by human capital. This perspective finds its theoretical justification in the well known literature on endogenous growth a la Romer or Lucas. Economic policy implications are obvious and supported, for example, by the World Bank for various developing countries: education and training become a medium-term productive investment, the trigger for a sustained development process.

The purpose of this paper is to suggest that industrial growth and human capital are dynamically interrelated. In other words–proposed by Nelson–they *co-evolve*. Following this approach, it is fairly simple to detect path-dependence and to describe tales of rapid success as well as of unexpected decline. The model was inspired by the following historical events. The success-stories of the first industrial revolution were based on steel and steam power. A country like England found itself blessed with various comparative advantages, in particular, high-quality coal to be used in the steel production process and cheap low-quality coal to be burned as fuel.

On the other hand, Italy did not have such natural resources and could not benefit from a similar technological push[1]. What we would like to stress is, however, that when later on the industrial use of electricity was developed and hydro-electric power was found to be a cheap and efficient way to produce energy, Italy found itself in a theoretically favourable position. The country is certainly rich in rivers and mountains that make the building of dams a relatively easy technical option.

Certainly, at that point, England would have appeared to be less fortunate. What happened, however, was that England built a much larger number of idro-electric power plants than Italy and ironically–it might appear–Italian enterprises had to buy electricity-powered plants and machinery from England. The reason, we want to argue, is that England, thanks to its precocious technological development, had accumulated a stock of human capital (engineers) that gave it a deeper comparative advantage than natural resources could offer.

Next section will describe the model. Section 3 will present some preliminary results, and we will conclude in section 4. with some questions that could be addressed inside the same framework.

2.   THE MODEL

The mechanism employed to obtain the co-evolution dynamics can certainly be reduced to a generalized Polya's urn, but we add enough structure to render it a credible metaphor. Recently Luna has proposed a neural-net constructive algorithm to describe the spontaneous emergence of institutions in general and firms in particular[2]. The trigger for this event is given by an induction process that is too complex for each element of a population taken singularly.

Among the results reached by that model, we stress that the successful firms created have very different structures. Only a few of them are efficient in the sense of solving the induction problem with the smallest possible number of "workers". In that model, however, the learning process of each actor was based exclusively on the individual confrontation with the environment. In other words, *imitation* was not an alternative available to the would-be entrepreneur.

Here, rather than introducing explicitly "imitation" in the set of alternatives available to would-be entrepreneurs, we strictly separate workers from entrepreneurs and give the imitation option only to workers. A worker is the expression of a particular skill, some well specified *human capital*. He lives in a neighborhood inhabited by various other workers possibly endowed with very different skills. On a logically different level, the entrepreneurs represent each a particular firm-structure. Equivalently, each entrepreneur is characterized by an *idea*, that is a particular way of organizing her firm.

2.1   WORKERS AND HUMAN CAPITAL

Technically, each worker is characterized as an automaton which simulates a simple linearly separable two-argument Boolean function. There are twelve such functions which are presented in table 11.1

f(A, B)	Instances			
	$\{1, 1\}$	$\{1, -1\}$	$\{-1, 1\}$	$\{-1, -1\}$
A	1	1	-1	-1
B	1	-1	1	-1
$\overline{A}$	-1	-1	1	1
$\overline{B}$	-1	1	-1	1
$A \wedge B$	1	-1	-1	-1
$A \wedge \overline{B}$	-1	1	-1	-1
$\overline{A} \wedge B$	-1	-1	1	-1
$\overline{A} \wedge \overline{B}$	-1	-1	-1	1
$A \vee B$	1	1	1	-1
$A \vee \overline{B}$	1	1	-1	1
$\overline{A} \vee B$	1	-1	1	1
$\overline{A} \vee \overline{B}$	1	1	1	-1
XOR	**-1**	**1**	**1**	**-1**

Table 11.1   Look-up table

The first column lists the twelve functions. All of them are defined on the same domain which obviously includes only four points, identified as *Instances* in the table. They are: $\{1, 1\}$, $\{1, -1\}$, $\{-1, 1\}$, $\{-1, -1\}$. For example, $\{1, 1\}$ means that both variables A and B are *TRUE*. Now if $\{1, 1\}$ is input to the function $f(A, B) := A$, the output will be *TRUE* or, as recorded in the look-up table, 1. However, the same input will be mapped by the sixth function of the list ($f(A, B) := A \wedge \overline{B}$) as a -1 since the Boolean function is not verified by that pair of values for A and B.

The last row of table 11.1 concerns another two-argument Boolean function, the *Exclusive OR*. This function is defined on the same "four-point" domain, but it is not *linearly separable*[3]. Figure 11.1 gives reason for such an expression: there is no way to draw a *straight line* to *separate* the positive instances[4] from the negative ones.

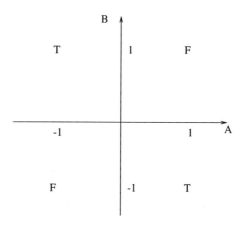

Figure 11.1   The *Exclusive OR* function

Our workers/artisans inhabit a torus and each of them is surrounded by eight neighbors. Initially, skills (or human capital) are distributed randomly among workers. Time is divided in *days* and *months*. Every day each worker receives an input that he transforms according to his ability; he will "produce" a 1 or a -1 depending on whether the Boolean function he simulates is verified or not by that particular input.

His reward, however, depends–continuing in the similarities with Bruun and Luna–on his output satisfying some consumer demand represented by the *XOR* function described above.

At the end of the month, workers count their successes and compare them with those obtained by their neighbors. At that point, everyone decides whether he wants to stick to his specialization or to *imitate* the most successful of his neighbors. Hence, the distribution of skills in the population evolves over time due to this process of imitation.

2.2   ENTREPRENEURS AND FIRM ORGANIZATION

An entrepreneur is characterized by an *idea* of how to construct her firm. In particular, she decides *ex ante* how many workers she will hire. The spectrum of possible dimensions we give is relatively limited[5] and goes from a minimum of 2 workers to a maximum of 6. Workers are chosen randomly among those who are available (not working for some other firm).

The entrepreneur collects and elaborates the workers' output. Her goal is to maximize the number of satisfied customers: her sales. That clearly requires her to infer the law behind the demand signals. In her induction chore she operates as a neural network. Each worker–Boolean function–reacts to the input $\{\alpha, \beta\}$ [6] demand signal. These "semi-products" are received by the entrepreneur neurode and weighted to produce the final output (a 1 or a -1) which is then compared to the *consumer's expected reply* represented by $XOR(\alpha, \beta)$

The learning algorithm employed by the entrepreneurs is the "simple perceptron" algorithm. It is easy to show that the smallest number of workers necessary to achieve an *effective* organization is two. An example is given in figure 11.2.

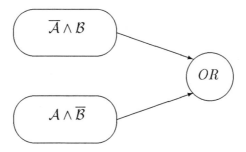

Figure 11.2 Simplest effective organization

In this case the function performed by the entrepreneur to coordinate successfully her workers is a simple *OR*. One worker will signal whether A and only A is *TRUE*, whereas the other will signal whether B and only B is *TRUE*. Hence, it is sufficient to receive a "positive" signal from either one of the workers to reply 1: *TRUE*. By a process of trial and error she adapts the weights associated with each "semi-product". For example, assigning a weight equal to 1 to each link and to the threshold, the output neurode simulates the *OR* function on the processed signals, but the whole organization will simulate the *XOR* function with respect to the initial input instances.

If at the end of the month a new enterprise is not effective, it goes bankrupt, it disappears from the scene, and its workers lose their "job". If, on the other hand, the organization is successful, it keeps on operating and its workers partake of the same perfect rate of success. Hence, their skills become more likely to be adopted in the population changing the overall human capital distribution.

Similarly, the following "generation" of entrepreneurs will find the *environment* modified and perhaps the chances of their idea of an organization more easily implemented. If the proportion of $\mathcal{A} \wedge \overline{\mathcal{B}}$ and $\overline{\mathcal{A}} \wedge \mathcal{B}$ workers increases, also the chances of an entrepreneur who is betting on a two-worker firm increase.

2.3   A BENCHMARK FOR THE COEVOLUTION

As in the story of the English engineers—initially trained because of the need of a particular technological innovation—who become the essential comparative advantage in the introduction of the next-generation technology, in our model human capital and the structure of firms would seem to interact in their evolution. It becomes essential to verify such hypothesis and, if possible, to appreciate its extent. This requires establishing a benchmark, a reference point to ascertain and "measure" changes.

Initially, we had thought of constructing such benchmark by determining with a grid search all successful organizations composed of 2, 3, 4, 5, 6, 7, and 8 workers systematically taken from the 12 different functions. In each case the neural-network entrepreneur would be built with weights taking, one after the other, all values in the set {-5, -4, -3, -2, -1, 0, 1, 2, 3, 4, 5} for each link plus the threshold. In particular, each candidate network[7] would be input the four instances and its output compared with the *XOR*'s output. All candidates which simulated correctly the *XOR* function were considered successful and counted. Furthermore, for each of these successful organizations, we also recorded the composition (in terms of human capital) so that an "absolute" index for the "most valuable" workers could be determined.

Unfortunately, the original plan could not be accomplished. The computation time grew exponentially so that finding all successful structures composed of 6 elements took almost 24 hours and the estimated time for case "7" was over two weeks[8] so we stopped and decided to choose as human capital pool only a subset of the twelve functions described in table 11.1.

The pool for our analysis is hence composed of: $\mathcal{A}$, $\mathcal{B}$, $\mathcal{A} \wedge \mathcal{B}$, $\overline{\mathcal{A}} \wedge \overline{\mathcal{B}}$, $\mathcal{A} \vee \overline{\mathcal{B}}$, and $\overline{\mathcal{A}} \vee \mathcal{B}$. The results obtained for this pool are recorded in table 11.2

From these results we also calculated the probability of an organization being successful conditional of having a particular structure. P(successful organization | organization cardinality = n)≡ P(suc|n)

Firms	A	B	$A \wedge B$	$A \vee \overline{B}$	$\overline{A} \wedge \overline{B}$	$\overline{A} \vee B$
			Human capital			
2-worker	0	0	65	65	65	65
3-worker	1260	1260	4470	4470	4470	4470
4-worker	78330	78330	187602	187602	187602	187602
5-worker	2962881	2962881	5970967	5970967	5970967	5970967
6-worker	87399099	87399099	159642873	159642873	159642873	159642873

Table 11.2 Grid-search results

$$P(suc|n) = \frac{\sum_{i=1}^{6} x_{ni}/n}{11^{n+1} \cdot \frac{6 \cdot (6+1) \cdot \ldots \cdot (6+n-1)}{n!}}$$

Where the numerator is simply the number of recorded successful organizations and the denominator indicates the total number of cases examined. $\sum_{i=1}^{6} x_{ni}$ is the sum along the *n-worker* firm row. These conditional probabilities are $P(suc|2) = 0.004651$, $P(suc|3) = 0.008294$, $P(suc|4) = 0.011175$, $P(suc|5) = 0.013354$, $P(suc|6) = 0.015057$. That is, a firm composed of two workers has an *ex ante* probability of success of about 0.4 percent, whereas an organization composed of 6 elements has a probability of being successful of about 1.5%. Since the probability distribution over the entrepreneur's *ideas* is uniform, the *ex ante* probability of the creation of a successful enterprise is the sum of the conditional probabilities above divided by 5 and roughly equal to 1%. That is, on average, one in every hundred new firms will turn out to be successful.

For future reference, figure 11.3 summarizes in a histogram the conditional probabilities $P(n|suc)$, that is, the probability that a successful organization has size equal to "n".

At least three things are worth mentioning. First, these probabilities hold in case the six different skills are uniformly distributed in the population. Second, it is not really surprising to see that the larger the organization the higher its probability of success. In fact, smaller successful firms are nested in larger ones when a zero weight is attached to the "unessential" links. However, finally, these higher probabilities do not take into consideration the fact that the search process may take longer for a larger organization, so that a potentially successful large firm may not reach effectiveness before going bankrupt.

Similarly, from table 11.2 it is also possible to calculate the probability of a particular skill being part of a successful enterprise conditional

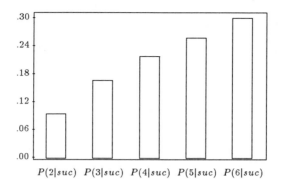

Figure 11.3 Probability Distribution of Successful Firms by Size

on the organization being of a given size. Table 11.3 records these probabilities.

Firms	Human capital					
	$\mathcal{A}$	$\mathcal{B}$	$\mathcal{A} \wedge \mathcal{B}$	$\mathcal{A} \vee \overline{\mathcal{B}}$	$\overline{\mathcal{A}} \wedge \overline{\mathcal{B}}$	$\overline{\mathcal{A}} \vee \mathcal{B}$
2-worker	0	0	.006976	.006976	.006976	.006976
3-worker	.003073	.003073	.010903	.010903	.010903	.010903
4-worker	.00579	.00579	.013867	.013867	.013867	.013867
5-worker	.007964	.007964	.016049	.016049	.016049	.016049
6-worker	.009707	.009707	.017732	.017732	.017732	.017732

Table 11.3 Conditional probabilities of success

In case the arrival of new entrepreneurs is uniformly distributed over the firm size, and the pool of human capital is uniformly distributed over all skills, we can easily calculate the probability of a particular skill being part of a successful enterprise in general. Again we summarize such results with a histogram in figure 11.4

We are now equipped to recognize the changes caused by the imitation process among workers on the distribution of skills and on the firm-size distribution.

3.   PRELIMINARY RESULTS

First of all, we want to check how our model replicates the theoretical results when the imitation process is prevented. To this purpose we set up the parameters as shown in figure 11.5

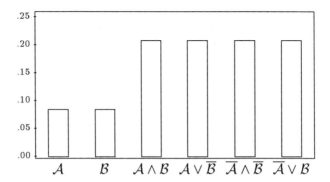

Figure 11.4 "Most valuable Players"

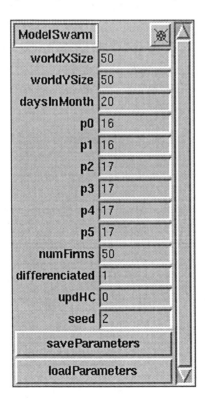

Figure 11.5 The Initial Set-up

Where `worldXSize` and `worldYSize` determine the dimension of the grid, `daysInMonth` defines the duration of each month, `p0` to `p5` determine the probability associated with each skill; i.e. `p0` = 16 implies that, on average, 16% of the population will be endowed with skill $\mathcal{A}$. `numFirms` indicates the number of new entrepreneurs who "try their

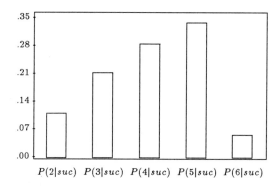

Figure 11.6 Average Distribution of Successful Firms by Size in 100 runs with parameters value defined in figure 11.5

luck" each month. The switch `differenciated` refers to the possibility of giving each worker an individual signal (`differenciated = 1`), or of inputing the same signal to the whole population. `updHC` triggers the imitation process among workers if it is set to 1; `seed` refers to the seed of a random number generator which, as explained in the tutorial, can, in general, take any integer value between 0 and 2,147,483,647 on microcomputers which allocate 32 bits for an integer. The buttons `saveParameters` and `loadParameters` allow the user to save a particular configuration and to re-load it when a new run is to be performed. Each parameter in this probe can be modified just before the beginning of the simulation: click on the particular value to be changed, input the new number, and remember to confirm your selection by hitting `Enter`.

We performed one hundred simulations (100 different seeds) for the set-up in figure 11.5 and the results are summarized in figure 11.6 and 11.7.

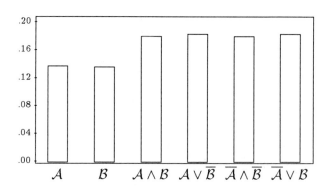

Figure 11.7 Average observed distribution of skills in the population of employed workers

The differences with the theoretical distributions are obvious. We suggest two reasons[9] without trying to verify our hypotheses and we leave this task as the first exercise for the interested reader.

The most striking divergence from the expected firm size distribution is related to enterprises composed of 6 workers. They form the smallest group in the simulation, whereas they should be the largest one according to the theoretical result. The reason we want to suggest is in line with the remark we made in the previous section. Large enterprises may require longer to reach effectiveness even when they are potentially successful. Penrose[10], substantiating her arguments with direct observation, suggests that when a firm grows–either by merger or by hiring new workers–its new human capital has to undergo a specific "on-the-job" training which may even cause the overall enterprise effectiveness to drop substantially.

One way to verify this hypothesis is to increase the size of the market, so that each organization will have to deal with more stimuli each period. In this way its units will acquire "experience" more rapidly. To this end, we have employed the `differenciated` switch performing the following experiment. We a have run two identical simulations one with `differenciated = 0`, and the other with the switch set to 1[11]. It is clear that the variety of stimuli reaching each would-be entrepreneur is greater when the switch is on. We expect to find a larger overall number of firms and a greater proportion of big firms in this latter case.

The results seem to confirm our hypothesis, with the number of size-6 firms doubling in the two experiments and with the first successful enterprise of that size appearing after 70 months in the non-differentiated case and after only 5 months in the other case. This experiment was performed just for one particular seed and the reader is invited to run a series of such experiments to check whether the tendency is confirmed on average.

The second obvious difference between the expected result and the recorded outcome is the "fatter" tail of the distribution of skills in successful enterprises. More precisely, the frequency of skill A and B are much higher than expected. We believe that the difference is due to the fact that our "grid" search for successful organizations is equivalent to a series of independent experiments on a population with uniformly distributed skills and with arrivals of entrepreneurs uniformly distributed over the space of organizations.

In our case, uniformly distributed arrivals of new entrepreneurs are guaranteed exogenously. However, since workers hired by one entrepreneur cannot work for anybody else, the distribution of *available* workers tends to become, month after month, more and more biased in favour of skills A and B as they become proportionally more numerous while other skills are hired and "exit the market". As a second exercise we invite the reader to track the evolution of this distribution in the initial stages of the emergence of successful firms so as to obtain a better approximation of the "independent experiments" set-up. Alternatively, one can remove the mechanism that currently prevents workers to be hired by more than one entrepreneur. In this way, the initial distribution of skills will be maintained for all new firms.

We can now introduce imitation among workers as the first step towards the analysis of coevolution between human capital and industrial structure. What would the reader expect the result to be? We must confess we were taken aback by the outcome of the first simulation. With initial uniform distribution of skills, the workers shift to either skill A or B in a matter of two to three months. In case no successful firm has been created in that short span, the economy is trapped in a suboptimal equilibrium.

Why does this happen? The reason is simple enough. Just look few pages back at table 11.1. Compare the outcome produced by the six skills selected for our human capital pool with the expected output represented by the **XOR** row. It is clear that A and B will be on average correct on 50% of the stimuli received, whereas all the other skills will be right only 25% of the times. It is, hence, most rational from an individual point of view to select either one those two skills. The creation of a 100% correct organization is a positive externality linked to the heterogeneity of the population which cannot be internalized by these simple automata.

In such a circumstance, it comes as no surprise that the "Invisible Hand" fails to lead the system towards a higher level of coordination. This is an example of "lock-in phenomena" studied in development economics. Such a *status quo* cannot be overcome counting only on endogenous resources. This result raises interesting questions about the sustainability of certain growth paths as pointed out by that strand of literature which recognizes in over-specialization a risk for the system and a source of inherent fragility.

As for our model, it may seem inadequate to tackle the original issue since the imitation mechanism imposes a dynamic which basically prevents any other more interesting phenomenon. However, this shortcoming may be corrected in a number of ways. First of all, the number of daring would-be entrepreneurs can be increased substantially. As we noted, one in every hundred firms should reach effectiveness on average. Another way would be to reduce drastically the number of "skill A and B" workers in the initial population in order to give "more time" for some successful firm to emerge. Naturally, in this case the benchmark has to be modified weighting the conditional probabilities of table 11.3 with the actual proportion of skills present in the population.

4.   UNANSWERED QUESTIONS

We propose now several other exercises related to the preliminary results presented in the previous section.

The version of this program (down-loadable from the net) enforces the sequence of events in a very inelegant way, without taking advantage of the class `Schedule`. The first exercise should be precisely to introduce a `daySchedule` and a `monthSchedule`.

The next exercise is simply to find in the code where the "genetic" pool of skills is recorded and to modify it as to introduce any one of the unused linearly separable Boolean functions appearing in table 11.1. If, for example, the skill $A \lor B$ were to be one of the "genes" in the pool, what is the expected dynamic for an initial population with a uniform distribution of skills?

Among the preliminary results we saw that the firm-size distribution is substantially different from the theoretical one with respect to the recorded frequency of size-6 enterprises. We suggested that the reduced "size of the market" may be one of the reasons. We proposed a test based on the use of the switch `differentiated`. Another way to check the hypothesis is to increase the length of each month as to allow for a larger number of stimuli to reach the entrepreneurs.

The *lock-in* episode we encountered suggests an exercise linked with the "transition" process currently experienced by former socialist economies. It has been argued that the variety in the degree of success shown by these countries could be explained by their geographical distance from the heart of the European market economy. Stanley Fischer and other researchers at the IMF have recently proposed a peculiar econometric study. Apparently the distance of each transition-economy capital-city from Bruxelles has a strong statistical significance in explaining the average growth rate of that country in the last ten years.

The exercise we propose is to create a sub-area of the workers' world to be considered as the transition economy. Here, the restructuring process[12] is to take place at the beginning of the transition and no successful firm exists yet. We have seen that the imitation process will normally lead the initial heterogeneity of workers to disappear leaving the system in an inferior "equilibrium". Possibly, however, if the imitation could expand beyond the country's geographic borders some pool of precious skills may still be found by entrepreneurs entering that market.

In our model, given the mechanism for imitation which involves immediate neighbors, it is obvious that only workers contiguous to the border
could initially have the chance of acquiring a valuable skill copying it
from a colleague across the border. It is also natural to expect that
the longer the border shared with a developed economy, the speedier
the transition. As a matter of fact, the Chinese experiment with well
identified market-economy areas is the real-world analog to our proposed
exercise.

Finally, it is clear that the issue of co-evolution has only been marginally touched. The analysis should be more detailed. In particular,
it may not be enough to keep track of the total number of firms of a
particular size, but it may be necessary to distinguish among the various
compositions of successful enterprises of that size. It is easy to see that
there are only two possible structures which lead to an effective size-2
firm. The first one involves $A \wedge B$ and $\overline{A} \wedge \overline{B}$. The second one is composed
of $\overline{A} \vee B$ and $A \vee \overline{B}$. However, how many different successful 3-worker
structures are there? Which of these employs one or more of the above
mentioned skills? This is important to know if we want to identify some
sort of evolutionary branch taken by the system. This is obviously a
very complex task to embark in and may require the design of a set of
tools different from the ones we used for this preliminary investigation
(basically histograms to record the observed frequency distributions).
We are confident that Swarm will provide suitable building blocks for
these new and more sophisticated tools.

Notes

1. Clearly, we are not suggesting that the delay in the Italian development was solely due
to the lack of readily available coal, only that it certainly played a role

2. See Bruun and Luna in this volume for a brief description of that model and the
relevant reference

3. The term is imported from the neural-network literature

4. Those instances for which the function is *TRUE*

5. We will explain this constraint momentarily.

6. One of the instances in table 11.1 where α is the value taken by the variable A and β
is the value taken by the variable B.

7. A particular structure and one set of weights

8. Initially the program had been written in Mathematica. Then we re-wrote the same
routine in C with great gains in performance, but we could reach only the results for 6-worker
organizations in an acceptable time

9. There is obviously always a third possibility: a mistake in the code. Rather than
excluding this event superciliously, we suggest that such an elusive "bug" might have been
introduced on purpose by the wicked mind of these authors as a challenge for the reader.

10. Penrose, E. 1959, *The Theory of the Growth of the Firm*, Oxford University Press,
Oxford

11. The other parameters were set as follows: updHC = 0, seed = 50, daysInMonth = 20.

12. represented by our mechanism for the creation of enterprises

Index

Advances in Computational Economics

1. A. Nagurney: *Network Economics*. A Variational Inequality Approach. 1993
    ISBN 0-7923-9293-0
2. A.K. Duraiappah: *Global Warming and Economic Development*. A Holistic Approach to International Policy Co-operation and Co-ordination. 1993
    ISBN 0-7923-2149-9
3. D.A. Belsley (ed.): *Computational Techniques for Econometrics and Economic Analysis*. 1993   ISBN 0-7923-2356-4
4. W.W. Cooper and A.B. Whinston (eds.): *New Directions in Computational Economics*. 1994   ISBN 0-7923-2539-7
5. M. Gilli (ed.): *Computational Economic Systems*. Models, Methods & Econometrics. 1996   ISBN 0-7923-3869-3
6. H. Amman, B. Rustem, A. Whinston (eds.): *Computational Approaches to Economic Problems*. 1997   ISBN 0-7923-4397-2
7. G. Pauletto: *Computational Solutions of Large-Scale Macroeconometric Models*. 1997   ISBN 0-7923-4656-4
8. R.D. Herbert: *Observers and Macroeconomic Systems*. Computation of Policy Trajectories with Separate Model Based Control. 1998   ISBN 0-7923-8239-0
9. D. Ho and T. Schneeweis (eds.): *Applications in Finance, Investments, and Banking*. 1999   ISBN 0-7923-8294-3
10. A. Nagurney: *Network Economics: A Variational Inequality Approach*. Revised second edition. 1999   ISBN 0-7923-8350-8
11. T. Brenner: *Computational Techniques for Modelling Learning in Economics*. 1999
    ISBN 0-7923-8503-9
12. A. Hughes Hallett and P. McAdam (eds.): *Analysis in Macroeconomic Modelling*. 1999   ISBN 0-7923-8598-5
13. R.A. McCain: *Agent-Based Computer Simulation of Dichotomous Economic Growth*. 1999   ISBN 0-7923-8688-4
14. F. Luna and B. Stefansson (eds.): *Economic Simulations in Swarm*. Agent-Based Modelling and Object Oriented Programming. 1999   ISBN 0-7923-8665-5
15. E.J. Kontoghiorghes: *Parallel Algorithms for Linear Models*. Numerical Methods and Estimation Problem. 1999   ISBN 0-7923-7720-6

KLUWER ACADEMIC PUBLISHERS – DORDRECHT / BOSTON / LONDON